Universities Remembering Europe

UNIVERSITIES REMEMBERING EUROPE

Nations, Culture, and Higher Education

EDITED BY FRANCIS CRAWLEY, PAUL SMEYERS, AND PAUL STANDISH

Berghahn Books
New York • Oxford

First published in 2000 by **Berghahn Books**

www.berghahnbooks.com

Library of Congress Cataloging-in-Publication Data

Universities remembering Europe : nations, culture and higher education / edited by Francis Crawley, Paul Standish, and Paul Smeyers

p. cm.

Includes bibliographical references.

ISBN 1-57181-957-6 (alk. paper)

1. Education, Higher--European Union countries. 2. Nationalism and education--European Union countries. 3. Multiculturalism--European Union countries. I. Crawley, Francis. II. Standish, Paul, 1949- III. Smeyers, Paul

LA628.U67 1999

378. 4 21--dc21

99-045863

British Library Cataloguing in Publication Data
A catalogue record for this book is available from the British Library.

Printed in the United States on acid-free paper.

ISBN -57181-957-6 (hardback)

Contents

List of Contributors

Jorge V. Arregui taught for ten years at the University of Navarra. He now teaches philosophy at the University of Málaga. He has been Academic Visitor at Oxford University, Honorary Research Fellow in Glasgow University, and Visiting Research Fellow in the University of St Andrews. His books include *Acción y sentido en Wittgenstein* (Eunsa, Pamplona, 1984), *Filosofía del hombre* (Rialp, Madrid, 1991), *El horror de morir*, (Tibidabo, Barcelona, 1992) and *Inventar la sexualidad: sexo, naturaleza y cultura* (Rialp, Madrid, 1996).

Nigel Blake works in the Institute of Educational Technology at the Open University and is Chair of the Philosophy of Education Society of Great Britain. His principal interests are in the politics and economics of higher education, the politics of educational discourse, and problems of modernity and postmodernity, with particular reference to the Critical Theory of Jürgen Habermas and Lyotard. He has published numerous articles and is joint author of *Thinking Again: Education after Postmodernism* (1998) and *The Universities We Need: Higher Education after Dearing* (1998).

Francis P. Crawley teaches rhetoric and history at the Vrije Universiteit Brussels. His primary interests lie in philosophy of education, focused particularly on European higher education, and issues concerned with education and ethics in biomedical research.

Joseph Dunne teaches philosophy of education at St. Patrick's College, Dublin City University, where he is also coordinator of Human Development, an interdisciplinary subject in the Humanities programme. He has spoken and published on philosophical and educational topics in Ireland and abroad. He is author of *Back to the Rough Ground: Phronesis and Techne in Modern Philosophy and in Aristotle* (Notre Dame and London: University of Notre Dame Press, 1993; new paperback edition, 1997).

Bas Levering lectures in philosophy and history of education at the University of Utrecht. He is Chair of the Philosophy and History Department of the Dutch Association of Pedagogues. He received his Ph.D. in the philosophy of education from the University of Utrecht in 1988. He is the author of *Values in Education and in the Science of Education. A Plea for a Challenging Pedagogy* (in Dutch) and of *Childhood's Secrets: Intimacy, Privacy and the Self Reconsidered* (co-authored by Max van Manen).

Terence H. McLaughlin is University Lecturer in Education in the University of Cambridge and Fellow of St Edmund's College, Cambridge, where he is Director of Studies in Philosophy and has also held the posts of Admissions Tutor and Senior Tutor. He is currently Vice-Chair of the Philosophy of Education Society of Great Britain and Chair of the Steering Committee of the International Network of Philosophers of Education. He has written on various aspects of the relationship between culture, nationality, identity, and education. He has recently published a collection of philosophical papers on moral education, *Education in Morality* (co-edited with J Mark Halstead).

Susan Mendus is Professor of Politics and Director of the Morrell Studies in Toleration programme at the University of York. Her main areas of research interest are liberal political theory, feminist theory, philosophy of education, and the philosophy of Kant. She has written and edited a number of works on questions of toleration and education in multicultural societies.

Richard Smith is Reader in Education at the University of Durham, where he is currently Director of Combined Social Science, and Editor of the *Journal of Philosophy of Education*. He teaches Environmental Ethics and theory of Social Science as well as various aspects of Education. His books include *Thinking Again: Education after Postmodernism* (co-authored with Blake, Smeyers, and Standish).

Paul Smeyers is Professor of Education at the Katholieke Universiteit Leuven, Belgium, where he teaches philosophy of education and methodology of the *Geisteswissenschaften*. He has held visiting appointments at Randse Afrikaanse Universiteit (Johannesburg, RSA), Auckland University (New Zealand), and at the Universidad de Lima (Peru). His many published articles address issues such as the justification of the content of education, philosophical issues of child-rearing, the importance of commitment, and the ethics of care, with particular reference to the work of Wittgenstein. With Jim Marshall he co-edited *Philosophy and Education: Accepting Wittgenstein's Challenge* (1995). He is the Editor of the Journal *Pedagogisch Tijdschrift* based in the Netherlands. Work in progress includes *Education in an Age of Nihilism* (co-authored with Blake, Smith, and Standish) and *The Blackwell Guide to Philosophy of Education* (co-edited with Blake, Smith, and Standish).

Paul Standish is Senior Lecturer in Education at the University of Dundee. His main research interest is in the relationship between analytical and Continental philosophy and its significance for education. His publications include *Beyond the Self: Wittgenstein, Heidegger, and the Limits of Language*; *Teaching Right and Wrong: Moral Education in the Balance* (co-edited with Richard Smith); *Thinking Again: Education after Postmodernism* (co-authored with Blake, Smeyers, and Smith); and *The Universities We Need: Higher Education after Dearing* (co-authored with Blake, Smeyers, and Smith). He is Assistant Editor of the *Journal of Philosophy of Education.*

Ido Weijers lectures at the University of Utrecht, Department of Educational Sciences. He studied political and social sciences at the University of Amsterdam, and gained his PhD from the Erasmus University of Rotterdam. His publications include a book on the future of the university (1995). He is currently preparing a book on juvenile justice.

Kevin Williams is President of the Educational Studies Association of Ireland and lectures in Mater Dei Institute, Dublin. His research interests include the philosophy of school subjects, especially foreign language education. Among his publications are *Assessment: A Discussion Paper*, and the two recent collections *The Future of Religion in Irish Education* and *Words Alone: The Teaching of English in Ireland* of which he is joint editor.

Foreword

The project 'Nations and Cultures in European Higher Education' which is the origin of this book emerged out of a network of friendship founded and promoted by the very generous and open atmosphere of the Philosophy of Education Society of Great Britain. Those who collaborated on this project shared the desire to contribute to the discussion on the 'new Europe' from the point of view of philosophy of education.

The project began in the autumn of 1995 with a discussion of European policies on universities and other institutions of higher education. In December 1995 the authors met for four days in London to analyse and critique a first set of essays. In the year that followed all of the contributions were rewritten. In May 1997, just following the change of government in the United Kingdom and around the time of the Inter-Governmental Conference in Amsterdam, editorial revisions were made.

On behalf of our contributors we would like to thank The British Council and the Nationaal Fonds voor Wetenschappelijk Onderzoek (the Belgian National Fund for Scientific Research) for generous financial support and our individual institutions for logistic support.

Francis P. Crawley
Paul Smeyers
Paul Standish

Introduction: The Implications of European Policies for Higher Education

> The Community shall contribute to the development of quality education by encouraging cooperation between Member-States and, if necessary, by supporting and supplementing their action, while fully respecting the responsibility of the Member-States for the content of teaching and the organization of education systems and linguistic diversity. (Treaty on European Union, Art. 126)

Since the signing of the Treaty on European Union in Maastricht on 7 February 1992, and its subsequent ratification by the individual member-states, the citizens of fifteen European countries have officially become citizens of the European Union. The enactment of new commitments and new loyalties revives fundamental questions regarding the place of traditional historical and cultural icons in our social and human identity. Undoubtedly this is a decisive period for Europe economically, socially, and politically as it confronts its past with a renewed vision of the future. A key instrument for the development of this emerging 'European dimension' in the hearts and minds of these newly won citizens is taken to be education. The concept of a 'new Europe' raises new questions against the background of the traditional role of education in passing on the cultural inheritance of a society and ensuring the proper formation of citizens. The time-honoured bastions of higher learning in Europe (the universities) as well as their more recent counterparts (the various institutions of higher education) have been called upon to participate in revising our understanding of nations and cultures in the light of the exigencies of a new European dimension in our economic, social, and political interactions. Places of higher learning in Europe are gradually assenting to their role in the construction of a 'new Europe' by offering intercultural, international education programmes aimed at a common commitment.

Forty years after Italy, France, Germany, and the Benelux countries signed the Treaty of Rome, the now fifteen member-states of the European Union face new challenges to their identity. The citizens of these nation-states have mixed identities taunted regularly by the forces of globalisation, Europeanisation, and regionalisation. The nation-state itself, the modern ideal of civic identity, seems to be losing out on all fronts. The once inalienable sovereignty of the nation-state is increasingly limited today by the technocracy of global communication and exchange. The unquestioned control of the nation-state over geographical territory dissolves in the face of a global market-place whose logic surpasses the frontiers of border controls. Most tellingly, the institutionalised power of the nation-state no longer guarantees the imposition of the social, political, and economic order feigned in the social contract of our Western democracies. The loyalty to one's national identity is repeatedly surmounted by one's commitment to professional, group, or circumstantial engagements.

The challenges to the loyalties of citizenship, however, go beyond concerns with sovereignty, geographic control, and even power. Similarly, the commitments to blood, race, ethnicity, culture, and tradition may never be more than partial aspects of a civic identity. At root there needs to be a commitment to shared values, a commitment to how we do things together and in what way things matter. The movement from a world organised around nation-states to a world economic structure poses anew the questions of civic identity: not just questions of the United Kingdom's identity, Ireland's identity, Norway's identity, or Europe's identity, but in the first place questions of the identity of the *citoyen français*, the Welsh intellectual, the Juventus football supporter, the Greek farmer, and the European citizen. How we arrange our affairs depends very much upon the manner in which these questions are addressed. Loyalty to an established order and commitment to one's engagements need to be harmoniously reconciled in all essential areas of a democratic civic community. Higher education in a democratic society should not only pass on the cultural inheritance in which these loyalties and commitments were formed but also provide a living critique of the values underlying these loyalties and commitments. Such a critique should never be a purely cerebral analysis of disembodied values; rather, it should be a genuine engagement with the activities in which those values are expressed.

During the latter part of the 1980s European universities and other institutions of higher education began (at a steadily increasing rate) to extend their relationships with one another through various research and exchange agreements developed under the different Framework Programmes of the European Commission. Included in these programmes were the Lingua Programme, the Eurydice Programme, the Comett Programme, the Iris Programme, and the very famous and successful Erasmus Programme. With the academic year 1989–90 the European Community Course Credit Transfer System (ECTS) was implemented as a Pilot Scheme, laying the foundation for increased student mobility based on the mutual recognition of course work between higher education institutions in different member-states. Then on 5 November 1991 the European Commission published the *Memorandum on Higher Education in the European Community*, which outlined basic building blocks for the creation of a 'European education'. The *Memorandum*, followed by the enormous set of responses it provoked, provided a watershed for a more focused reflection on the implications of policies directed at the 'Europeanisation' of higher education.

Since the *Memorandum*, and with the support of the Maastricht Treaty, these policies have become more focused while at the same time increasing their scope. While the original mandate for action at the European level in higher education was based nearly exclusively on economic concerns, since 1992 this mandate has extended into the area of culture and is steadily reaching toward nearly all areas of the social. However we are disposed to evaluate these developments, as either positive or negative in general for the peoples of Europe, there remains a need to understand their implications on social, moral, cultural, and intellectual values. These values support the fundamental identities we have with groups and peoples, ultimately influencing the commitments we make at the local, regional, national, and supranational levels. What values are realised in education, and how these values are realised, is an underlying concern for the philosophy of education.

It is the task of philosophy to reflect on the activities of persons and society in their present situation. As a reflective activity, philosophy is necessarily historical, looking back on the past in order to understand the origin of present moral and intellectual values. At the same time, an analysis of the present situation requires an orientation, even a disposition, toward the future. In order to discern properly the motivations underlying the activities of persons and society, the engagement of philosophy requires a consideration of both what appears as foundational and what appears as ephemeral. The challenge to the European philosopher today is enormous, particularly as it regards our institutions of higher education.

The contributors to this volume approached their analysis of the implications of the 'new Europe' on the values of higher education largely through a critical evaluation of documents on higher education emerging either directly from the European Commission or through support of the Commission. Of course, the vast majority of these documents are primarily political and their composition is very often best described as 'technocratic' (some prefer the more direct expression 'Eurocratic'). Their aim is, necessarily, rational and even calculative in the first instance. They are directed at achieving general agreement by harmonising difference and avoiding confrontation. These documents – programme descriptions, official and non-official reports; memoranda; white papers and green papers; guidelines, directives, and decisions; and, of course, the treaties themselves – offer a wide variety of rhetorical styles in accordance with their varying purposes. They generally rely on the building of a consensus in the development of a positive disposition toward the new Europe.

The essays in this book present a philosophical analysis of the potential implications for values in higher education brought about by the invitation to establish a European dimension in the curriculum. The project emerged out of a widely felt need to understand the implications of the 'new Europe' on higher education, not only from the perspectives of economics and politics, but also more fundamentally from the perspective of philosophy and education. In this period of transition regarding the national and cultural values of Europeans, and their expression in institutions of higher education, it is essential that a sustained philosophical reflection be developed on the role of institutions of higher education in European society. The authors collaborated on a study of the core documents and programmes emerging from the European Commission concerning the role of higher education in the formation of European citizens. They examined the implications of these policies and programmes on the moral, intellectual, and spiritual values of higher education.

The challenge to the philosophy of education presented by this enormous volume of literature lies in sifting through the obviously rhetorical aspects in order to lay bare the very serious and demanding engagement that supports this dynamic. The role of philosophy here is, at least in the first place, to attain conceptual clarity. However, this can only be achieved if the arguments and concepts presented in these very political documents enunciating European policy are placed in a wider context of writings and activities impinging on European higher education. Philosophy needs to chafe through the surface ambiguities, the apparent (and real) contradictions, and the wide lacunae of what has been left unsaid – because it was thought to be too controversial, or too early in the discussion, or too wrongheaded, or (perhaps) simply too evident. The underlying economic and political motivations of this quickening drive to involve higher education in the construction of a European civic community are underpinned by a complex dialogue on cultural, social, psychological, and spiritual values in both their traditional and contemporary forms. In order to appreciate the real impact of European policy on higher education, one needs to clarify the essential concepts of this dialogue through an active engagement.

The evolving 'European dimension' of the economic, social, and political spheres of the 'new Europe', and its resulting expression or promotion in education, adds an exciting aspect – though it may not always be evident – to the engagements of persons, groups, and nations in Europe today. While the 'idea of Europe' is primarily an orientation toward the future – what Europe might/could/should become – it is an idea with a long and burdened past. At the same time, its present expression – in treaties, institutions, and laws, as well as in economic, political, and social actions – is unique. And, of course, 'Europe' is not all that is happening here – would that our philosophical reflections could remain so focused. The new Europe is partly a response to the ongoing globalisation of the marketplace, to the demise of communism in central and eastern Europe, and to the increasing importance of technology and communication. The new Europe is also partly a response to the increased importance being placed on regional and linguistic identity within all European nations today, to recurring and evidently deepening crises in the social sphere (particularly concerning employment, health, and social security), and to an increased sense of a 'democratic deficit' in the political sphere.

The place of nations and cultures in European higher education is today no simple matter. Still it is a place requiring analysis and appreciation, and this not simply by the Eurocrats and national ministries of education. Nor is it a matter only for professional educators. The heart of a constructive attitude is a critical disposition. At stake in the analysis is a deepened and more critical understanding not only of the 'new Europe', but also, and perhaps more centrally, of the evolving role of the universities and their partner institutions of higher education in passing on the cultural inheritance of *Homo Europeanus*. Higher education provides the capstone to the formation of the citizen and the professional: it builds on the product of primary and secondary education, and prepares the student (in a very contemporary and European sense) for a lifetime of learning. However, this is only possible where higher education is mindful of the underlying concerns of society, going beyond the requirements of citizenship and professionalism to the fundamental moral, intellectual, and spiritual values of nations and cultures.

This book presents twelve contributions, each focusing on different aspects of the implications of European policy on higher education. They represent a wide variety of approaches and perspectives within philosophy of education. In several instances there are overlapping concerns and themes, as one would expect. However, the interest of each author arises out of a unique context oriented by specific aims.

The editors have sought to preserve the diversity of the European project in the manner and presentation of the contributions. Terence McLaughlin focuses on the *Memorandum on Higher Education*, that pivotal and transitional document in the development of European higher education policy. Francis Crawley and Kevin Williams present differing perspectives on the implications for citizenship of European policy on higher education. Susan Mendus, Jorge Arregui, and Paul Smeyers examine European policy on higher education within the framework of multiculturalism, a partial concern for Joseph Dunne and Paul Standish as well. Ido Weijers and Nigel Blake examine higher education in the context of the demands for skills and vocationally related expertise. Joe Dunne presents an analysis of the roles of culture and citizenship in a higher education context increasingly challenged by the demands of the global market-place. In questioning the extent to which European higher education is truly democratic, Richard Smith explores new conceptions of learning. Bas Levering examines the psychological and social implications for the student leaving home for higher education, and Paul Standish looks at the idea of the university's mission in circumstances of multiculturalism.

Finally, the concluding chapter sets forth twelve statements derived by the editors from the project of the book. The editors believe that philosophy should provide not only commentary on higher education policy but also a well-formulated contribution to policy development in this important facet of European life. The aim of this project was to examine critically the implications of European policy for higher education from the perspective of philosophy. The value of the critical explorations and analyses that follow lies, we are convinced, in their ability to contribute constructively to the ongoing debate on the role of higher education in European society.

Part I

The Idea of the European Dimension

Chapter 1

The European Dimension of Higher Education:

Neglected Claims and Concepts

Terence H. McLaughlin

I consider here a number of claims and concepts relating to the European dimension of higher education that are neglected in both the recent *Memorandum* published by the European Commission on the future of higher education in Europe and in the subsequently reported discussions of the document. I here argue that inattention to these claims and concepts may lead to unjustifiable educational influence of various kinds. I offer an account of acceptable forms of educational influence that can be derived from defensible interpretations of the 'claims and concepts' with reference to school-level education. I conclude that a failure to offer an adequate analysis of the 'claims and concepts' is a significant obstacle to reflection and debate on European higher education as well as to the implementation of justifiable educational policies, which the *Memorandum* seeks to stimulate.

The *Memorandum on Higher Education* published by the European Commission in 1991 (Commission of the European Communities 1991) was produced in order to stimulate reflection and debate on many aspects of the future of higher education in Europe in the context of the extensive political and other changes and developments in recent years. Yet the *Memorandum* itself, and the responses to it which the commission has published (Commission of the European Communities 1993a; Commission of the European Communities 1993b), display a marked inattention to a number of matters of fundamental principle and value which any adequate reflection and debate on the future of higher education in Europe must address. This inattention concerns especially, but not exclusively, the specifically 'European' distinctiveness which is urged upon higher education. A failure to interrogate clearly what is involved in this distinctiveness can have several effects. At one level, there is a danger that the various claims relating to distinctiveness will be regarded as mere rhetoric, attention being focused on the details of particular programmes, policies, and strategies. More seriously, however, there is a danger that highly contentious aims and values may be imposed upon European higher education without appropriate critical assessment.

One way of illustrating this neglect by the *Memorandum* of such fundamental questions is by pointing to a number of distortions in the document. One distortion is the somewhat uncritical salience that is given to economic and employment considerations in relation to higher education. For example, in the 'executive summary' of the document, the first five of the seven paragraphs relating to 'The Role of Higher Education' concern economic and employment matters. The opening sentence of the summary sets the tone for what follows: 'The population of the European Community is ageing and declining and the labour market is demanding more people with higher levels of knowledge and skill in order to support an expanding knowledge-based economy' (Commission of the European Communities 1991: p. I). The document proper begins with a sentence referring to the 'strategic importance' of higher education in making the Internal Market work (Commission of the European Communities 1991: para. 1). Numerous further illustrations could be given of the unargued priority and emphasis given to economic and employment matters throughout the document. For example, the first reason cited for the need to increase participation in higher education is the need to raise the level of knowledge and skills required by the European work-force in order for it to remain competitive (Commission of the European Communities 1991: para. 60).

The criticism offered here is not, of course, that economic and employment considerations are unimportant in higher education. Nor is it being claimed that the *Memorandum* is wholly unbalanced with respect to these matters. A careful reading of the document reveals several paragraphs that attempt to add qualification and balance. We find, for example, an insistence that higher education in Europe has a role not merely in relation to vocational and professional training, but also in the wider responsibility of cultural maintenance, development, and transmission, in the advancement of knowledge in the humanities as well as in science and technology, and in the fostering of wide ranging independent judgement, creativity, and 'esprit critique' (Commission of the European Communities 1991: para. 4). Further, for example, the document acknowledges that research must not be governed by economic considerations alone but must include the pursuit of knowledge for its own sake (Commission of the European Communities 1991: para. 24). These 'balancing' elements of the document are important. However, they are insufficiently developed to reassure readers that the 'cultural' dimension of higher education is not being seen as a 'bolt-on' to dominant economic purposes. (It is, of course, important to recognise the close interrelationship between cultural and economic considerations. Any assumption of the dominance of economic purposes is – at least in part – a cultural matter.)

The complaint here is rather that the document fails to offer, and to situate its discussion within, a sustained and systematic overall view of the proper aims, purposes, and values of higher education. The document therefore contributes to a prevalent failure that Ronald Barnett claims is characteristic of much contemporary discussion of higher education: a failure, arising in part from the general unavailability of adequate theoretical resources, to develop and articulate an overall view of higher education in specifically educational terms (Barnett 1990). The document is therefore in an important sense 'mis-shapen'. This can be further illustrated by, and is indeed exacerbated by, pointing to a second kind of distortion. In relation to a number of questions, the document has a tendency to move too quickly into a consideration of matters of detail whilst neglecting the need for a prior overall perspective on the matters at stake. For example, the section of the document dealing with the crucial question of the 'European Community Dimension' of higher education devotes its first two subsections to student mobility within the EC (Commission of the European Communities 1991: paras 99–111) and to cooperation between institutions at European level (Commission of the European Communities 1991: paras 112–18) respectively. Yet such matters ought surely to be considered only after a prior extended examination of what this 'dimension' might actually mean in some overall sense, and how it might be justified.

The inattention of the *Memorandum* to matters of fundamental principle and value does not merely have a distorting effect upon the document. It also has the effect, as we shall see, of leaving some of its important claims and concepts seriously unclear, underanalysed, and (for at least these reasons) neglected.

The *Memorandum* does not, of course, pretend to offer a fundamental, philosophically sophisticated treatment of the matters with which it deals, and it would be unrealistic to expect such a treatment in a document of this kind. It would be unfair to criticise the document as if it were offering an academically rigorous statement of its claims and concepts. The document aimed to stimulate a wide-ranging general discussion among a group of parties with varying backgrounds and interests, and an overly philosophical approach might well have inhibited this aim. A further difficulty for the document is that of attempting to articulate, beyond the level of rhetoric, general principles for highly diverse systems of higher education across the European Community. However, despite the need to avoid subjecting the document to an unfairly rigorous academic criticism, it should be remembered that we are told that the *Memorandum* was discussed at around eighty meetings at national and European level, with more than 8,000 people taking part (Commission of the European Communities 1993a: p. 7). It might therefore be expected that in this process of debate the deficiencies of the document would have been identified and addressed and some analytical rigour applied to some fundamental questions. On the evidence of the published responses to the *Memorandum*, however, this has taken place only to a limited extent. For example, there is extensive discussion in the responses of the need to 'reverse the priorities' of the *Memorandum* so that economic and employment considerations should be seen in the perspective of the primary and overriding cultural role of higher education (Commission of the European Communities 1993a: section 2). However, despite the extensive debate, a number of central claims and concepts in the *Memorandum* remain significantly out of focus. Indeed, the published responses may well have contributed to this problem by introducing new ill-focused claims and concepts. For example, 'firm agreement' is reported in the responses that 'the secular nature of the humanist tradition in European higher education should be maintained' (Commission of the European Communities 1993a: para. 2.3). The meaning of the 'secular' nature which is referred to here (a notion not found in the *Memorandum*) is wholly unclear and, when properly focused, potentially highly contentious. It gives rise to a host of complex questions, not least of the sort that Susan Mendus addresses in her contribution to this volume (see Hume 1994). At the empirical level alone, it is not clear that claims about the secular character of the humanist tradition in European higher education are well grounded, as the contribution of Paul Smeyers to this volume makes clear. Indeed, depending on how it is to be interpreted, a commitment to the 'secular' nature of the humanist tradition could well be in conflict with the commitment of the European Commission to the diversity – including the cultural diversity – of higher education provision across the Community (Commission of the European Communities 1991: para. 147; Commission of the European Communities 1993a: para. 2.3.4).

In the next section of this chapter, attention is focused upon a prominent family of claims and concepts in the *Memorandum* that escape the sort of critical scrutiny that one might expect to find in the discussions reported in the published responses. These claims and concepts all relate to the 'European Dimension' of higher education, which the *Memorandum* recommends as becoming 'much more ... a feature of the planning and functioning of higher education throughout the community' (Commission of the European Communities 1991: section II).

The European Dimension of Higher Education: Fundamental Claims and Concepts

The *Memorandum* argues that 'a concerted effort' is needed to produce a 'fundamental change' in the attitude of higher education institutions towards the 'European Dimension' of their work. This dimension, the document claims, must embrace, and become a 'basic element' in, the academic planning and policies of the institutions, must lead to 'greatly enhanced' cooperation between higher education institutions at European level across the full range of academic disciplines, and must result in the adoption of 'institutional "European" policies covering all aspects of academic life' (Commission of the European Communities 1991: para. 113). As indicated earlier, much of what is recommended here is of a practical nature, relating to student mobility schemes, policies for the achievement of mutual recognition of qualifications, and the like. However, embodied within many of the proposals are the neglected fundamental claims and concepts with which I am concerned.

In the published responses to the *Memorandum* we learn that the *Memorandum*'s proposals with regard to the 'European Dimension' of higher education was seen as of crucial importance by many respondents, and that the 'dimension' secured a great degree of support and wide ranging consensus. The 'various actors' in higher education, we are told, are 'clearly committed' to 'enhanced Europeanisation'. With regard to the fundamental claims and concepts to which I am alluding, the respondents are, however, largely silent. Indeed, we learn that, on the whole, the respondents felt that further 'conceptual refinement' of the notion of the 'European Dimension' was unnecessary. The most prominent misgiving registered by respondents concerned matters of finance (Commission of the European Communities 1993b: Introduction and section 1). This suggests that their attention was mainly focused on the more practical aspects of the 'European Dimension' such as the Community programmes and the practical issues and strategies referred to earlier.

The lack of recognition by the respondents of the need for further 'conceptual refinement' of the 'European Dimension' as a whole is surprising and worrying, as is the fact that most (but not all) of the respondents found the claims and concepts that I am about to address unproblematic. Even when some respondents did raise critical questions about these matters, the issues at stake are not pursued in the published response document. The fundamental claims (and the concepts involved in them) are as follows:

i. the claim (the truth of which is reported as 'obvious') that higher education systems should play an 'active part' in helping to achieve 'the goals of European integration' (Commission of the European Communities 1993a: para. 1.1);
ii. the claim (against which it is reported that 'no-one argued') that 'passing on the European cultural heritage' is a key element in the 'European integration process whose foundation was basically cultural' (Commission of the European Communities 1993a: para. 2.3.2);
iii. the claim that the 'European Dimension' is an important means of confirming 'European Identity' (Commission of the European Communities 1993a: para. 2.3.2), and that higher education should cultivate a 'European affiliation' in students;
iv. the claim that the 'European Dimension' is importantly related to the development of European citizenship (Commission of the European Communities 1993a: Foreword).

As earlier, the criticism here is not that these claims and concepts, which can be interestingly compared to the Resolution on the European Dimension in Education adopted by the EC Ministers of Education on 24 May 1988, are necessarily false or unjustifiable. It is rather that they are under analysed and under explored by the respondents, and in discussion of European higher education in general. Depending on how they are interpreted, these 'claims and concepts' are potentially rich in implication for European higher education. These implications relate to such matters as the content of the curriculum (for example, the sort of history and literature which should be taught) and curriculum continuity, balance, and control. In addition, implications arise for questions of access, student location, and mobility. The implications also extend to the sorts of outcomes that should be expected of higher education institutions both directly and indirectly and the sort of role they should play with respect to society. However, it is difficult to discern and evaluate these implications in the absence of an analysis of the complexities not addressed in the claims and concepts. Some of the complexities not addressed are the following:

(i) the claim that higher education should play a role in achieving the goals of European integration gives rise to at least three questions. First, how precisely is 'European integration' being understood here? The *Memorandum* nowhere explicitly addresses this central question, and no attempt is made to draw even the most basic distinctions between (say) economic, political, and cultural senses of the term. In two successive paragraphs, for example, the *Memorandum* uses the term 'integration' in the first paragraph and 'unification' in the second without exploring whether or not the terms are to be understood equivalently (Commission of the European Communities 1991: paras 41, 42). In the absence of important distinctions such as these, it is impossible to understand what might be meant by 'the goals of European integration', let alone the meaning and justifiability of the role of higher education in relation to them. Reference to higher education being invited to help realise 'Community objectives' (Commission of the European Communities 1991: para. 49) seems to suggest that it is being given a very specific agenda to achieve, to which the Treaty on European Union is a guide. The second question arises from the important point that many aspects of European integration are the subject of deep-seated and well-grounded controversy. The claim that higher education has a role in *achieving* European integration (in whatever sense) seems to sit ill with the acknowledgement in the *Memorandum* of the responsibility of higher education to foster independent judgement and the spirit of criticism (Commission of the European Communities 1991: para. 4). This acknowledgement is at least in significant tension with the observation elsewhere in the same document that in higher education 'the age and experience of the students ... better enables them to be responsive to a grand political design' (Commission of the European Communities 1991: para. 44) and the reference to 'the importance of the support which young people can bring to European integration' (Commission of the European Communities 1991: para. 41). These matters need to be related in a much more nuanced way to an account of the proper role of education in relation to them (see Commission of the European Communities 1991: paras 42, 43). It seems clear that higher education has an important responsibility to offer a reasoned critique of aspects of European integration, and to allow room for a range of considered views on the matter. The concern expressed by some respondents that 'Euro-ideology' not be forcibly introduced into higher education courses accurately identifies a central worry here (Commission of the European Communities 1993b: p. E-103). The third question concerns whether it is appropriate to see higher education as having an extrinsic aim of whatever kind. This stands in conflict with the deeply rooted tradition that higher education is not *for* any extrinsic end.

(ii) the claim that culture and its transmission are central to the process of European integration is clearly impossible to understand and evaluate in the absence of the sort of clear analysis of the notion of 'integration' that has been called for. The reported perception of 'most respondents' to the *Memorandum* that the foundation for a united Europe is 'basically cultural' (Commission of the European Communities 1993a: para. 2; see also 7) is, to put it mildly, unclear. Interpreted as implying that Europe could benefit from a shared *political* culture in the sense of a commitment to democratic values, procedures and institutions, the perception has much to commend it. It is perhaps this sense of 'culture' that lies behind the observation in the Synthesis report that Europe needs a 'general, comprehensive culture' that can 'absorb' the historical, cultural, economic and social tensions that beset European society and threaten to destroy its social fabric (Commission of the European Communities 1993a: para. 2.3). The claim that the 'European cultural heritage' can strengthen the spirit of citizenship in 'a democratic and caring' society (Commission of the European Communities 1993a: para. 2.1) also seems to invite a political interpretation of 'culture'. In other places, however, 'culture' in a fuller sense seems to be invoked. In relation to this broader notion a host of questions arise. What is the nature of its 'heritage'? In what sense is it 'common' to Europe? Might an emphasis on it be restrictive with respect to the wider and more global perspective that is needed on many matters, as Paul Smeyers suggests in his contribution to this volume? What role precisely does it play in relation to 'integration'? The commitment in the *Memorandum* to preserving the 'diversity' of this 'heritage' calls into question the ability of the 'heritage' to help with matters of integration as well as raising questions about the sense in which it is common to Europe (Commission of the European Communities 1991: paras 40, 41; see Commission of the European Communities 1993a: para. 2.3.2). Questions of this kind are not illuminated by references such as that in the *Memorandum* to an unspecified 'cultural progress' which characterises the 'increasingly integrated' European Community (Commission of the European Communities 1991: para. 60). A full discussion of all these matters is required.

The complex questions that arise in relation to the notion of 'European culture' present themselves in a similar form in the context of the claim that higher education should help to form a 'European identity', claim (iii) above. Again, the primary question here is one of meaning. What is meant by the claim that higher education should promote 'a European identity and commitment' (Commission of the European Communities 1991: para. 49)? Again, this claim is ambiguous as between a political sense of identity and one that is more full. In the case of the former, does 'European identity' include an act of explicit commitment to the aims and values of the EC, or does it involve a more passive 'identity' arising from, say, the fact of holding a passport? In the case of the latter fuller sense of identity, in what does it consist, and how distinctive, important, and salient can it be (questions explored from a sceptical point of view by Kevin Williams in his contribution to this volume)? Williams's argument should lead us to be cautious about the claim that the development of a 'European identity' is a necessary 'first step' for many people in embarking on the international dimension of higher education (Commission of the European Communities 1993b: p. E-88). A recently published study of pupils' perceptions of Europe in different member countries of the EU is relevant here. Of the sample of fourteen to sixteen year-olds interviewed, 90 percent of interviewees in the Netherlands described themselves as 'totally European', whilst the figure fell to 42 percent of French participants in the study and only 19 percent of interviewees in England. Further, 40 percent of the English interviewees did not think of themselves as European (Convery, Evans, Green, Macaro, and Mellor 1997). The fact that the *Memorandum* places an inverted comma around 'identity' at one point shows that it is unsure about quite how the term should be used (Commission of the European Communities 1991: para. 87). Yet this renders opaque the various claims made throughout the document that invoke the notion, not least those relating to how the educational development of a 'European Identity' can be construed and justified. It is important to note that the *Memorandum* concedes that European identity can and should coexist with regional and national allegiances (Commission of the European Communities 1991: para. 49). It is occasionally unclear, however, how 'Europe' is to be understood. Does it refer merely to the member-states of the European Community or the larger European continent? (On this see, for example, Commission of the European Communities 1991: para. 152.) Again, one is confronted by a host of issues requiring attention.

The claim in (iv) above, concerning the relationship between the 'European Dimension' and the development of European citizenship, is equally difficult to bring clearly into focus. The *Memorandum* merely alludes to the topic in a vague way. For example, reference is made to the 'higher educational attainments' that are needed 'in order to put people in a position to ... exercise their citizen's responsibilities within a wider Europe'(Commission of the European Communities 1991: para. 60), but the nature of these attainments is never illuminated and neither is the concept of 'European citizenship' itself. In a later point in the document there is a reference to the potential of open and distance education to teach about the European Commission and its laws, institutions, and policies, but the significance of this kind of learning for 'education for citizenship' is undeveloped (Commission of the European Communities 1991: para. 93). The *Memorandum* contains a number of other undeveloped hints relevant to the notion of citizenship – for example, a comment about the significance for the future of the European Community of 'the understanding and commitment which support significant political transformations', including the achievement of 'cohesiveness' among Community citizens (Commission of the European Communities 1991: Foreword). The Green Paper on the European Dimension of Education recently published by the European Commission does not offer very much more on this topic (Commission of the European Communities 1993c: paras 13–15). Again, we find an important example of claims and concepts that are not properly explored and articulated.

This neglect of some of the central claims and concepts implicit within the notion of the 'European Dimension' of higher education should lead the respondents to the *Memorandum* to be more qualified in their acceptance of that dimension. For example, it is not clear that the proposal that higher education institutions should have clear and carefully monitored policies for 'Europeanising' their activities (Commission of the European Communities 1993a: para. 7) should escape detailed analysis.

It seems that the claims and concepts which have been discussed tend to play a merely rhetorical function in the discourse of the 'European Dimension'. Attention is focused on the immediate and tangible realities of Community programmes, policies, and strategies. The degree of unanimity about the 'European Dimension' in the responses arises in part because the term is constantly being employed 'in its broadest sense' (Commission of the European Communities 1993a: para. 1.2.3) and the underlying central claims and concepts are seen as marking vague realities which can perhaps be realised as a by-product of the programmes, policies, and strategies rather than by clarity of vision (at least on these matters). However, inadequate conceptualisation of the sort that has been referred to can both lead to harmful, and inhibit good educational practice. Critical attention to claims and concepts is therefore important.

(For one reported response which was exceptional in criticising ambiguity, see Commission of the European Communities 1993b: p. E-87). One of the main difficulties with the claims and concepts (i) to (iv) discussed above is that, at least on some interpretations, they might be thought to involve unjustifiable educational influence of two kinds. First, unjustifiable influence may be exerted upon institutions of higher education to transform their work in various ways. Second, this transformation may involve forms of unjustifiable educational influence upon students. For example, in relation to (i) students may be influenced to adopt a particular view on the controversial question of 'European integration'; in relation to (ii) they may be subjected to an ill-conceived and inappropriate form of cultural influence; (iii) may lead to an unduly particular 'identity' being formed in them; and in relation to (iv) they may be invited to assume a potentially problematic 'European citizenship'.

Different aspects of the various questions raised by these matters are discussed by other contributors to this volume. In what follows, I will seek to illuminate one aspect of the question of unjustifiable educational influence upon students by focusing in the next section upon what might be thought to be acceptable in this regard for students up to the age of eighteen ('school students'). After looking at the issues at this level, I shall attempt to draw out the implications of the discussion for higher education.

Education and Democracy: General and Particular Influence

The societies which make up the European Union are, to a greater or lesser extent, pluralist liberal democracies. We can therefore use as a reference point for our discussion of acceptable influence upon school students the principles and values typically associated with liberal democracy, and a conception of education typically associated with such societies. Despite the imprecision involved in a brief account, I trust that this general conception both of society and of education will be familiar enough, at least in general outline, from what follows. I shall offer some reflections about education in general in the first instance, and will address specific questions relating to higher education in due course.

Any conception of education based on liberal democratic principles is suspicious of unduly particular influence, especially when the particularity involved concerns the shaping of individuals in ways which presuppose values and commitments that are, from a democratic point of view, significantly controversial. The sort of education attempted in totalitarian societies is seen as objectionable from a democratic perspective on precisely these grounds. In the pre-*perestroika* Soviet Union, for example, education attempted to shape a particular identity in students based on a significantly controversial theory of the good. This education was designed to bring about the sort of unified, detailed, moral formation contained in the notion of *vospitanie*. In this process, individuality, criticism, and variety were subordinated to Marxist–Leninist theory, which determined the aims and methods of a monolithic and centralised system of schools. These schools, together with youth organisations and the media, all conspired in a coordinated way to develop the ideal communist person, complete with collectivist and atheistic beliefs and qualities of character (see, for example, Halstead 1994).

In contrast, education based on liberal democratic principles seeks to avoid such a particularistic formation. It might be argued, of course, that a 'liberal democratic' form of education is itself based on a theory of the good which is 'particular' and 'significantly controversial'. Such an education, it might be claimed, also tries to shape a certain sort of person, and to impart a 'particular' individual identity. In reply, a proponent of 'liberal democratic' education will argue that, whilst there is some truth in these objections, education based on democratic principles seeks to reduce particularistic influence to a minimum. Further, the proponent will claim that a liberal democratic form of education is committed to an underlying theory of the good which is maximally hospitable to individual autonomy and to differences of view. Whilst a full articulation and evaluation of a 'liberal democratic' conception of education is beyond the scope of this chapter, its general character can be briefly sketched in the following way (see, for example, Gutmann 1987; McLaughlin 1992; McLaughlin 1995).

The task of education in pluralistic liberal democratic societies is conceptualised in the light of two important realities. First, education of whatever form is inherently value-laden, the values involved being of many different kinds. No form of education can be value-free or value-neutral. The question which arises for education is therefore not *whether* it should be based on and should transmit values but *which* values should be invoked. The second reality is the well-grounded, deep-seated, and perhaps ineradicable difference of view concerning many questions of value that is characteristic of pluralistic liberal democratic societies. This is not to suggest that such societies are entirely bereft of value agreement and consensus. If this were so, it would be hard to see how these societies could achieve stability and coherence, much less satisfy the value commitments and demands implicit in democracy, such as justice, freedom, and personal autonomy. There are, however, large areas of disagreement about many questions, most notably about overall views of life as a whole, or 'comprehensive' theories of the good.

In the light of these two realities, public education of school students in pluralistic liberal democratic societies, at least in common schools attended by students from all backgrounds, seeks to base its substantial value influence on principles broadly acceptable to the citizens of society as a whole. This requires that this form of education cannot assume the truth of, or promote, any particular, comprehensive, or all-embracing, vision of the good life. Rather, it aims at a complex twofold influence. On matters which are widely agreed and which can be regarded as part of the common or basic values of the society, education seeks to achieve a strong, substantial influence on the beliefs of students and their wider development as persons. It is unhesitating, for example, in promoting the values of basic 'social morality' and democratic 'civic virtue' more generally. Involved here is the notion of 'an education adequate to serve the life of a free and equal citizen in any modern democracy' (Gutmann 1992: p.14) which includes the notions of both education for a significant form of personal autonomy and for democratic citizenship (see McLaughlin 1992). On matters of serious disagreement, however, where scope for a legitimate diversity of view is acknowledged, education seeks to achieve a principled forbearance of influence: it seeks not to shape either the beliefs or the personal qualities of students in the light of any substantial or 'comprehensive' conception of the good which is significantly controversial. Instead, public education either is silent about such matters or encourages students to come to their own reflective decisions about them. One way of expressing in an overall way the nature of educational influence on this view is that it exerts a complex combination of centripetal (unifying) and centrifugal (diversifying) forces on students and on society itself.

On this view, therefore, instead of encouraging students to become committed to any one substantial view of life as a whole, education is charged with encouraging students to engage in independent critical reflection and to achieve, at least to a significant extent, an appropriate form of self-directness and personal autonomy consistent with the demands of democratic citizenship. It is not merely 'substantial views of life as whole' that education of this kind is suspicious of. It also calls into question the sorts of potentially unjustifiable educational influence in relation to the 'claims and concepts' discussed above. With regard to (i) for example, the claim that education must help to achieve the goals of 'European integration' is confronted by an insistence that students must be helped to come to their own critical assessment of the matters at stake. (ii), the claim that the transmission of 'European culture' has a role in achieving integration, adds to this insistence a concern that the notion of 'European culture' be carefully interrogated and that tendencies to artificial and arbitrary conceptualisation and imposition be resisted. In addition, there is a concern that 'culture' should not be used for an extrinsic end. The claims in (iii) and (iv) – that education should confirm 'European identity' and 'European citizenship' respectively – give rise to worries about unduly specific influence and shaping in these matters. The general or universalistic thrust in the liberal democratic conception of education is well captured in Charles Bailey's insistence that liberal education must lead students 'beyond the present and the particular', including the 'incestuous ties of clan and soil' (Bailey 1984: pp. 20–22).

The difficulties involved in articulating and defending a form of education with these general and universalistic emphases are considerable, particularly given, say, the undermining of some of the foundations of this kind of educational influence by the sorts of post modern perspectives discussed by other contributors to this volume. In the context of higher education, for example, some of the responses to the *Memorandum* draw attention to the question of whether higher education can continue to be based on notions of reason, universality, and good citizenship. The question is posed in this way: 'Do these values still hold good in a society which tends to glorify local origins and cultures, encouraging emotional reactions and the cult of the individual, and which sometimes calls into question the need for progress, education and even humanism' (Commission of the European Communities 1993a: para. 2.3.1). Leaving aside challenging questions of this kind at this point, it is important to note, and to explore, the significance, even within the terms of the 'liberal democratic' conception of education, of 'the demands of particularity'.

Education and the Significance of Particularity

Education and schooling, however much it might seek to transcend particularities, cannot escape from them. Education cannot take place in a vacuum. It is necessarily conducted in particular social, political, and cultural contexts. The schools of a liberal democratic society cannot therefore avoid transmitting some norms which are culturally distinctive in that they selectively favour some beliefs, practices, and values in ways that go beyond what could be justified from a strictly neutral or 'global' point of view. Amy Gutmann notes that in the U.S.A. local communities have been given the democratic right to shape their schools in their own cultural image, within principled liberal democratic constraints (Gutmann 1987:

pp. 41–47, 71–75). But within these limits, the shared beliefs and cultural practices which are particular to communities can be transmitted and maintained.

The identity which is developed in students by the educational process is (to a significant extent) therefore inevitably concrete and particular, shaped by the specificity of the social, political, and cultural context in which this process takes place. Education may seek to transcend these particularities, but they cannot be avoided. Education for citizenship, for example, involves the student coming to understand matters of general democratic principle. But, since there is no abstract 'democratic citizen' who is not the citizen of a particular place, this process cannot be wholly general. This point is well summed up in De Maistre's remark that 'I have seen, in my times, Frenchmen, Italians and Russians ... but as for Man, I declare I have never met him in my life' (quoted in Tamir 1993: p.13). The ingredients of a local identity formed by education are wide ranging and include such matters as language, literature, custom, and sensibility. The significance of such local and substantial ingredients for personal identity, recognition, and flourishing have been acknowledged by many writers, including the communitarian critics of liberalism (on these critics, see, for example, Mulhall and Swift 1996: especially Part 1). Nor can such local and substantial identities be seen as opposed to autonomy and freedom. On the contrary, as Yael Tamir insists, 'no individual can be context-free, but ... all can be free within a context' (Tamir 1993: p.14). Such a context is indeed a prerequisite for freedom.

What appropriate forms of local and substantial commitment should education in a liberal democratic society seek to develop in students? In matters of broadly political identity, it has been suggested that students could be encouraged to develop a certain sort of patriotism focused on an imaginatively enriched concern for the community as a whole (see Callan 1991; Callan 1994). To what extent, however, should the development of the sorts of 'European' commitment and identity discussed earlier be seen as appropriate and desirable? It is useful to approach this matter via consideration of the appropriateness and desirability of developing a national identity in students.

The Nature and Value of National Identity

David Miller, in his recent philosophical defence of the concept of nationality, offers an account of it which involves eight interconnected propositions (Miller 1993). These are presented here in a slightly reordered form.

i. National identity may be a constitutive part of personal identity ('may' is important for Miller here, since he does not advance the implausible claim that personal identity *requires* a national identity).
ii. Nations are ethical communities in the sense that 'nationality' generates distinctive ethical obligations and expectations. We may have, for example, fuller duties to fellow nationals than we do to human beings as such.
iii. National communities are constituted by *belief*: 'a nationality exists when its members believe that it does' (Miller 1993: p. 6) rather than simply by any common attribute such as race or language. Examples of the shared beliefs at stake here include a conviction that its members belong together and that they wish to continue their life in common. Miller agrees with Benedict Anderson's claim that nations are 'imaginary' in that they are sustained by acts of the individual and collective imagination (Anderson 1983).
iv. Members of a nation must, however, share certain distinctive traits. These may be varied in character, and include cultural features.
v. Nations must embody historical continuity, generating depth of involvement and obligation in ways not found in more transitory groupings.
vi. Nations are related to a particular geographical place.
vii. Nations are 'active' in the sense that 'they' do things, take decisions, and so on.
viii. Nations must be, at least in aspiration, political communities. People who form a national community have a good claim to political self-determination, although not necessarily via a sovereign state. The actions of nations must therefore include at least seeking to control 'a chunk of the earth's surface'(Miller 1993: p. 7). The validity of this claim has, however, been challenged. Yael Tamir, for example, argues that a nation may be a cultural community without necessarily any political dimensions (Tamir 1993: ch. 3).

A number of important distinctions relating to national identity require acknowledgement here. A nation is not to be identified with a state. A state is a legal and political entity with authority of a specific form (sovereignty), resources of power of various kinds, and a well-defined territory. Some nations do not have a state, and many modern states, in view of their cultural heterogeneity, cannot be identified with a national society. Many states are multinational in that they contain a number of national communities and cultures. Further, nationality should be distinguished from nationalism. Helpful here is Michael Ignatieff's distinction between 'civic' and 'ethnic' nationalism (Ignatieff 1994: pp. 3–6). Civic nationalism is democratic in character, envisaging the nation as a community of equal, rights-bearing citizens, patriotically attached to a shared set of political practices and values. In contrast, ethnic nationalism sees national identity as based on ethnicity rather than citizenship and law. Whilst civic nationalism can be rational, flexible, pluralistic, and morally rich, ethnic nationalism is tempted by irrationality, fanaticism, and authoritarianism. It is more likely to be 'nationalistic' in the sense of the term which implies the inherent superiority of one nation over others. The distinction between 'civic' and 'ethnic' nationalism is further illuminated by the distinction, which Tamir draws, between 'citizenship' and 'nationhood'. Citizenship is a primarily legal concept referring to the relationship between a state and its formal members, embracing such matters as entitlements, rights, and liberties. Nationhood involves a sense of membership in an imagined community, and the adoption and practice of a particular imagined cultural and communal identity. In Ignatieff's 'civic' nationalism, 'nationhood' embraces 'citizenship' and does not contradict it.

What is the value of nationality? The general benefits of nationality include affiliation, attachment, embeddedness, belonging and communal identity, and solidarity, all of which resonate with the communitarian themes alluded to earlier. Nationality is clearly a significant element in the formation of personal identity.

The question of whether a European identity could provide an alternative or supplementary source of these benefits is an important question.

The Importance of Civic Attachments

What, however, is the value of nationality, or indeed any equivalent attachment, from the perspective of democratic principles and values, and from the perspective of the 'liberal democratic' conception of education that is under discussion? The tension between 'ethnic' nationalism and these principles and values is readily apparent. This is less so in the case of 'civic' nationalism. In 'civic' nationalism, democratic principles and values may be 'clothed' by features of nationality, and not submerged by them. It is this sort of nationalism which Miller has in mind in his claim that one of the benefits of nationalism is that it is a *de facto* source of the large-scale solidarity that is needed in complex societies if social atomisation is to be avoided and collective goods secured. Nations can provide an 'overarching sense of community' of the sort that facilitates this. Since in Miller's view national identity has a flexible, because partly mythic, character, it is capable of accommodating a number of different points of political view, and is therefore open to cultural pluralism and to criticism (Miller 1993). These emphases upon flexibility, pluralism, and criticism are important features of 'civic' nationalism. It is in the light of considerations such as these that John White argues that the notion of 'British' identity and nationality needs to be reworked to make it acceptable in terms of democratic criteria (White 1996; see Enslin 1993/94).

The educational implications of 'civic' nationalism are wide ranging. Although these implications cannot be explored in any detail at this point, education for nationality in the 'civic' sense must clearly be conducted in close connection with education for personal autonomy and for democratic citizenship. With regard to the development of personal autonomy, Tamir notes that 'civic' nationalism is compatible with the 'elective' aspects of our personal identity, which is an important democratic emphasis. Our lives should not be determined by history and fate, and significant possibilities for reflective choice should be insisted upon (Tamir 1993: ch. 1). With regard to the development of democratic citizenship, the significance of 'civic' nationality for appropriate forms of solidarity is important. One important aspect of the educational development of a 'civic' national identity is the significance of the development in students of capacities for broad critical reflection and understanding, informed by a political and general education of some substance (see, for example, McLaughlin 1992; Williams 1995b). This involves amongst other things a study of the political and other principles relevant to democracy: the study of the western European philosophical political tradition. The task of developing a 'civic' national identity is not, however, unproblematic, not least because of the corrosive effects upon it of the liberal democratic demands of criticism, justification, and transparency.

The important point to note here is the significance of civic attachments from a democratic point of view. They may be associated with, or 'clothed by', particular substantive attachments and identities, such as those distinctive of 'civic nationalism', but offer, and insist upon, a more general identity that is derived from the values and demands of democracy. The question of whether a 'European identity' of some kind could provide an alternative or supplementary source of the benefits of national identity in general is an important question which is addressed by a number of other contributors to this volume. However, a more precise question raised by the present discussion concerns the meaning and possibility of a 'civic' form of European identity – one based on a shared liberal democratic political tradition of thought and practice. A foundation for such a form of European identity is the western European philosophical and political tradition relating to democracy that has already been alluded to. Another foundation is the determination to promote democratic principles and values throughout the member states of the EC, not least with the aim of preventing the re-emergence of the conflicts that have bedevilled Europe in the past. On this view a European identity is seen as a 'portmanteau' identity constituted primarily by liberal democratic commitments. Educational influence in the formation of a European identity in this 'civic' sense is well grounded, and can be defended in the face of the sorts of concerns about unduly specific educational influence of the sort outlined above. However, it is important to note that the development of a 'civic' European identity leaves open and does not foreclose a number of central issues relating to the four 'claims and concepts' discussed earlier. With regard to (iii) for example, the sort of 'European identity' that is being shaped in students is seen in precisely 'civic' terms, rather than in a more contentious way. This means that a critical eye needs to be cast upon materials for school students that invite them to adopt a 'European identity' in a fuller sense (see, for example, Couloubaritsis, De Leeuw, Noel, and Sterckx 1993). In relation to (i), the whole question of the nature and value of 'European integration' is left open for critical assessment. With regard to (ii) the concept of 'European culture' involved is seen primarily in political terms. As Joseph Dunne suggests in this volume, a shared European political culture is compatible with, and is enhanced by, a diversity of other aspects of culture throughout Europe. In relation to (iv) the development of European citizenship is seen as primarily concerned with the formation and application of shared democratic values and principles relevant to Europe rather than with the formation of 'European citizens' in a way that prejudges certain controversial judgements relating to matters such as European integration. (On teaching for 'Citizenship in Europe' see, for example, Osler, Rathenow, and Starkey 1995.)

The Role of Higher Education

The extent to which schools throughout the European Community are orientated towards European questions varies considerably (on the neglect of these matters in schools in England see, for example, Morrell 1996). However, in the previous section, an indication has been offered of the sorts of principles that might be invoked to determine appropriate educational influence on school students with regard to the four 'claims and concepts' that have been identified.

What are the implications of this discussion for higher education? In considering this question it is useful to return to the two sorts of potentially unjustifiable educational influence mentioned earlier arising from the 'claims and concepts'.The discussion in the last section has been concerned with the second of these – influence upon students. It is appropriate to begin this part of the discussion, however, by addressing at the outset the first sort of influence mentioned – influence upon educational institutions.

It might be thought appropriate to invite, or even require, schools to exercise influence over their students with respect to the issues relating to the four 'claims and concepts'in a way that it would it not be appropriate to invite institutions of higher education. The influence upon students that is involved, it might be argued, forms a part of school-level education in a way that it does not form part of higher education. Given that both schools and institutions of higher education are concerned with education it can be assumed that it is defensible influence upon students of the sort outlined in the previous section that is at issue. The question, however, is whether an expectation that institutions of higher education will necessarily address these matters in any way is inappropriate. For example, the *Memorandum* gives a number of reasons why higher education should be seen as having a particular role with respect to European integration: the range of studies it offers, its responsibility in educating for the cultural professions, and its commitment through developing as well as transmitting cultural heritage (Commission of the European Communities 1991: para. 43). However, such views confront the objection that such tasks related to European integration are not appropriate ones for higher education to undertake. The tasks may be achieved as an indirect result of higher education, it will be replied, but they are not ones that higher education exists to perform. A resolution of this matter requires a detailed consideration of the proper aims and values of higher education, and of how we should understand the notion of a 'university' (for a bibliographical essay on the idea of the university in scholarly literature see Pelikan 1992: ch. 18). Prominent among the themes requiring attention here is the adequacy of the tradition, associated particularly with Michael Oakeshott, of seeing the aims and values of higher education as being unrelated to extrinsic purpose of any kind (see Fuller 1989). Some of the emphases of the 'liberal democratic' conception of education outlined earlier are deeply rooted in the notion of higher education. Ronald Barnett, for example, notes that while the idea of higher education has a long history of development and change, and that it is to some extent inevitably culturally specific, there is a strong level of agreement about what its 'cognitive core' is: about what is to count as higher education (Barnett 1990: ch. 2). For Barnett this is:

> a general allegiance to the university having as its dominant idea a community of individuals collaborating in a particular form of life, namely an inquiry into knowledge and truth ... an inquiry which is sensitive to the interconnectedness of different domains of knowledge, and the difficulties of obtaining real knowledge ... conducted in a critical spirit, having as an outcome new ways of perceiving the familiar. A fundamental condition of the process of higher education is a lessening of the taken-for-grantedness of the individual's hold on the world. It is in this sense that higher education essentially embodies a liberal outlook or ... an emancipatory concept of education. (Barnett 1990: p. 23).

For Barnett, higher education must preserve its emancipatory character, even if, for various reasons, it cannot properly be seen as an 'ivory tower' with respect to society (Barnett 1990: ch. 5), and its central cultural influence upon society must be seen not as the transmission of any elusive (and possible elitist) 'common culture' but as strengthening the culture of critical discourse (Barnett 1990: chs 7, 12). The defensibility of seeing part of the 'emancipatory' role of higher education as embracing a responsibility to promote the values and wellbeing of liberal democratic societies has been developed by a number of writers. Michael Luntley, for example, considers that universities have an important role to play in the renovation of political culture (see Luntley 1996; see also Brecher, Fleischmann, and Halliday 1996). Given the arguments developed in the last section, it might be argued that part of this role might extend to the developing in students of a 'civic' European identity, political culture, and citizenship of the sort that has been delineated.

Even if this role for higher education was accepted in principle, however, it should be noted that any attempt to exert influence on institutions of higher education in Europe to fulfil this role is fraught with difficulty. One of the major problems here is the diversity of the European higher education system, which is taken to include all general and specialised education beyond secondary school level (Commission of the European Communities 1993a: para. 2.2). The *Memorandum* informs us that there are over 3,500 diverse higher education institutions in the member-states, serving around 6.75 million students (Commission of the European Communities 1991: paras 48, 141). This difficulty is enhanced by the fact that the diversity which is characteristic of the system is regarded as a positive value (Commission of the European Communities 1991: para. 147). It is hard to see how unity of purpose in any substantial sense could be agreed for institutions across the European Community as a whole.

With regard to the second potentially unjustifiable educational influence mentioned earlier, influence upon students, there are also important differences between schools and institutions of higher education. One of the major differences here is that schools can embody their influence in a core curriculum which is offered to all students, and in the life of an institution as a whole which can demand a degree of consistency of engagement and experience. These conditions do not obtain so readily in institutions of higher education. The specialised nature of course and study programmes inhibits the sorts of planned 'core' learning for all students at higher education level to which the demands of European civic education might be thought to give rise. There is support for the development of 'core' curriculum elements related to the 'European Dimension' (Commission of the European Communities 1993a: p. E-103; see Commission of the European Communities 1991: paras 116, 119–20), and the *Memorandum* gives its support to discussions about curriculum balance (Commission of the European Communities 1991: para. 52). It might be thought, however, that such discussions and initiatives are naive with respect to what can be achieved in these matters, not least because of suspicion of the role of the EC in curriculum planning. Increasingly, even within individual higher education institutions, the academic community and the experiences offered to its students are diverse. Clark Kerr considers 'multiversity' a better description of contemporary higher education institutions than 'university' and offers his famous observation that they have become 'a series of individual faculty entrepreneurs held together by a common grievance over parking' (quoted in Barnett 1990: p. 97). A further contrast between the educational influence exerted upon students by schools and by institutions of higher education relates to the much higher salience of critical questioning in the latter. Francis Crawley, in this volume, draws attention to the inherently corrosive effect of criticism in institutions of higher education upon any attempt to develop relevant forms of solidarity in education for European citizenship.

For various reasons, therefore, the two sorts of potentially unjustifiable educational influence arising from the 'claims and concepts' are much more easily realised in schools than in institutions of higher education. Schools as institutions, and the educational experience they offer to their students, are (arguably) more readily controlled and are more susceptible to the imposition of potentially objectionable interpretations of the 'claims and concepts'. This is why a discussion of the sorts of principles relevant to appropriate forms of educational influence in these matters is so important. Institutions of higher education are less susceptible to the imposition of these potentially objectionable interpretations and are likely to respond in a piecemeal way to invitations to embrace the 'European dimension', focusing in the way suggested earlier upon the immediate and tangible realities of Community programmes, policies, and strategies, and seeing the 'claims and concepts' as having merely rhetorical significance. Many of these programmes, policies, and strategies have considerable value in themselves, and do not depend upon any potentially objectionable interpretations of the 'claims and concepts'. Many of these initiatives embody, or at least leave room for, precisely the critical attitude to the 'claims and concepts' that has been called for. Examples here include the Erasmus Curriculum Development project, 'Education for Citizenship in a New Europe: Learning Democracy, Social Justice, Global Responsibility and Respect for Human Rights' (see Osler, Rathenow, and Starkey 1995), and EC-funded research in several European universities on the different 'discourses' of citizenship engaged in by teachers in a number of different member states (see Arnot, Araujo, Deliyanni-Kouimtzi, Rowe, and Tome 1996).

The failure of the *Memorandum* adequately to analyse its 'claims and concepts' is, however, important. This is not just for the negative reason that vigilance is needed with respect to the possibility of unjustifiable educational influence, but also for the positive reason of attempting to discern what justifiable educational influence higher education institutions should exert in these matters. For example, the claim that higher education has a role in engaging in a form of 'European civic education' is a controversial one. However, in the light of the discussion in the last section about the sorts of defensible educational influence that can be exerted upon students arising from an appropriate interpretation of the 'claims and concepts', it might be thought that such a proposal is worthy of consideration. In the absence of an adequate analysis of the 'claims and concepts', however, such a consideration is greatly inhibited.

Chapter 2

The Myth of a European Identity:
The Role of the Universities in the Formation of European Citizens

Francis P. Crawley

However we are disposed to approach university education today, whatever vantage point we should decide to take when reflecting on the role of the European university, it appears to be inescapable that we stand on the threshold of changes that are without precedent for this institution rooted in (and rooting) European culture. It is the task of the philosopher of education to reflect on the practices that define the institution of education at a particular point in time, both those practices acting within and those impinging from without. The aim of this essay is to describe the role of the university in European society today, focusing particularly on the role it plays in the formation of European citizens. The concept of citizenship has become more laden philosophically and more complex politically than perhaps at any other time in European history.[1] To add the qualification 'European' to our embedded notions of citizenship only further complicates the problematic and invites controversy. The controversy is heightened when education, especially university education, is employed as a means for achieving 'European citizenship' through the development of a 'European dimension' in education. Since the signing of the Treaty on European Union in Maastricht (1992), education has become an overt vehicle for achieving a common political community of citizens. We need to understand both the threat and the promise of this 'European dimension' if we are to grasp how education is perceived to act in the formation of 'the idea of European citizenship'.[2]

For most philosophers (perhaps all) the university stands at the heart of their activity, and it establishes the commanding perspective from which proceeds their reflection on society. It is the place from which a reflective grasp of history, science, literature, and culture is made possible. However, this strategic locale for reflecting on (and passing on) the icons of social intercourse is not simply a mirroring of a pre-delineated activity; a university (and its education) is more than simply an instance for echoing an external activity. According to Jaroslav Pelikan, 'a modern society is unthinkable without the university.' This is because the university not only holds a 'critical position' regarding government, industry, technology, and societal relations; but perhaps more importantly because the university is at the same time able to put into question the institutions and values that underlie our practices. 'If,' writes Pelikan echoing Voltaire, 'the university did not exist, it would be necessary to invent it' (Pelikan 1992: p. 17). Without the university we would lose the special place in our society that offers us room for reflection and critique, a place that makes it possible for society to conceptualise and express a certain concern regarding its activities and engagements. The unique force of the university in our societies is its capacity to provide an integrated discourse that projects the prejudices, rationality, and concerns expressed in the differing activities of our communities.

The Place of the Universities in European Culture

Oakeshott calls the engagement of the university 'a conversational encounter' with 'particular adventures in human self-understanding' (Oakeshott 1989: pp. 28–29). The project of the university is not, and never has been, the achievement or establishment of a singular rational or scientific voice. As 'encounter' the university is a place of meeting, of engagement, of exchange, and of reflection. Its utterances are the transformations of certain human activities into the idiom of a discursive understanding, guided by a specific understanding of truth and science. Oakeshott calls the underlying structure of this discursive understanding a conversation because he wants to emphasise that there is no sovereign or absolute point of view directing the quest for self-understanding and truth to which the university responds. The conversational structure of the university's discourse represents a wide variety of voices, each expressed in its own respective modality and register, and each similarly engaged in the pursuit of self-knowledge. This is never a purely logical or systematic structure; it embraces equally the rhetoric of metaphor and the ambivalence of emotion. At the same time, it is a dislocated conversation, a conversation separated from the immediacy of the idiomatic activities to which it gives expression. The reflective engagement of the university is made possible by the imposition of an interval separating human conduct from reflective thought.

The university is that place in our society where we come to an understanding of ourselves as individuals committed to specific projects within a community having a recognisable culture and a shared identity. This is the role, not so much for which the university was designed, but which it created for itself. From its origin in medieval society the university enacted a place to theorise the contingencies of the human situation, to assemble theory into the coherence and unity of science, and to initiate the next generation of scholars and citizens into the discourse appropriate to the engagements of society. Higher learning entails, in part, coming to see the commitment to individual projects as a form of participation in the expression and development of a society's culture. Oakeshott, in explaining the structure of a university's conversation, defines 'culture' as follows:

> It is useful to have a word which stands for the whole of what an associated set of human beings have created for themselves beyond the evanescent satisfaction of their wants, but we must not be misled by it. A culture is not a doctrine or a set of consistent teachings or conclusions about a human life. It is not something we can see before ourselves as the subject of learning, any more than we can set self-understanding before ourselves as something to be learned: it is that which is learned in everything we may learn. A culture, particularly one such as ours, is a continuity of feelings, perceptions, ideas, engagements, attitudes and so forth, pulling in different directions, often critical of one another and contingently related to one another. (Oakeshott 1989: p. 28)

Culture is neither an established standard nor a devised end for the education provided by a university. Rather culture is the achievement of the adventure called education; it is the wavering goal in the journey toward self-understanding expressed in the epithet 'know thyself'. It is not, though, an achievement simply lying at the end of a pilgrimage waiting to be recovered. Culture is part and partial of the journey itself. It is there at the beginning and informs the journey throughout. The end of the journey is death, which is always singular and unique. However, the accomplishments of the journey remain in the iconography of expressions that the participants have created.

Culture might be defined as what Neils Bohr called 'the background that we loosely refer to as "ourselves"' (quoted in Petersen

1985: p. 310). An individual's or a society's culture is the inventory of actions and expressions resulting from the specific engagements and commitments undertaken. Education opens up the possibilities for action based on an understanding (self-understanding) of this background. As such, culture is the product of education. In education we are confronted with (and, to a certain extent, released from) the ambiguities of our conceptual understanding, further enabling the conversation between the individual and society, as well as the conversation within the institutions of society itself, and the conversation between societies. Ever since its origins in the *studium generale* the university has taken on a special role in the conversation, concerned not only to educate the citizens of a particular (European) society, but also to develop a discourse on science, truth, and affections that extended beyond the interests of the individual as citizen and member of a specific social/political community. The university opened up a special place in society where the various expressions of a society's culture could be represented in a reflective discourse, reformulated according to scientific principles, and critically passed on from one generation to the next. The university belonged wholly to the society in which it was situated, but in a special way. It belonged as a place set apart for a discursive encounter with the artefacts and engagements of the society.

In the 'Explanatory Memorandum' attached to the European Commission's proposal for the establishment of the Socrates Programmes, the objective of 'the gradual establishment of an open European area for education and training' guides the thinking behind the establishment of a foundation for further European action in higher education. The focus is on the development of a place, an 'area', in higher education for 'building up a European culture'. As is well accepted, a united Europe must be constructed. A Europe based on the concept of a shared citizenship will not come about of its own accord; it needs to be created. This formation of 'European identity and citizenship' requires that new areas be opened up in our institutions in order to make place for the development of a new conceptual understanding of citizenship. This conceptual understanding is to be constructed on the basis of what is seen to have lain dormant for so long in the cultural heritage of Europe, in the idea of Europe still pregnant with its ownmost possibilities. It is not simply a matter of reorganising syllabi and increasing student mobility that will generate the 'European dimension' necessary to realise 'the spirit of citizenship in a democratic and caring society based on Europe's cultural heritage'. Rather, European unity can only be achieved through a reformation that creates a new dimension, a new ontological place, in education[3] for a 'European culture' under construction (Commission of the European Communities 1994: pp. 2–4). A new dimension to European society is needed to realise the potential of a two-thousand-year-old idea of Europe.

This new area in the structure of a European university is certainly in no way limited to a purely economic dimension of higher education in society. Although the legitimisation of action at the European level is rooted in the strictly economic mandate of the European Community prior to the Treaty on European Union, the development of a 'European dimension'[4] in higher education has never been limited to such a narrow focus: 'To examine education and training in the context of employment does not mean reducing them simply to a means of obtaining qualifications. The essential aim of education and training has always been personal development and the successful integration of Europeans into society through the sharing of common values, the passing on of cultural heritage and the teaching of self-reliance' (European Commission 1995: p. 3). The 'European dimension' of higher education may have its political origin in the commonly agreed upon end of invigorating Europe's economic force in today's world; however, it clearly encompasses a complete revision of the concept of a European culture that goes beyond the narrow concept of a 'shared heritage': 'It is in the European dimension that a forward-looking society can be built' (European Commission 1995: p. 47). The 'European dimension' in higher education is nothing less than the focal point for the construction of a new concept of European culture. There is a conscious and deliberate attempt to shape the future against the background of a certain mythic understanding of the past and the responsibility of the present toward a haunting and elusive idea of what Europe, for so long, 'ought to be'. What needs to be achieved in the new space of a European dimension is precisely the potential of an idea inherent in the common European cultural heritage.

A concern with European culture, politics, and the role of the university is addressed in T.S. Eliot's *Notes Towards the Definition of Culture*. Writing some fifty years ago, Eliot similarly finds the impetus for his essay in a proposal for the construction of a new concept of culture through education. He begins the 'Introduction' to this essay by quoting Article I of the August 1945 draft constitution for a United Nations Educational Scientific and Cultural Organisation. He focuses on the use of the word 'culture' and (what appears to him as) its ambiguous and unexamined employment in the document.[5] The essay itself might be seen as an attempt to found a critical and argued definition of the word in order to inform and perhaps provide some guidance to the political world. Eliot argues for the existence of a European culture, based in Christianity, that is, a unified culture.

Although the fundamental features of this culture are rooted in 'the identities which we can discover in the various national cultures' (Eliot 1948: p. 121), its unity transcends the boundaries of politics: 'The unity of culture, in contrast to the unity of political organisation, does not require us all to have only one loyalty: it means that there will be a variety of loyalties. It is wrong that the only duty of the individual should be held to be towards the State; it is fantastic to hold that the supreme duty of every individual should be towards a Super-State' (Eliot 1948: p. 121). One's duty, the conception of one's moral and political obligations, is the outcome of an education whose background is culture. Although one prominent feature of culture is place or locality, culture can neither be limited, nor satisfactorily defined, by reference to geographical (or political) boundaries.

The special character of culture as a unity extends beyond the boundaries of political organisations or national identities. For Eliot, this transcendent character of culture is best represented in education, particularly university education:

> No university ought to be merely a national institution, even if it is supported by the nation. The universities of Europe should have their common ideals, they should have their obligations towards each other. They should be independent of the governments of the countries in which they are situated. They should not be institutions for the training of an efficient bureaucracy, or for equipping scientists to get the better of foreign scientists; they should stand for the preservation of learning, for the pursuit of truth, and in so far as men are capable of it, the attainment of wisdom. (Eliot 1948: p. 123)

The idea of culture (and here specifically, the idea of European culture) goes beyond the immediacy of the present and the givenness of the past. The unity of culture cannot be expressed wholly in the singularity of an individual nor in the identity of a nation. Culture is not simply received by young minds, nor is it the mere re-enactment of past events through education. Culture is also much more than simply the backdrop to the myriad economic, scientific, artistic, and religious expressions of a society. For Eliot, culture ('the culture of Europe') is the driving force behind the continued pursuit of truth, knowledge, and artistic expression. It is that to which education is an invitation and to which education must respond.

The Universities in the Construction of European Citizens

The goal of the construction of a new concept of European culture within the European dimension of higher education is that of citizenship: 'Every person holding the nationality of a member-state shall be a citizen of the Union' (Committee on Institutional Affairs 1993: Article 3). What would it mean to be a citizen of the European Union? From whence this idea of citizenship? How might the nature and the character of today's university contribute to the building of such a citizenry? A necessary step in the realisation of European citizenship lies, according to the Study Group on Education and Training, in orienting the cultural heritage of the past towards future values: 'education and training must become a positive ally in making progress towards European citizenship' (Study Group on Education and Training 1996: p. 16). The European dimension of higher education moves beyond the limited concern with the passing on of cultural artefacts and the achievement of scientific truths: higher education has become an ally in constructing the politically and culturally weighted concept of 'citizen'.

The concept of citizenship in our western democracies has a twofold root. On the one hand, it has been used to indicate members of a nation (*natio*) who, according to birth and lineage, share a common origin and a common ethos. Citizens, according to this definition, are people joined together in a shared social enterprise due to their participation in a common culture: a shared language, customs, and traditions that provide a basis for a sense of sameness and identity. This is what Habermas calls the 'prepolitical' concept of citizenship: 'the idea of belonging to a prepolitical community integrated on the basis of descent, a shared tradition and a common language' (Habermas 1995: pp. 258–59). The bonds on which the nation-state are built are not, in the first place, political. The underlying basis for community and for government is the shared identity of a common social, historiographic, cultural background. The justification for the nation-state lies in an understanding of politics as primarily the means for organising the relationships between members of an extended clan (*demos*) sharing a common descent and, thus, a common set of cultural artefacts and values.

On the other hand, the concept of citizenship in today's Europe developed equally from the modern idea of the individual as free and autonomous. Citizenship here is a purely political term: a citizen is one who freely and wilfully identifies herself with the nation-state: 'The nation of citizens does not derive its identity from some common ethnic and cultural properties, but rather from the *praxis* of citizens who actively exercise their civil rights' (Habermas 1995: p. 258). Citizenry is the result of self-determination where each member wilfully agrees on a principle of mutual recognition in which her will attains rights and duties accorded to it through the recognition of similar rights and duties accorded to others. This Habermas refers to as 'the republican meaning of citizenship'. Following Rousseau and Kant, Habermas stresses the importance here of the identification of the will of the individual with the authority of the state. Freedom and equality, as fundamental democratic values, are not the inherent birthright of the citizen, but a rational conclusion based on the mutual recognition of the legitimisation of the nation-state being rooted in the self-determination of each individual citizen.

These two very different notions of citizenship have been commingled in the history of western democracies. The competing tension between the two is at the root of the many political (and even philosophical) differences in understanding today. This tension is apparent throughout the debate on multiculturalism, the debate on the hegemony of European culture, and (partially in) the debates on gender, race, and sexuality. The tension also appears in political debates between the (far) right and the (far) left, between established parties and new parties. It reappears in the more philosophical debate between liberalism and communitarianism. Habermas has sought a way out of this tension through his idea of 'constitutional patriotism' based on 'communicative pluralism'. He wants to avoid the one-sidedness expressed in the more limited concepts of liberalism and communitarianism. At the same time he is anxious not to take an all too simplified middle ground. Rather, he is intent on retrieving a description of citizenry that appropriately reflects both the current situation of our Western liberal democracies as well as their historical background.

At stake for Habermas is the fact of an increasing Europeanisation of politics in the nation-states of Europe against the background of German unification and the democratisation of the east central European states[6]:

> That nation-states constitute a problem along the thorny path to a European Union is, however, due less to their insurmountable claims to sovereignty than to another fact: democratic processes have hitherto only functioned within national borders. So far the political sphere is fragmented into national units. The question thus arises whether there can ever be such a thing as European citizenry. And by this I mean not only the possibilities for collective political action across national borders but also the consciousness of 'an obligation toward the European common-weal'. (Habermas 1995: p. 266)

Habermas's concern with Europe is primarily a practical concern, one nonetheless requiring a critical, structured (procedural) response. The question 'whether there can ever be such a thing as European citizenship' arises at the moment one looks for the possibility of active participation by 'European citizens' in supra-national or trans-national political decision-making processes. To what extent have the institutions of the nation-state been transformed to allow for an identification of both individual will and local national culture with the action of government at the European level? This is a question that one sees repeatedly asked in the documents issuing from the European Commission regarding proposals for higher education, and the question has been posed with increasing force in the period leading up to the Treaty on European Union as well as during the debate concerning its ratification and its implementation. The 'European dimension' is not just a political necessity in the formation of a new concept of European citizenship; rather, it is an ontological necessity if there is ever to be a true identification of 'the hearts and minds' of the European peoples with a loyalty extending beyond the homeland of the nation-state.

Habermas's proposal of a 'communicative pluralism' is intended to foster a particular concept of European identity: if there is a chance for a future European citizenship it lies in the possibility of individuals maintaining their attachments to the identities of the nation's prepolitical cultural artefacts and values while effective communication networks are established for the expression of a common political will at the European level. The solution requires the loosening of the historical bonds between the nation and the state in order to maintain the plurality of European culture (primarily in historiography, artistic expression, and languages) while expanding an area for common responses to political interests that transcend the traditional nation-state. However, this loosening of the bonds also requires, at the same time, the construction of a new sort of community space: 'With the construction of a "new Europe", citizenship accretes a new space for expression, a space that inserts itself into existing ideas of citizenship but does not replace them' (Study Group on Education and Training 1996: p. 14). The concept of European citizenship requires the opening up of a place in society (a European dimension) where the cognitive, emotional, and communicative practices of the Community interface between the individual, the state, and the community in all its engagements. The development of a European dimension cannot be a wholly political or institutional structure; rather, it must be developed throughout the entire range of networks of public communication such that there arises a self-conscious understanding among the citizenry of the rights and obligations adhering to those who belong to (identify with) the European Union.[7]

Legitimising European Citizenship

Neither Habermas nor the many and various authors driving the concept of European citizenship conceive of European culture as a singular or identifiable whole. Rather, the notion of a common European culture is most often used to collate interlinked artefacts and family resemblances in various (differing) forms of expression. For example, in the halls of the European Commission or the European Parliament, it is politically incorrect to speak about the 'European people'; rather, one hears (and reads) discussions regarding the 'peoples of Europe'. There is really nowhere in Europe the sense of a 'melting pot' effect leading to a common (multi)cultural identity, either within the individual nation-states or between nation-states. That Europe is multicultural at nearly all levels, no sensible European is wanting to deny (though the far right has difficulty coming to terms with this fact of the European cultural heritage). However, it is a multiculturalism of identity through difference, where difference is the norm. Indeed, one of the trump cards of Brussels has been its ability to promote an increased sense of cultural and linguistic identity among minority cultures throughout the member-states. The normative value of difference is re-enforced (once again) through the explicit recognition of plurality in the Treaty on European Union. 'The Community shall contribute to the flowering of the cultures of the Member States, while respecting their national and regional diversity and at the same time bringing the common cultural heritage to the fore' (Treaty on European Union 1992: Article 128). The supranational structure of the European Union precedents itself on cultural difference and fosters difference in its own development of an *acquis communautaire*, of a European identity.

The European identity that is to become a shared commodity among the new European citizens remains deferent to the cultural diversity of Europe, while pooling together elements of this plurality into a common cultural inheritance. However, this identity continues to appear elusive and we are wont to ask: 'By what authority?' This determining cultural phenomena shows itself to be artificially constructed from bits and pieces of a spurious history. And, there should be no doubt, the universities have been called to foster this creation: according to the authors of this idea, it is the role of university education to contribute to the moulding of the '"*Homo Europeanus* – both citizen and professional" … . "We are invited to construct the European Union on the basis of shared values, fundamental rights and a sense of belonging." … "[T]he Europe of the peoples must be built on hearts and minds as well as products and technologies."' (Smith and Schink 1993: p. E-88). What authority, what ground, shores up this call for political (and moral) commitment in education to the supranational government of the European Union? By what right, dare we ask, is the citizen of an individual member-state called upon to become, with her 'heart and mind', *Homo Europeanus*?

The legitimisation of the state in the eyes of the citizen is based on the intuition that the artefacts and values of the society, in the varying practices in which they are expressed, are respected and represented by the actions of the political institutions. In the idea of an *acquis communautaire*, of a state and its citizens under construction, the grounds for the legitimisation of the political realm come under more exacting scrutiny: 'Persons, and legal persons as well [citizens], become individualised only through a process of socialisation. A correctly understood theory of rights requires a politics of recognition that protects the integrity of the individual in the life contexts in which his or her identity is formed' (Habermas 1994: p. 113). Habermas argues, somewhat along the lines of Wittgenstein, that our individual understandings of who and what we are find their roots in a form of life ('life context') that itself does not come up for challenge. The linguistic, artistic, scientific, historiographic, and economic activities of a people – in short, a people's culture – is the expression of a certain habituation, way of living, or form of life. While perhaps any one or any several cultural practices or expressions may come up for questioning, for appraisal, and even for rebuke, neither the whole of a culture nor the underlying form of life can ever come up for review. However, the underlying support for the interactions between the individual and society, between the citizen and the state, is the general recognition that the form(s) of life is (are) respected. The ultimate ground for the legitimisation of political institutions lies in their being true to the form(s) of life for which they are (in part) an expression.

Habermas's reply to Charles Taylor is telling in this context:

> The same thing [full public recognition as equal citizens] holds, of course, for *Gastarbeiter* [foreign workers] and other foreigners in Germany, for Croats in Serbia, Russians in the Ukraine, and Kurds in Turkey; for the disabled, homosexuals, and so on. The demand for respect is aimed not so much at equalizing living conditions as it is at protecting the integrity of the traditions and forms of life in which members of groups that have been discriminated against can recognize themselves. (Habermas 1994: p. 110)

In the area of the political community, political equality is not fully achieved by a simple recognition of difference (often expressed as indifference) and an attitude of *laissez-faire* by the majority of citizens (or the state itself) towards a minority culture. The challenge of creating a common political environment for Germany, France, Bavaria, Scotland, Sicily, Limbourg, Italy, and Great Britain bears similarities with the need to create a common political culture for immigrant workers, homosexuals, and EU bureaucrats living in

Brussels. A cohesive and fully democratic European society requires the mutual recognition of the forms of life themselves, alongside their differing cultural expressions. That European, Canadian, and American societies are becoming increasingly porous, as are so many other societies today, should not imply that the character of their multicultural communities can be addressed with the same political measures, as Charles Taylor seems to suggest (see Taylor 1994). What is needed is that each society should search for its own (not necessarily unique) approach for integrating individual autonomy and public autonomy into a shared form of life.

The development of a European dimension, primarily through (higher) education, provides a basis for the realisation of a legitimating ground for a common political ethos. The idea of a European state and European citizenship is constructed on the back of firmly ingrained histories, artistic expressions, and national identities that are not easily loosened from their attachment to linguistic expression and locality. The forms of life that underlie the various peoples of Europe are not everywhere the same, and they are far from being mutually understood. Still the requirement remains: full citizenship on the part of the peoples of Europe (and thus full statehood on the part of the European Union) depends on full mutual recognition of these varying forms of life. Thus, rather than insisting on a certain all-encompassing cultural identity pre-existing the European state, but for which the European state would provide a long needed political expression, the 'architects of Europe' chose to construct a new area in the lives of the European peoples that the different forms of life could share in without giving up the fundamental identities found in their various cultural expressions. The European dimension neither replaces nor subdues any particular form of life. It has been introduced as an additional (economic, social, and political) sphere for the enhancement of existing forms of life.

If the legitimisation of the state and its activities requires the pooling of individual autonomy and public autonomy in a shared area of interaction, then it is perhaps easier to see how education can be called on to undertake the role of caretaker in the construction of the European polis. Indeed, education will have to come front and centre in a society where the very concept of citizenship, now existing only in 'an ambiguous, contradictory conceptual space', is under construction. Through the rites of passage that characterise the 'conversational encounter', the adventure of education is correctly understood as the initiation into a cultural inheritance that can neither be ignored nor directly appropriated. A form of life has no specific content that determines it and neither has it finely defined boundaries that are perceivable from within nor, should one say, from without. A form of life can neither be theorised nor transcribed; rather, it is inherent in the practices, engagements, beliefs, dispositions, and refusals of those sharing a common experience. There is no particular cultural expression nor grouping of cultural expressions that one might point to in conversation or argument as identifying a form of life. A form of life hangs silently in the background. The metaleptic imagery Wittgenstein used to speak of a form of life points in the direction of the literary distinction between the 'world of the text' and the 'world about which one writes'. It is the elliptical 'about which' that remains so elusive to all attempts at thematisation. A form of life is an entirely figurative backdrop for actions and expressions; and, as a contextualising trope, it figures in all we do and say. We might adapt a particularly apt figure of Stanley Cavell's in order to construe what is intended in the expression 'form of life': 'a matter of orientation, of bearings, of the ability to keep to a course and to move in natural paths from any point to any other' (Cavell 1979: p. 65). It is a habit of directing or orienting practices, a habit that lends itself neither to expression nor description because it is itself what makes expression and description possible. 'There is nothing,' we are wont to believe, 'but shared forms of life to keep us, as it were, on the rails' (McDowell 1979: p. 339). The shared forms of life in Europe are what ultimately orient the choices (and their expressions) of individuals and society. Certainly a form of life is not a deliberate construction and neither is it easily affected by deliberative actions.

At the same time, a form of life is never simply given, never simply inherited or passed on uncritically from one generation to the next (no matter how tempting this picture might appear to some). As peculiar as it may be, a human being needs to be initiated into a form of life, this form rather than that, although never (wholly) consciously or deliberately. The initiation into a form of life is itself a moment in the form of life, the creation of *ein Bildungsstand*. The primary role of education is to ensure that the cultural inheritance of a society remains animated by the form of life that underlies it, ensuring its meaning, founding the practices and beliefs already engaged. Education is an initiation, not just into particular forms of cultural expression, but (perhaps more importantly) into a certain background or framework for orientating ourselves through the interconnection of meanings and symbols supporting the particular self-understanding of an individual and a society. At the same time, this initiation is also the great challenge of an education: to impart not only the overt considerations of the artefacts and values belonging to a particular cultural identity, but also to ensure the connection of these cultural expressions with their underlying force, which enlivens these expressions, making them meaningful for a given people. Education is unavoidable for us precisely because it connects individual, cultural, and political forms of identity with meaning, albeit that this meaning is grounded in the groundlessness of our form of life. At the same time, we must be especially careful in education in any attempt to prefigure the grounds for our actions, institutions, and political instances. In engaging in the design and promulgation of a shared educational project, the European community takes on a particular responsibility vis-à-vis the life forms of the European cultures. As Derrida has already warned us, there is a delicate balancing act needed today to hold education (the university) on the precipice, and the abyss [*Abgrund*] looms large beside the *arche*.[8] Education, especially university education, cannot serve an illegitimate master. All too readily the precarious nature of the relationship between a culture and its form of life becomes apparent in the enlightenment of an education. What we eventually learn in education is that neither politics, nor science, nor history, nor morals, nor education itself guides or orientates the individual in society. Orientation, finding one's natural way about, is rooted in a form of life. Education, like politics, science, history, art, and so many other cultural expressions, at best provides a fitting response to this orientation which legitimises. A European project in education will only succeed if it heeds an orientation pre-existing in its society.

In reflecting on Thoreau's search for self-understanding and the grounds for legitimacy in the then young American political sphere, Cavell writes: 'The work of humanization is still to be done. While men believe in the infinite some ponds will be thought to be bottomless… . There is a solid bottom everywhere. But how are we going to weigh toward it, arrive at confident conclusions from which we can reverse direction, spring an arch, choose our lives, and go about our business' (Cavell 1979: p. 76). The same question can be asked again of today's construction of the concept of a European state and its citizenry: How are we to weigh toward the solid ground that will allow us to get on with our business in a united Europe? In what way might education connect a European dimension (an economic, social, political dimension) to the various forms of life supporting the European cultural heritage? And is education rightly called upon to join together the concept of European citizenship with 'conduct *inter homines*' (see Oakeshott 1991) in the construction of the *Homo Europeanus*?

The Power of Myth in Education

Forms of life seem to be shaky grounds on which to wager our stakes, especially if the stakes include the education of our children and the future of our communities (and the link between the two). We justifiably require something more to found our trust and secure confidence in decisions and actions in which we invest what is most dear to ourselves:

> We learn and teach words in certain contexts, and then we are expected, and expect others, to be able to project them into further contexts. Nothing ensures that this projection will take place (in particular, not the grasping of universals nor the grasping of books of rules), just as nothing ensures that we will make, and understand, the same projections. That on the whole we do is a matter of our sharing routes of interest and feeling, modes of response, senses of humour and of significance and of fulfilment, of what is outrageous, of what is similar to what else, what a rebuke, what forgiveness, of when an utterance is an assertion, when an appeal, when an explanation – all the whirl of organism Wittgenstein calls 'forms of life'. Human speech and activity, sanity and community, rest upon nothing more, but nothing less, than this. It is a vision as simple as it is difficult, and as difficult as it is (and because it is) terrifying. (Cavell 1969: p. 52)

Cavell's insistence on the 'nothing more' is perhaps more suggestive than it is limiting. The acceptance of the notion of a form of life as a footing for a common European cultural inheritance, or a common European identity, does not appear to satisfy completely our commitment to a ground of legitimacy. This is especially the case in a multicultural society that precedents identity on difference. The question we need to pose here concerns how we are to understand a form of life as a support for our educational and political practices? More specifically, how can a form of life support an educational commitment that aims at a distant political construction?

In the end, what is at stake in our discussion of a form of life is meaning. A form of life is in the last analysis that backdrop to a severance by which the meaning of signs or words is echoed. Our form of life holds us 'on the rails' by connecting the expressions of a self-understanding to the framework of meanings supporting that understanding. However, an awareness that it is a form of life that supports our engagements entails also the realisation of the contingent objectivity by which we rule our practices. This is especially the case in areas such as education and politics, where there appears to be no ground beyond the repetition of what we perceive to be our appropriate tradition. And, perhaps strangely, this is in itself usually satisfying for us. Yet the real problem arises when we attempt to reconcile the satisfaction we find in meaning (meaningful speech, meaningful practice, meaningful engagement) with the demand for certainty in truth. The conflict between meaning and truth taunts us, not only in philosophy but also in the everydayness of our engagements.[9] The idea of a truth that transcends our form of life (and thus transcends the meaningful) is referred to by McDowell as follows: 'This composite idea is not the perception of some truth, but a consoling myth, elicited by our inability to endure the vertigo' (McDowell 1979: p. 339). 'The vertigo' describes the experience one has while standing on the bedrock of the precipice and looking out (looking abroad, the British might say) over the gorge (the severance, the English Channel).

The idea of Europe is not a creation of the European Community, and no less is it a creation of the university nor any other historical institution. The origin of the idea of Europe has to be recovered from an archaeological excavation of the variety of historical meanings inherent in the word 'Europa', in particular those of liberty, Christendom, and civilisation (see den Boer 1993). Underlying this idea and its manifold meanings is a myth that has constantly needed to be re-made, re-invented, and emancipated from its own forms of historical contextualisation. In the 1470s, the Florentine scholar-poet Angelo Poliziano recast Ovid's description of the relief sculptures beside the door of an imagined palace of Venus as follows:

> On the other side of the door, Jove, transformed for love into a handsome white bull, is seen carrying off his sweet rich treasure, and she turns her face towards the lost shore with a terrified gesture: in the contrary wind her lovely golden hair plays over her breasts; her garment waves in the wind and blows behind her, one hand grasps his back, the other his horn.
>
> She gathers in her bare feet as if fearing the sea wash over her: in such a pose of fear and grief, she seems to call in vain to her dear companions; they, left behind among flowers and leaves, each mournfully cry for Europa, 'Europa' the shore resounds, 'Europa, come back,' the bull swims on, and now and then kisses her feet. (Quint 1979)

Ovid goes on in his *Metamorphoses*, further retelling the ancient Greek myth, describing how Europa now marooned on the isle of Crete, away from her homeland of Asia, is raped by the great god and begets the Europeans. Surrounding this story is an enormous mythology that has repeatedly transformed itself in an endeavour to achieve the promise of its realisation.

The strength of the idea of Europe, which underlies the European dimension of university education, an education unabashedly aimed at a new concept of European citizenship, lies in the power of a myth. The idea of university education as the achievement of self-understanding through an ongoing conversational encounter, both for the individual and society, receives its force from the institution's collusion with myth. All known cultures have produced networks of narratives wedded to myth in which they express their evolving self-understanding: 'Myth constitutes the culture's effort to retain through the exercise of memory its knowledge of itself' (Vickery 1993: p. 806). Myths are concerned to tell us how our gods came into existence, how the world was formed, and what the ultimate purpose of a culture and its people is. A myth stretches beyond history, beyond memory, beyond culture. 'Cultural pluralism and historical stratification rather than geographical or ethnic purity condition both myth and literature' (Vickery 1993: p. 807). A myth belongs to the present and constantly needs to be told and told again – and reshaped in the telling – if it is to figure in our futures.

Of course, the wise among us discount myth. Quite evidently there is a whole range of explanations for our practices and beliefs. And the matter of a myth is all but evident. Witness Socrates at the onset of the *Phaedrus*:

> The wise are doubtful, and if, like them, I also doubted, there would be nothing very strange in that. I might have a rational explanation that Orithyia was playing with Pharmacia, when a northern gust carried her over the neighbouring rocks; and this being the manner of her death, she was said to have been carried away by Boreas. There is a discrepancy, however, about the locality, as according to another version of the story she was taken from the Areopagus, and not from this place. Now I quite acknowledge that these explanations are very nice, but he is not to be envied who has to give them; much labor and ingenuity will be required of him; and when he has once begun, he must go on and rehabilitate centaurs and chimeras alike. Gorgons and winged steeds flow in apace, and numberless other inconceivable and impossible monstrosities and marvels of nature. And if he is sceptical about them, and would fain reduce them all to the rules of probability, this sort of crude philosophy will take up all his time. Now I have certainly not time for this; shall I tell you why? I must first know myself, as the Delphian inscription says; and I should be absurd indeed, if while I am still in ignorance of myself I were to be curious about that which is not my business. And therefore I say farewell to all this; the common opinion is enough for me. For, as I was saying, I want to know not about this, but about myself. Am I a wonder more complicated and swollen with passion than the serpent Typho, or a creature of a gentler and simpler sort, to whom Nature has given a diviner and lowlier destiny? (Plato nd: pp. 382–83)

Just what the proper matter of a myth is and where it is to be located is a curious, even spurious concern. Socrates realises this as he recalls a myth close to the heart of the Athenians, and yet nearly forgotten. The untangling of a myth, he tells us, is a merciless and intriguing affair. Historical, scientific, religious, and ideological explanations are all possible for any contingency of a myth. However, substitutions for contingencies can only one for one abate the 'inconceivable and impossible monstrosities and marvels of nature'. In this dialogue concerned with self-knowledge, the engagement of an education, the embattlement of explanation with *mythos* seems somehow quite beside the point. The dutiful wagging of natural explanation in the face of mystery falls short of what is required for criticism, instruction, and self-understanding. At the same time, natural explanation is required in education because it is precisely this attempt to go beyond common opinion that rehabilitates and revitalises myth, that ensures that the narratives of a myth do not become fixed icons speaking only of past memories. Still, the monstrosities and marvels of our natural situation seem to require even more than the explanations we are now and again satisfied to express alongside a complex web of stories. Ritual, sacrifice, and the occasional libation punctuate those narratives, keeping at bay the contingent profaning of the sacred.

The power of a myth lies in its ability to continually inform and respond to the diffusion of culture and its interaction with other cultures. The role of education in society cannot be limited, on this view, simply to the transmission of cultural icons from one generation to the next. Education provides an arena for the telling and retelling of myth. At the same time, edification requires that the telling and retelling both instructs and explains: 'And he who can not rise above his own compilations and compositions, which he has been long patching and piecing, adding some and taking away some, may be justly called poet or speech-maker or lawmaker' (Plato nd: p. 448). The natural limitation of our self-understanding is myth. In education we do not escape the narratives of our culture; however, in education we are able to transcend the immediacy of our self-understanding through the power of myth. The Eurocrats in Brussels put their finger on something sacred in our societies by involving education in the formation of European citizens. Myth is that self-sustaining structure of a society's culture, essential to its conception of reality and beliefs regarding its ownmost possibilities. The institutions of education are the caretakers of a society's commitment to myth, to the possibilities of self-understanding and self-transcendence. Cavell is right to insist that there is 'nothing more' than a form of life orienting our actions and convictions. However, we should not be deceived by this into thinking that the metaleptic character of a form of life is empty, that there would be a complete (ontological) severance between meaning and expression. A form of life is the underlying structure supporting the cultural expression of its self-understanding at a particular (geographical) place and (historical) time.

Conclusion

The myth of Europa recalls the harrowing and alienating memory of a people, whose birthright is exile and violence, who live caught between heaven and earth in their struggle for identity, all the while hearing the distant echo 'come back'. We should not be surprised that so much of what is being asked for in the European dimension of higher education relies on the sense of a not yet ripe cultural heritage. The construction of the European citizen through education is really 'nothing more' than the realisation of a distant promise of Europe's mythic memory. It is in the nature of myth, as McDowell points out, that it consoles. And it does so because it provides a sense of belonging. It is in a myth that we can locate the identity of a people, both as that which has been achieved and that which extends itself as a promise.

A myth is the construction *par excellence*. It is without author, belonging as much to its audience as it does to the storyteller. The power of a myth is its ability to characterise and enact in the artefacts and expressions of a culture those figures that are important to us, those figures about which we care. Myth allows us to transcend the immediacy of our situation by extending self-understanding beyond historical memory and making it possible to prefigure the future in imagination. It is this power of transcendence that can, and does, allow us to escape the contingency of our form of life. 'The suggestion that a person may be in some sense liberated through acceding to a power which is not subject to his immediate voluntary control is among the most ancient and persistent themes of our moral and religious tradition' (Frankfurt 1988: p. 89). The creation of European citizens through the establishment of a European dimension in higher education is really 'nothing more' than the expression of our contemporary form of life in yet another attempt to embrace the haunting myth of Europa.

Notes

1. 'What does it mean for citizens with different identities, often based on ethnicity, race, gender, or religion, to recognize ourselves as equals in the way we are treated in politics? In the way our children are educated in public schools? In the curricula and social policy of liberal arts colleges and universities?' (Amy Gutmann, 1992: p. 3; see also Habermas 1995).
2. 'The idea of the European dimension was one which was received uncritically in all responses although there was a variety of interpretations as to its meaning… . Its aim was identified variously … [including] as part of the concept of European Citizenship and European mentality (F, GR, IRL).' (Callaghan 1993: p. 47)

3. According to the Danish government, 'The European Dimension means an extension of the dimension of learning – not a narrowing – i.e., an increased freedom of choice, creating the basis for a broader, common framework of understanding within the European area' (Smith and Schink 1993: p. E-89).
4. For a discussion of the historical background to the notion of the 'European dimension' in higher education and its development, see Mulcahy 1993: pp. 58f.
5. Eliot writes in a footnote, with some lamentation, that the word 'culture' is all too often bantered about without serious consideration or genuine understanding: 'The pursuit of politics is incompatible with a strict attention to exact meanings on all occasions' (Eliot 1948: p. 15). Eliot regrets that political language is not informed with the same attention to exactitude and objectivity as, say, the language of philosophy or science. While Eliot's statement is certainly true, Eliot does not seem to grasp that its truth is founded in a kind of necessity: political language could not be otherwise. The role of political discourse is to provide expression for generally held beliefs among individuals having (often sharply) differing opinions regarding the enactments of those beliefs. It would be unwise (and readily impossible) to proceed in political discourse with exacting definitions and linearly structured arguments. Such a means of expression becomes all too rapidly the identifiable possession of the individual, not the expression of a generally realisable outcome of an ongoing discourse within a community.
6. An identical concern is expressed in 'The Commentary' introducing the *Draft Report on the Constitution of the European Union*:

   > Until recently, Europe has been able to progress without the active participation of its citizens although requiring their tacit consent, because the ideas of peace and prosperity for which it is a vehicle, and the feeling of protection which it gave in the face of threats from the Soviet Empire, confirmed them in this attitude of benevolent tolerance. The collapse of the Soviet system, Europe's impotence in the Yugoslavian crisis, the economic crisis and unemployment, instead of the prosperity promised by the Single Market, and the absence of generally accepted Community leadership, have completely altered this attitude of benevolent consent as has been shown by the debate on the ratification of the Maastricht Treaty. Progress toward European Union is no longer self-evident. (Committee on Institutional Affairs 1993: p. 6)

7. The Study Group goes on to indicate a fundamental challenge for education: 'the European dimension of citizenship is very underdeveloped, which is not surprising, given that European citizenship is an ambiguous, contradictory conceptual space' (Study Group on Education and Training 1996: p. 14). A major challenge for institutions of (higher) education in Europe is the development of a clear understanding in the minds of the youth of that space in our societies in which European citizenship is enacted and thus receives a well-defined conceptual understanding.
8. 'Il y a là un double geste, une double postulation … dans la pensée la plus abyssale de ce qui fonde l'Université' (Derrida 1990: p. 491). In the same vein Derrida writes in the footnote introducing the French edition of this text: 'Que faut-il faire pour éviter qu'on ne se précipite au fond de la gorge? Est-elle responsable de tous ces suicides? Faut-il construire des clôtures?' (Derrida 1990: p. 461) Derrida asks us to consider the final responsibility of (university) education regarding its opening to the construction of a ground that legitimates. How can the university guarantee us safe passage to the grounds of our convictions? And, if safe passage cannot be guaranteed, should we perhaps not turn back? And, further still (though a question we cannot pose with any force here), who is responsible for those who undertake the passage?
9. For this reason some philosophers have argued that the 'realm of meaning' and the 'realm of truth' need to be kept (and understood) separately. See Burms and De Dijn 1986.

CHAPTER 3

REALISM, RATIONALISM, AND THE EUROPEAN PROJECT

Kevin Williams

Before addressing the place of nations and culture in higher education in Europe, it is wise to engage in some preliminary conceptual investigation and this chapter is an attempt to set in train such an investigation by exploring critically the notions of nation, culture, and Europe. By the European project, which is the concern of this chapter, I mean the promotion of a united Europe or 'New Europe', that is, a unitary European state 'which is economically, socially, politically and culturally integrated' (Vanbergen 1988: p. 5). The European project refers therefore to the political aspiration to vest fiscal, foreign, and defence policy in a supra-national authority as well as the extravagant aspiration to integrate the culture of the nation-states of Europe. The chapter takes issue with both aspects of the European project and also with the consensus about its desirability as this is reflected in the official literature.

The degree of consensus on the pursuit of a united Europe which is to be found in this literature is quite extraordinary. In recent documentation on higher education the term 'consensus' recurs and is emphasised by association with the adjectives 'widespread' and 'strong' (see Smith and Schink 1993: pp. E-87, E-88, E-90, E-116) and there is also much reference to shared agreement and commitment (see Smith and Schink 1993: pp. E-87, E-89; Jallade 1993: p.16). This widely shared consensus stands in urgent need of philosophical scrutiny. As with any consensus which remains unquestioned, its 'dust', like the dust of custom, may come to 'lie unswept, / And mountainous error be too highly heaped / For truth to o'er-peer' (Shakespeare *Coriolanus*, act 2, sc. 3, lines 121-24).

To be sure, the consensus reflected in the official literature is not universally shared because the relationship between European institutions and the continent's nation-states is a contentious political issue. It is also one of those issues which prompts polarised feelings and a tendency to see things in stark either/or terms. Advocates of opposing views tend to see one another in uncomplimentary terms: on the one side, as irredentist nationalists and, on the other side, as cosmopolitan idealists. Although the European project has its left-wing critics, its opponents tend to be ultraconservative. I am concerned at the monopoly of this critique by the voices of conservatism as well as the assumption that one is chauvinistic and unappreciative of the cultures of other European countries unless one also supports a united Europe. While many anti-Europeans are nationalistic in a narrow illiberal sense, to be a Eurosceptic is not to be a xenophobic moral reprobate. Philosophical reflection on the issues surrounding European unity will show us that we do not have to choose between extremes: between anti-national Europhilia and anti-European chauvinism. This reflection might also help us to avoid 'that old business of theorising, taking up a position, planting the flag of identity and self-esteem, then fighting all comers to the end' (McEwan 1988: p. 80).

At the outset there are some matters which require clarification and qualification. In spite of talk of a 'democratic deficit' between European institutions and citizens, the trend towards the construction of a united Europe is not undemocratic. Involvement in Europe has been endorsed in many countries by national referenda; furthermore, the institutions of the European Community are governed by democratic procedures. In the second place, commitment to a united Europe does not imply a renunciation of national identity as it is fairly obvious that a person can be Danish or Dutch or Spanish or Portuguese or Irish or British as well as being European. What I wish to call into question is the fabrication of a further layer of political allegiance for citizens of nations that already have long civic traditions of their own. This is why I argue that the emphasis in civic education should be on the cultivation of more local loyalties (sometimes regional or ethnic, but often national) which are liberal, generous, critical, inclusive, and expansive[1] rather than on the rationalistic cosmopolitan ideal represented by the united 'New Europe'. In challenging the appropriation of education to promote the European project, I am, of course, aware that education served an explicitly political and civic function in the creation of the current nation-states of Europe. But whatever may be our attitude towards nation-states, for better or worse we are now stuck with them and we simply do not require another focus for people's political allegiance and identity. While in certain respects the notion of a unitary European state is a positive ideal, such a state is unlikely to provide 'the sort of clarity that individuals require if they are to be able to identify their fellow citizens and experience the laws which govern them as of their own creation' (Brown 1994: p.181; and see also Hutchinson 1994: pp. 160-61). Although it is not impossible that the inhabitants of the various states of Europe may come to think of themselves as citizens of a single European state, this outcome seems to me to be both unlikely and, most of all, unnecessary.

Although my reservations about the European project are significant, the project has positive and realistic features which it is reasonable and appropriate to seek to promote. Before drawing attention to the questionable aspects of the project, I wish to try to define its positive features.

The Realistic Dimension of the European Project

The documents on higher education that have just been quoted reflect some of the spirit of the European project, which is the subject of the critique offered in this paper. These documents in turn reflect the thrust of official policy on the subject, which is worth elaborating in more detail. The Resolution adopted by the Council of Ministers illustrates fairly dramatically the scope and spirit of what is involved (Council and the Ministers of Education Meeting within the Council 1988). The aims of this resolution can be identified as follows:

- to strengthen in young people a sense of European identity and make clear to them the value of European civilisation and of the foundations on which the European peoples intend to base their development today, that is in particular the safeguarding of the principles of democracy, social justice and respect for human rights (Copenhagen Declaration, April 1978);
- to prepare young people to take part in the economic and social development of the Community and in making concrete progress towards European union, as stipulated in the European Single Act;
- to make young people aware of the advantages which the Community represents, but also of the challenges it involves, in opening up an enlarged economic and social area to them;
- to improve their knowledge of the Community and its Member-States in their historical, cultural, economic, and social aspects and bring home to them the significance of the cooperation of the

Member-States of the European Community with other countries of Europe and the world.

The following are among the measures that member-states are required that member-states to 'make every effort' to implement:

- to include the European dimension explicitly in their school curricula in all appropriate disciplines, for example, literature, languages, history, geography, social sciences, economics, and the arts;
- to make arrangements so that teaching material takes account of the common objective of promoting the European dimension;
- [to] give greater emphasis to the European dimension in teachers' initial and in-service training;
- [to] offer some teachers from other Member-States certain in-service training activities, which would constitute the practical expression of belonging to Europe and a significant means of favouring the integration process;
- to give a new stimulus in the perspective of 1992 to the strengthening of the image of Europe in education ... [by] opening up new paths for the strengthening of the European dimension;
- to make authors and publishers of teaching material more aware of the need to include the European dimension in their production;
- to examine the possibilities of reinforcing the European dimension in education by using audio-visual means at European level.

In this resolution there are elements which are commendable. The wish to engender cooperation between nations and peoples is reasonable and appropriate. It would be most unwise to fail to acknowledge the place of international forums with specific, practical remits. For example, there is everything to be said for supporting international cooperation between governments or other organisations to protect the environment and to combat crime. Reasonable and appropriate also is the aspiration to emphasise and to promote the principles of democracy, social justice, and respect for human rights, which are accepted by many European nations. No sensible person could find fault with this affirmation of the value of shared moral sentiments and practices.

Moreover, many previous and current initiatives of the European Community are also realistic and appropriate. These initiatives are wide-ranging and have contained a commendable emphasis on provision for the disadvantaged.[2] Although many of the initiatives concentrate on vocational education and on courses dealing with the transition from school to working life, it is untrue to claim that EU initiatives are exclusively functional or utilitarian. Some of the courses developed for the EU Transition from School to Working Life programmes are examples of how the school can make a positive, direct, and genuinely educational contribution to preparing young people for working life. There may well be vested bureaucratic and business interests within the 'New Europe' which envisage schools, colleges, and universities primarily as an arena in which young people are offered an apprenticeship to industrial and commercial life in the 'New Europe' through the '[s]ystematic cultivation of a "European" mentality' (Smith and Schink 1993: p. E-88). But this would probably be an unfairly reductionist view of the entire educational policy of the EU. The various initiatives such as Lingua, Erasmus, and Socrates to encourage contact between students and staff of institutions of higher education are also to be welcomed. Such contact is enriching both to the students who go abroad and to the host institutions.

Yet in spite of all that is positive in European cooperation, we need not have the slightest desire to share political loyalties with the citizens of the nations with whom we cooperate in certain practical matters and with whom we share particular moral values. Moreover, I am not persuaded that the conception of civic and cultural identity underlying the notion of European citizenship is sufficiently robust or thick to animate a notion of citizenship capable of sustaining shared political loyalty and allegiance.

Rationalism and the 'New Europe'

Identifying the elements of a civic culture which would be capable of providing the basis of a shared citizenship is more problematic than is often appreciated (see Williams 1996b). For example, the affirmation in the Resolution of the Council of Ministers of the principles of democracy, social justice, and respect for human rights serves to draw attention to one of the difficulties in any endeavour to provide a conceptualisation of a peculiarly European political culture. This is the difficulty of specifying the relationship between the notions of western civilisation itself (which embraces the American continent and the Antipodes) and what is exclusive and peculiar to Europe. For example, among fundamental principles of European states are freedom of speech and a distinction between religious laws and civil laws or between sin and crime. Respect for freedom of expression entails a willingness to tolerate criticism of the government and the existence of pornography; acceptance of the distinction between sin and crime leaves the regulation of sexual behaviour as largely a private matter.

Subscription to these principles certainly distinguishes the political culture of European states from the civic culture of states governed by Islamic law. But these principles are features of the civic life in other western states, such as Canada, the United States, Australia, and New Zealand. The values here are western rather than peculiarly European: they are the values which link western civilisation to what Isaiah Berlin, in an essay entitled 'European Unity and Its Vicissitudes', describes as 'the habits, traditions, above all the common notions of good and evil, which reunite us to our Greek and Hebrew and Christian and humanist past' (Berlin 1990: p. 205).

Furthermore, the transnational bonds which link European nations to other countries outside Europe may well have much deeper roots in the lives of the inhabitants of Europe than any bonds which they may have with one another. For example, there are people on the western seaboard of Ireland who would feel more at home in Boston than in Dublin. For these individuals Brussels and the other major European cities are distant foreign places which are irrelevant to their lives in any cultural sense. During the 1995 fishing dispute between Spain and Canada the sympathies of Irish fishermen and of the Irish public were with the Newfoundlanders rather than with their 'partners' in the European Community. There were two reasons for this sympathy. The first was a joint hostility towards Spain as the common commercial enemy for fishing within national waters and the second was the cultural affinity which Irish people felt with Newfoundlanders. In fact, the cultural practices of individual European countries may have more in common with those to be found in North America, South America, or Australia than with those of other European nations. This point is well illustrated in the comments of David Corson, editor of a book on the relationship between education and work. Introducing the volume Corson explains that the book's scope is limited to 'the English-speaking countries ... that make up North America, Britain and Australasia'. This is because these countries are 'linguistically and culturally similar' and 'are broadly alike in the knowledge, beliefs and experiences of their peoples' (Corson 1991: pp. 8, 11). These comments capture a mind set that is not uncommon in the anglophone world and which *mutatis mutandis* is replicated in the French, Spanish, and Portuguese speaking worlds. The role of language in cultural identification should not be underestimated. As a graduate student in France I was struck by the extent to which students from francophone Africa were gallicised and by the extent to which the anglophone world had a homogeneous quality in the minds of many French people. Indeed, Chirac, the current President of France, has portrayed the attempts of Greenpeace to prevent French nuclear testing as an arm of an Anglo-Saxon conspiracy (see

Hone 1995). This is why we need to consider whether the bonds which join European nations to non-European countries that are linguistically and culturally similar are more important than whatever bonds the nations of Europe may have with one another. Moreover, language is not the only basis of transcontinental bonding, for example, the relationships of the Mediterranean coasts of Italy, France, and Spain with North Africa, of Greece and Cyprus with Asia Minor arguably have a significance to the Europeans of these regions greater than any intra-European relationship.

Finally, there is the role of class relationships which strike me as more significant than any relationship based merely on geographical propinquity. For example, in the novels of Henry James much is made of the distinction made between American and European sensibility and the potential for misunderstanding between the 'New World' and the 'Old World'. But James's Europeans are generally members of a privileged elite whose *Lebenswelt* and sensibility would have had little in common with that of peasants, small farmers, landless labourers, and the urban working class of their native countries. In both 'New World' and 'Old World' social and economic status is likely to have a more significant bearing on the development of sensibility than geography. 'The conquests of learning and taste, the general fabric of civilisation as we know it', remarks Hyacinth Robinson in James's novel, *The Princess Casamassima*, are 'based ... upon all the despotisms, the cruelties, the exclusions, the monopolies, and the rapacities of the past' (quoted in Allen 1968: p. 271). Whatever generalisations we can make about citizens of other countries, it seems to me that those made without reference to social class are incomplete. Let me add here that class-based divisions within society will not be eliminated by shared allegiance to a nation: individual citizens may share the same national allegiance without sharing the same class interests. It is worth noting that commitment to the European project tends to be the monopoly of a largely middle class cadre (and their offspring) of academics, professionals, business persons, and civil servants (see Hutchinson 1994: p. 140). We should also remember the literature in support of a united Europe is produced mainly by this cadre which could be said to have a vested interest in the success of the European project.

Rationalism and Education

These are among some of the considerations (see also Williams 1996b) which lead me to argue that the idea of a 'New Europe' can be described as rationalistic. It is a theoretical construct without roots in the ecology of existing civic cultures. In this respect it offers a close parallel to what Oakeshott (1981: p. 35) calls the 'morality of the Rationalist' for whom moral life consists in the self-conscious pursuit of moral ideals and the application of moral rules. For the political 'rationalist', politics consists in the implementation of a premeditated ideology that specifies ends thought to be desirable and fit to be pursued. This ideology is implemented by means of applied or technical knowledge of a scientific nature, for example, by the use of economics or psychology (Oakeshott 1981: pp. 116–223). The 'rationalist' version of civic education in support of the European project involves initiation into a premeditated ideal that specifies the end thought to be desirable (the realisation of a united Europe) together with the means for achieving it (education). Education, we are advised, has a 'vital' and 'key' role to play in achieving a united Europe (Government of Ireland 1995). Its first task will be to 'interest and inform people about Europe from a young age' and thus raise 'awareness of Europe from an early age' (Government of Ireland 1995) and then through the '[systematic] cultivation of a "European mentality", this awareness will come to assume a developed form among students at third level. The outcome of all this activity, or what the latter document calls the "product", will be what the French call "*Homo Europeanus*" both citizen and professional' (Smith and Schink 1993: p. E-88).

It is precisely because the European project is rationalistic that we find proponents of the project attributing to the school and institutions of higher education such a disconcertingly explicit ideological role in engineering loyalty to the 'New Europe' (see Williams 1996a; Williams 1996b). The ideological role which educational institutions are expected to embrace is very different from recognising the European dimension which the school curriculum in European countries has always and inevitably contained. This dimension is not something new; it is to be found in the teaching of Latin and Greek, in the teaching of both vernacular and modern European languages, and in the teaching of history, geography, civics, art, and religion. The conception of a European dimension in education as simply a new coat of educational varnish is not only pedagogically misguided, but also marks a failure to appreciate what actually happens in many schools and colleges in European countries. In these institutions the work of most teachers or lecturers is already concerned with European culture or else informed by its spirit, and advice to them not to 'ignore' the European 'cultural heritage' (Tabatoni 1993: p. 26) is therefore both patronising and otiose. But what is most objectionable is the identification of the European dimension exclusively with European integration and the appropriation of the curriculum as a vehicle of 'intellectual, psychological and occupational preparation' (Vanbergen 1988: p. 13) for this integration.

For example, in Ireland for many years now there has been an almost universally shared belief that educational institutions should be used to engineer a new political loyalty to the 'New Europe'. Government documents, such as the Green Paper and White Paper on education of 1992 and 1995 enthusiastically endorse this belief. Although the authors of responses to the Green Paper disagreed on many issues, most took the opportunity to deliver themselves of some exhortations in support of the 'New Europe'. These views are consistent with those to be found in the literature from the European Commission advocating the use of education to promote a united Europe. In the words of a resolution of the European Parliament, educational authorities must discharge 'their responsibility to prepare their citizens for European unification through education and training' (Commission of the European Communities 1991: p. 12). According to the *Memorandum* on higher education and the responses thereto, higher education will share responsibility with the school for the mission of evangelisation. To anyone who has kept a distance from Euro-ideology, the uncritical appropriation of the European project by higher education is striking. We are informed of 'widespread acknowledgement by ... higher education institutions of the need for strategies to develop a European dimension in the studies of all students ... [as] a sign of their commitment to the development of European citizenship' (O'Dwyer 1993: p. 6). We are told that 'no-one argued' with the view that 'passing on the European *cultural heritage*, especially through education, can be considered a cornerstone of any European integration process' (Tabatoni 1993: p. 16). 'Obviously' writes the author of this document, 'higher education systems should play an active part in achieving the goals of European integration (ibid., p. 9). ... The specific scientific and cultural missions of higher education are central to any changes brought about as a result of integration' (ibid., p. 26). The irony about all of this rhetoric is that it is to be found alongside platitudes on 'teaching people to have open, critical and creative minds' (ibid., p. 13).

As characterised in the literature, education for the 'New Europe' seems to me to be proselytising, manipulative, even indoctrinatory. It is like a form of religious education that seeks to secure from young people a commitment to a particular religion regardless of their own wishes in the matter, while at the same time inviting them to believe that they are being 'open' and 'critical'. The analogy with religion can be further developed. Just as we do not expect clergy to preach sermons on the merits of atheism, we should not expect academics evangelising on behalf of the 'New Europe' to offer a disinterested, genuinely critical view of this project. These peripatetic evangelists, who travel around the continent at the expense of the taxpayer (*heureux ceux qui, comme Ulysse, font de beaux voyages*), may well disagree on matters of emphasis and detail but on the essentials of European dogma, they are of one faith.

Education as a Means to an End

Underlying the conception of education upon which the European project is based, there is a misguided means-ends logic. According to this logic, which is by no means peculiar to the literature under consideration, education occurs as a result or by-product of engaging in particular activities. Conceived as 'essentially instrumental', education is viewed as a 'means both to fulfilment in the individual and to stability and progress in society ... a tool ... to achieve the aims which society sets before itself' rather than as an 'end in itself' (Garforth 1964: p. 25). Educational activities are seen as in some way neutral in respect of realising particular purposes. But, like other human activities which have their purposes built into them, educational activities should not be conceived in terms of means-ends logic. It is as inappropriate to apply this logic to educational activities as it would be, for example, to speak of hill walking, sailing or gardening as a means to the pleasurable end of enjoyment. The exhilaration, the sense of achievement, wellbeing, and closeness to nature which a person gets from hill walking are not ends to which certain physical movements are the means. From the enthusiastic and practised participant's point of view such feelings are what hill walking is for her; they are not ends which are instrumentally related to participation in the activity itself. Likewise, for example, feelings of increased sympathy towards others, an appreciation of, and a sense of outrage at, the damage wrought by unemployment are not ends, results, consequences, or effects which may or may not follow a sensitive reading of Walter Greenwood's novel *Love on the Dole*. Understanding the destructive power of sexual jealousy is not an end to which watching a performance of *Othello* is the means. Responding to novels and plays actually means having these and similar experiences. These experiences constitute the response. Education requires engagement in activities; it is not something which occurs as a byproduct of engaging in them.[3]

A further point is that the achievement of understanding and the experience of satisfactions are not to be conceived as slightly different extrinsic ends to education. To speak of these as extrinsic ends is similar to speaking of pleasure and stimulation as extrinsic ends of conversation. Personal enrichment is not an end at all; it is part of what being educated means. When we characterise an activity as educational, we focus primarily on what it contributes to enabling us to live fuller and richer lives. In the idiom of Michael Oakeshott, used elsewhere in this volume by Susan Mendus and others (see also Williams 1989), the educational character of an activity refers to the propensity of that activity to enrich the lives of those who accept the invitation to acquire facility in the metaphorical language in which it consists and to join in the conversation to which it lends its voice.

To treat education as a mechanism to realise extrinsically prescribed aims is then a matter of a certain conceptual confusion. Where the prescribed aims are of a politically controvertible character, however, educators must be alert to the danger of manipulation or indeed of indoctrination.

Citizens: Real and Aspirational

The main reason for conceiving of the European project in manipulative, means-ends terms is because the notion of a united Europe is in many senses an artificial ideal to which many ordinary citizens do not aspire. The notion of a united Europe is largely a contrived idea without roots in the hearts of people. Commitment to the 'New Europe' is not something which most people would ordinarily come to embrace through participation in the life of their communities or through their encounters with the normal school curriculum. To be sure, modern European nation-states are artificial rather than natural constructs and, as was pointed out earlier in this chapter, the appropriation of education in the mission of promoting a uniform civic identity has been an important feature in the development of nation-states. To a significant extent, many European nation-states could be described as 'hooped together, brought / under a rule, under the semblance of peace / by manifold illusions' (W.B. Yeats, 'Meru'). Unfortunately, too, these nation-states often include within their boundaries ethnic and other groups which do not share a sense of identity with the majority population of the nation-state into which they have been incorporated. Indeed, it could be said that the 'New Europe' will offer a context which will affirm the identity of groups, such as Catalans and Basques, who perceive themselves in terms of nationhood and who feel alienated from the nation-states (Spain and France) in which they find themselves. But nation-states may not always be considered objectionable by groups whose culture differs from that of the majority (see Williams 1995b). For example, the composition of international sports teams in such European countries as France, the Netherlands, and Britain provides some evidence of multi-ethnic and multicultural allegiance to these states. In any event, whether we like it or not, nation-states are the jurisdictional units in which we find ourselves.

Still in years to come the 'New Europe' may well no longer appear rationalistic. After all, identities and loyalties can be multiple and citizens of the individual nation-states of Europe may come to experience a sense of identity with and loyalty towards 'Europe', either together with or in place of any national, regional, or ethnic identity. Let me repeat that I do not understand the European project to require the abandonment of national allegiance and identity. All I can say is that emergence of a widely shared 'European' identity seems to me to be unlikely. Again I would draw attention to the sense of European identity possibly enjoyed by a largely middle class cadre (and their offspring) of academics, professionals, business persons and civil servants and contrast this with the sense of identity of ordinary citizens (see Hutchinson 1994: p. 140).

The rationalistic character of the 'New Europe' is well captured by David Marquand, a commentator who is in fact sympathetic to the project: 'All too often, the logic of the Europe-builders of the 1950s and 1960s echoed the logic of the state-builders of the previous two centuries. They spoke of rationality, modernity, progress, enlightenment, just as their state-building predecessors had done; and although they paid lip service to the cultural diversity of Europe, they did not sound as if they meant it. Partly as cause, and partly as consequence, they did not – and do not – have a reservoir of feeling and identity on which to draw' (Marquand 1993: p. 18). The presence on the part of the inhabitants of European states of any special feelings of identification with or loyalty towards one another because of their geographical propinquity is highly questionable. The main obstacle to a united Europe is not any 'democratic deficit' between European institutions and European citizens but rather the psychological implausibility of expecting people to identify with a large supranational political entity which exceeds so dramatically the scale of what Isaiah Berlin (1990: p. 258) describes as '"natural" units of "human" size'. Feelings of identity with and loyalty towards 'Europe' lack roots in the actual lives of most ordinary citizens of European countries and the absence of such feelings and loyalty is confirmed by the low turn-out at European elections. A strong or thick sense of civic identity must embrace a combination of cultural and psychological elements. These include, most importantly, a consciousness of membership of a living and historical community 'with a shared democratic culture involving obligations and responsibilities as well as rights, a sense of the common good, fraternity, and so on' (McLaughlin 1992: p. 236).

Let us take one important and very concrete area where such a conceptual framework may play a significant role in the animation and sustenance of civic culture. In their efforts to redistribute income in the interests of the less well-off, central government may draw upon citizens' perceptions of themselves as members of a living community with some sense of shared responsibility and obligation. A sense of belonging to a living, national community will tend to make somewhat more acceptable the efforts of central government to redistribute income through taxation. Each individual taxpayer does not have to be willing to share with the less well-off, but national civic culture normally presupposes acceptance of redistributive principles. This is expressed in acknowledgement of the authority of the government to make laws which levy taxes and this acknowledgement is a crucial feature of the civic culture of nation-states.

To be sure, it is precisely such a perception which advocates of the 'New Europe' are trying to promote. And it is the absence of such a perception which is exploited by conservative politicians. For example, former British minister Norman Tebbit has expressed exasperation at having to pay tax which allows the citizens of other nations 'to do nothing ... [but] sit there and sponge'.[4] Whatever reasons lie behind Tebbit's views – after all, he is unlikely to advocate much sharing with the less well-off in a national context either – his statement draws attention to the absence of that aspect of a shared identity which is conducive to an acceptance of redistributive principles. And although, by endorsing European treaties through referenda, various countries have been coming to recognise the authority of European political institutions to make laws, the notion of European citizenship does not seem to me to offer the subsoil of common identity which is conducive to an acceptance of redistributive principles and to a willingness to share goods. Let me stress once more that I appreciate that the possible emergence in the future of a notion of European citizenship in which redistributive principles are accepted cannot be ruled out in principle.

Loyalty and Economic Self-Interest

One reason why recognition of the authority of European political institutions is unlikely to lead to a willingness to share with others is because agreements like the Maastricht Treaty tend to be promoted on the grounds of what they offer to individuals in terms of their economic self-interest. Note here that I am not calling into question the necessity and value of productive economic activity. What I wish to challenge is a view of human beings which sees them primarily as self-interested consumers. Underlying the European project is a tendency to conceive of people in this way. Citizens of Europe are invited to enjoy 'a new vision of their future' based on 'an increase in the profitability of the productive apparatus as a result of the opening up of the market and increased competitiveness' (Vanbergen 1988: p. 13). In the realisation of the necessary competitiveness higher education will play a crucial role (Smith and Schink 1993: p. E-107; Tabatoni 1993: p. 16). Yet, somewhat ironically, if what ultimately gives purpose to the European project is an enhanced consumerist future, then what drives the 'New Europe' is the universal impulse for, in the words of Wordsworth, 'getting and spending', which is hardly exclusive to Europeans.

The last point does raise an interesting issue. If the notion of common bonds in any substantial sense is incapable of carrying the weight of European identity, can its citizens be said to share interests in a more pragmatic sense? After all, the new pan-Europeanism assumes a shared commitment to greater and more conspicuous consumption. There is little doubt that there is economic advantage for those Europeans who wish to sell goods or services in having access to enlarged markets where impediments of taxation and customs formalities and restrictions have been removed.[5] For European consumers there is also some advantage in gaining access to goods that can be produced more cheaply given the economies of scale that are facilitated by enlarged markets. As my concern is not with the economic benefits or otherwise of a united Europe, I shall simply note that economic arrangements form the basis only of an instrumental, prudential, or transactional relationship.

Based on prudence rather than on feelings of solidarity, the kind of interest on which economic arrangements build provides an insufficient basis for a sense of shared identity. To suggest that individuals should start to feel a shared identity or experience loyalty to one another for prudential reasons alone is inconsistent with the logic of the notions of identity and loyalty. It is as if one expected a professional footballer transferred from one club to another to feel the same kind of loyalty towards the clubs he plays for as that felt by lifelong supporters of these clubs. To take a political example, it is almost certainly a mistake to reduce the loyalty of Ulster Unionists to economic self-interest. Doubtless there is an element of self-interest in the loyalty of Unionists to the British Crown; but even if it were not in their economic interest, the national loyalty of Unionists to Britain would probably remain unchanged. For the same reason it flies in the face of the way human beings are in the world and feel about themselves to suggest that citizens of European nation-states should adopt a European identity simply because it is said to be in their economic self-interest to do so.

Realism and Imagination in Civic Education

Even if it were psychologically plausible, the idea of generating a 'reservoir of feeling and identity' (Marquand 1993: p. 18) on which to construct a shared European identity is hardly realistic. This is why I argue that the nation is a more appropriate focus of civic loyalty than the ideal of the 'New Europe'. Civic education normally needs to take place within a context of cultural rootedness and this context for many people is supplied by the nation-state. This is not to deny that regional, local, ethnic, or religious identity can play this role. For the purposes of my argument, all I wish to claim is that the nation-state can and does provide a peculiar sense of identity (see Tamir 1993) and satisfy for many individuals 'a craving for "natural" units of "human" size' (Berlin 1990: p. 258). Traditional nation-centred civic education, unlike the Europe-centred version, has roots deep in the subsoil of the actual loyalties of people. However, they may have emerged, and for all the regrettable absence of overlap in places between nation and state, loyalties to nation-states exist and are deeply and viscerally felt. Identification with and loyalty to the nation provides part of the stuff, the 'gross earthy mixture' (Hume 1978: p. 272), of the self-understanding of many human beings. Nation-states are the units in which we find ourselves and the loyalties which they engender cannot be readily abandoned. The nation is often, therefore, an appropriate focus of loyalty in civic education. Furthermore, as I have argued at length elsewhere (Williams 1995), nation-centred civic education, where generously conceived and imaginatively designed, can be hospitable to a genuinely critical spirit.

The main reason for endorsing nation-centred civic education is because the nation-state offers a strong or thick sense of civic identity which embraces not only cultural, but also social and psychological elements. Consequently national identity can promote a positive sense of belonging to a larger human community. In large cities and towns where the intercourse between citizens tends to be impersonal, anonymous, and transactional, national identity provides a basis for feelings of solidarity with other people. In this way, nation-centred civic education draws upon a reservoir of 'pre-existing sentiments' (Miller 1993: p. 9). Again let me repeat that roots of human identity do not have to be national in character: they may have their source in local, regional, ethnic, or religious attachments.

Roots and Moral Quagmires

Talk of roots, however, understandably strikes chords of great unease in the minds of many people. Local, ethnic, and national pieties can lead to a moral myopia in respect of obligations and duties which extend beyond geographical and political borders. Eva Hoffman draws attention to the ambivalent and somewhat negative feeling which some central Europeans have about national or ethnic self-identification, a feeling that such self-identification is a 'retrogression' (Hoffman 1994: p. 37). Yet Hoffman points out that, for example, the resistance to the communist regime of Helena Luczywo, a distinguished Polish intellectual, could not really be 'understood without the spur of solidarity and love of her country, without something like patriotism ... although she might be loath to use such words' (Hoffman 1994: p. 38). Likewise she writes that, although the playwright Agnieszka Osiecka 'would never speak about patriotism', for her Poland was 'truly a familiar, well-loved home' (Hoffman 1994: p. 66). Yet given the destructive influence of nationalism throughout this century and in our times, the reluctance of people to invoke national sentiment is understandable. The reprehensible dimension of national sentiment, which many find repellent, is captured in the remarks of Heinrich Himmler: 'only to members of our own race do we owe honesty, decency, comradeship, and loyalty, to no one else' (quoted in von Krockow 1993: p. 149). As Claudio Magris comments, loyalty can put down 'roots too deep to budge even when one's native soil has become a stinking quagmire' (Magris 1990: p. 71). In comments (which may or may not be justifiable) on Heidegger's claim to be a Black Forest peasant, Magris shows how it is possible to profane local piety. In Heidegger's 'over emphatic identification with a familiar and immediate community – its woods, its hearth, its dialect - there was', writes Magris:

> an implicit claim to a monopoly of authenticity, almost to an exclusive, patented trademark, as if his sincere attachment to his own soil allowed no room for the loyalties of other men towards other soils and other lands... . The inspired asperity with which he affirmed his loyalty led him to accept only the wood outside his own door as authentic, only those peasants whom he knew by name, only that particular gesture of raising an axe above a chopping-block, only that particular word in Alemannic dialect. Other peasants, woods or

> word, customs beyond the mountains or the seas, things he could not see or touch, but of which he could gain only second-hand knowledge, struck him as abstract, and unreal, as if they existed only in dry statistics and were the inventions of propaganda. These abstractions were not alive and tangible, made of flesh and blood ... he was unable to perceive them with his senses, as he could perceive the odour of the Black Forest. (Magris 1990: p. 45)

Magris goes on to claim that Heidegger's 'flirtation with Fascism' was related to this attitude, the 'attitude of someone who knows himself to be a good friend to his next-door neighbour, but fails to realize that other people can be equally good friends to their next-door neighbours' (Magris 1990: pp. 45-46). This attitude is like that of Eichmann who expressed horror on learning that the father of the Israeli officer who interrogated him, and who was respected by him greatly, had met his death in Auschwitz. This horror, observes Magris, derived from a 'lack of imagination [that] had prevented him from seeing the faces, the features, the expressions of real people behind the statistical lists of victims' (Magris 1990: p. 46). Himmler was well aware of the need to prevent people from confronting the human faces of their victims. 'Eighty million good Germans', he states, will each propose 'his own example of a decent Jew', while acknowledging that 'the rest are all animals, but this one here is a fine Jew' (quoted in von Krockow 1993: p. 149).

Part of the positive impulse behind the European project derives from revulsion at the destructive effects wrought by local loyalties, especially nationalism with its 'deep, dark sources' (Berlin 1990: p. 195). The authors of *The Outlook for Higher Education in the European Community* quite rightly draw attention to the dangerous tendency to 'glorify local origins and cultures' (Tabatoni 1993: p. 15).[6] In any case, moral myopia can also apply with regard to European-centred civic education. Even if it were possible to engender feelings of communitarian loyalty and solidarity on the part of European citizens towards one another, Europe is a narrow focus for such feelings. Civic education should have a focus of extra-national commitment, but the bonds of this commitment should extend far beyond the boundaries of Europe (see Williams 1996a; Williams 1996b). In fairness, commitment to the European project is unlikely to lead to the kind of morally reprehensible attachment which sometimes derives from excessive local and national loyalties. But where appropriately conceived and designed, nation-centred civic education can promote a sense of sympathetic imaginative engagement with the lives of citizens of other countries. Rather than seeking to replace it by the cosmopolitan ideal of the 'New Europe', we need to educate national and ethnic sentiment to an enlarged sense of human sympathy. The promotion of imaginative sympathy beyond the boundaries of the nation-state is likely to be more pedagogically effective if it has its basis in the local and the particular rather than in the benevolent but rationalistic cosmopolitan ideal underlying the European project. How then might we develop an imaginative sympathy which extends beyond the boundaries of the individual nation?

Internationalism and the Curriculum

In the task of educating the imagination and resisting ethnocentricity, many subjects have their place. History, geography, religion, philosophy, and the study of foreign languages can all have a role. One of the traditional grounds for studying foreign languages is in fact on account of the perspective which they offer on the peculiar psychological orientation of a people as articulated in the idiom of the language which they use (see Williams 1991). In German, for instance, understanding of the word *gemütlich* entails appreciation of the cultural loading of the expression in terms of the notions of cosiness, intimacy, and congeniality which are so valued in German culture. A different kind of example demonstrates what knowledge of linguistic idiom can illustrate about relationships between people: Irish young people are often baffled by the type of formality marked by the distinctions expressed in such pronominal forms as *tu/vous, du/Sie*, and their equivalents in other languages. The social distance which the terms express can appear odd to them (in the Irish language *tú* is the only form of address in the singular), but later they may come to appreciate the kind of intimacy which is communicated in the familiar form and come to see its value over the Irish form *tú* or over the even the more promiscuous English pronoun 'you'.

Literature, however, is perhaps the most potent avenue to a liberal civic education. More than any other area of the curriculum, literature can help us to learn that 'every other person is basically you'.[7] Part of the thrust of internationalism/pluralism/multiculturalism in civic education should be towards the cultivation of an empathy with the life of other human beings. This is not to treat literature merely as a means to enlarge civic sympathy. Literature is not conceived as simply instrumental to the cultivation of a sensitive, liberal, and generous civic imagination. For example, a sensitive reading of such novels as *The Past is Myself* by Christabel Bielenberg or *Hour of the Women* by Christian von Krockow actually involves increasing our understanding of and sympathy for the complexity of the dilemmas of personal and political loyalty in Nazi Germany. Likewise, part of what it means to respond to a performance of *Observe the Sons of Ulster Marching Towards the Somme* by Frank McGuinness is to understand something of the loyalties, beliefs, and commitments of Northern Irish unionists.

Recent advocacy in civic education of internationalism in general and of the European project in particular seems to have led some people to forget that the fostering of understanding between peoples has been a feature of the practice of teachers of many subjects as a normal part of their work. Most teachers do not need to be exhorted to embrace ideals of human solidarity: they rightly perceive that promoting these ideals is simply part of the educator's job. The authors of the platitudes in the European documents about the promotion through civic education of international understanding would have done better to have spared us their sermons.

Notes

1. See Williams 1995, where I attempt to show how nation-centred civic education might be conceived and conducted in terms which are liberal, critical, generous, and inclusive.
2. A survey of these initiatives can be found in *ATEE News* 1992/93: p. 23.
3. I am not denying that education can serve as a means to something else. A person might study Latin solely in order to meet a requirement for entry to a particular university – or just as she might work in a restaurant in order to earn the money to continue her studies. Indeed in a society where the demand for jobs exceeds supply, education is almost inevitably going to be invested with an instrumental or exchange value.
4. Quotation taken from a speech of Norman Tebbit, the British Conservative politician, at Southampton University as reported in the *Irish Times Weekend*, 26 June 1993.
5. The free market will, however, tend to have a negative effect on the small to medium-size businesses which do not have the resources to exploit the economies of scale available to larger companies.
6. This reasonable observation is followed, however, by the suggestion that this tendency 'sometimes calls into question the need for progress'. Heaven forbid that higher education in the 'New Europe' would do such a thing as call into question the need for progress.
7. Quoted in Callan 1992. This is the explanation of one man for his efforts to rescue Jewish victims of the Nazis.

Part II

The Challenge of Multiculturalism

CHAPTER 4

THICK AND THIN IN CULTURE AND HIGHER EDUCATION

Susan Mendus

At the risk of appearing to revert to a Neanderthal age of philosophical enquiry – the age of linguistic analysis – I want to concentrate here on what is implied by the terms 'culture' and 'higher education'. Consider, to begin with, the following two quotations: the first taken from *The Outlook for Higher Education in the European Community: Responses to the Memorandum*; the second taken from T.S. Eliot's *Notes towards the Definition of Culture*. Under the general heading 'Humanism and the European Cultural Heritage', the EU document declares: 'There is firm agreement that the secular nature of the humanist tradition in European higher education should be maintained. This tradition puts individuals, their personal and social relations with nature at the heart of their investigations and educational goals' (Callaghan 1993: p. 15). By contrast, in 'The Unity of European Culture', Eliot writes: 'The dominant force in creating a common culture between peoples each of which has its distinct culture, is religion… . It is in Christianity that our arts have developed; it is in Christianity that the laws of Europe have – until recently – been rooted… . I do not believe that the culture of Europe could survive the complete disappearance of the Christian faith. If Christianity goes, the whole of our culture goes' (Eliot 1948: p. 122). For Eliot, European culture is Christian or it is nothing; for the respondents to the *Memorandum*, by contrast, the European tradition, at least as it is conveyed through education, is essentially secular. In comparing these two quotations, the question which immediately arises is whether the two claims contradict one another, or whether they reflect different understandings of 'culture' and are therefore addressing separable, though doubtless related problems.

Similar difficulties arise in considering the nature and purpose of higher education. The authors of the EU document note that:

> For most respondents the role of higher education is first and foremost cultural, particularly as the foundation for a united Europe seemed to them to be basically cultural. This cultural role, they said, involved contributing to the furthering of knowledge through research, methodological training and the necessary specialisms. It meant teaching people to have open, critical and creative minds, and encouraging them to take initiatives, favour action and communicate effectively; it should strengthen the spirit of citizenship in a democratic and caring society, based on the 'European cultural heritage.' (Callaghan 1993: p. 13)

Here the role of higher education is intimately linked with creating a certain sort of person – someone who is critical, self-reflective and an active citizen of the democratic society which she inhabits. And it is the single, unifying culture which both informs and is informed by the university in its role as educator.

However, this too is a controversial and contested claim. Michael Oakeshott famously (or notoriously) denies that higher education is *for* anything: 'a university is not a machine for achieving a particular purpose or producing a particular result,' he says. 'It is a manner of human activity' (Fuller 1989: p. 96). Moreover, the appeal to culture in the attempt to justify higher education strikes him as ill-conceived and misguided: 'the pursuit of learning may have the appearance of a fragmentary enterprise... And some who feel most strongly about this are to be found filling in the interstices between the sciences with a sticky mess called "culture", in the belief that they are supplying a desperate need. But both the diagnosis and the remedy spring from a sad misconception' (Fuller 1989: p. 98). Higher education, then, needs no purpose or function and the attempt to provide it with a purpose by reference to 'culture' is doubly misguided.

The quotations that I have taken as my starting point highlight two difficulties in the task which confronts us: the first is to identify what exactly is meant by the term 'culture' in an educational context; the second is to consider what would be the implications of understanding higher education as a means of transmitting or reinforcing culture.

Culture and Higher Education

I begin, then, with the interpretation of 'culture' and my suggestion here is that the differences between the first two quotations reflect different understandings of what culture is. The respondents to the *Memorandum* adopt an understanding of culture which is fundamentally 'thin' and forward-looking, while Eliot adopts an understanding of culture which is 'thick' and backward-looking. Thus, in insisting that the European tradition of higher education is secular and humanist, the respondents to the *Memorandum* are reflecting the fact that, in modern times at any rate, provision of education generally and of higher education in particular, has not required that the student be an adherent of any religious belief.

The use of religious commitment as a form of 'entry test' to university was, of course, common in Britain and the United States in the eighteenth and early nineteenth centuries, but such tests have long since fallen into disrepute and been replaced by what, following Alasdair MacIntyre, we might refer to as 'liberal universities' (MacIntyre 1990: pp. 216–36). MacIntyre laments this change, construing it as one which confused the true belief that religious and other tests were potentially unjust and exclusionary with the false belief that the abandonment of all tests in favour of pure rationality would produce justice in entry and progress in enquiry.

In stating this objection to the liberal university, he has attracted considerable criticism: at some points he appears to be supporting the use of religious and other exclusionary tests as a price worth paying for the maintenance of that coherent intellectual background without which, he says, university education simply degenerates into a cacophony of competing voices. I have myself been critical of this aspect of MacIntyre's thought, but I now want to suggest that there is perhaps more to it than first appears (see Mendus 1992). One of the questions which MacIntyre is raising is whether it is possible to advocate secularism and humanism in the thin sense outlined above without at the same time advocating secularism and humanism in a thicker sense. I suggested earlier that all that is implied in the response to the *Memorandum* is that access to education should not depend upon subscription to a particular system of religious belief. On inspection, however, we may wonder whether the matter can be as simple as that. The recent, and much discussed, case of the wearing of the *chador* in French schools suggests that it is not merely the case that liberal educational institutions do not require any particular religious affiliation; it is also the case that (at least sometimes) they prohibit religious affiliation in educational contexts. Put differently, the secularism of French education is not evidence of its refusal to make religion relevant; it is evidence of its insistence on making irreligion compulsory (see Galeotti 1993; Galeotti 1994).

This is, of course, a provocative way of putting the matter, and it must be said that, in Britain at least, there is widespread incomprehension of the *chador* case, and a concomitant failure to see what could ground an insistence that the wearing of it be forbidden. Nevertheless, the case highlights a question which I take to be central to our concern, and that is whether the thin understanding of culture can consistently be sustained, or whether it also implies a thicker conception, one more akin to that implicit in Eliot's use of the term. As I understand it, the problem of the *chador* arises where and because secularism is understood in a stronger sense than that outlined earlier. The tradition of secularism in French education is long established and dies hard. Hence the prohibition on the wearing of the *chador,* which is construed (rightly or wrongly) as open defiance to a state policy of secularism in education and also as a rejection of the educational purpose of creating and sustaining a distinctively French national identity. Taking this point seriously, however, poses a problem because the *Memorandum*'s claim that there is a tradition of secularism in European education is ambivalent between the claim that religious affiliation is not required and the claim that religious affiliation is (in educational contexts) positively precluded, or at least something to be discouraged.

Doubtless there are differences between higher and secondary education here, but the *chador* case draws our attention to two ways in which secularism may be endorsed, and it is important to be clear about which of these ways is being advocated by the respondents to the *Memorandum*. Additionally, and most importantly for my purposes, it is crucial to be clear whether the original, thin, sense of secularism can be sustained without implicit appeal to a thicker sense of secularism and, concomitantly, whether the thin sense of culture does not require implicit appeal to a thicker sense if it is to be useful in explaining the purpose of higher education. Crudely, what I want to suggest is that the respondents to the *Memorandum* may be endorsing an understanding of secularism which commits them to prohibiting the wearing of the *chador* even though that is not their intention – nor indeed something they desire.

Thick and Thin

To recall, the respondents to the *Memorandum* see higher education as a means of 'teaching people to have open, creative and critical minds, and encouraging them to take initiatives, favour action and communicate effectively'. This notion of people as critical creators is familiar, and indeed dominant, in modern liberal political theory. On one level, it is unobjectionable, since the abilities to criticise, reflect and take initiatives are important skills, and ones without which the individual will fail to thrive in the modern world. However, and as Michael Walzer has recently pointed out, it also presents us with a particular understanding of the shape and direction which a human life should take and, in so doing, it precludes other conceptions. Walzer writes:

> Today we commonly think of our lives as projects, undertakings in which we ourselves are the undertakers, the entrepreneurs, the managers and organizers of our own activities. And the set of our activities, extended over time, planned in advance, aimed at a goal... this is what we mean by a *career*. The word first appears in English with this meaning in 1803; it obviously comes earlier in French, but probably not very much earlier. But this is a historically specific and peculiar understanding of a human life. Think of the alternatives: (1) an inherited life, where I simply take over the place and accomplishments of my parents and make them my own; (2) a socially regulated life, where I get precisely what is due to my birth or my virtue; (3) a spontaneous life, randomly constituted by circumstance and impulse; (4) a divinely ordained, or predestined life, where the plan is God's, not mine, and I obey his will in so far as I can make it out. (Walzer 1994b: pp. 23–24)

Two points are of importance here: the first is that the conception of the individual implicit in the response to the *Memorandum*, and widespread in modern political philosophy, is one which is essentially forward-looking: we have goals which we pursue, actions which we undertake, and careers which we embark upon. It is the future, and not the past, which is of prime importance to us. The second point is that such a conception is at odds with, and indeed positively precludes at least some alternative conceptions of what a life may be. Specifically, it precludes those understandings of life which make essential reference to the past, and those understandings of life which do not give centrality to individual choice. The general contrast is perhaps best expressed in MacIntyre's conception of a human life as having a narrative form: for MacIntyre, one of the major defects of modernity is precisely that it has encouraged (even required) us to view our lives as projects to be undertaken, and in so doing it has precluded any understanding of life as a narrative to be lived out within a context which is already given – a story in which each individual is but a part. The language of role, of status, and of virtue has yielded to the language of agency, individuality, and justice.

What follows from this is that the apparently thin conception of culture and of secularism invoked by the respondents to the *Memorandum* may have a thicker backdrop than at first appears. Or, to put the point paradoxically, the very rejection of thickness may itself be an indirect way of thickening the conception of secularism. By advocating secularism, and explaining it by reference to a conception of people as instigators of action, we marginalise what is given in people's lives. And part of what is given is their cultural heritage, the tradition into which they are born and which provides the vocabulary through which they lead their lives. To see this, we need only look again at Eliot's account of culture. Eliot writes: 'It is in Christianity that our arts have developed; it is in Christianity that the laws of Europe have – until recently – been rooted. I do not believe that the culture of Europe could survive the complete disappearance of the Christian faith. If Christianity goes, the whole of our culture goes' (Eliot 1948: p. 122). What I wish to draw attention to in this passage is the prominence of the past tense: for Eliot, culture involves essential reference to the past, whereas for the respondents to the *Memorandum*, culture is directed to the future. Its importance lies not in identifying the circumstances under which people operate, but rather in projecting those people into a future which is to be predominantly of their own making.

One further consequence follows from this distinction between thin and thick understandings of culture, and of secularism. This is that the role of the political is differently conceived by the two. And that, as the Marxists would say, is no accident. When the respondents to the *Memorandum* emphasise activity, initiative, and agency, they do not see themselves as advocating a specific ideal of human existence. Rather, they would claim, they are setting out the conditions under which people may pursue their own ideal. They are, however, and as we have seen, precluding certain competing ideals, notably those identified by Walzer under the four headings given above. One significant feature of those four ideals is that none of them makes direct reference to the political structure of society. By contrast, the respondents to the *Memorandum* yoke secular culture to democracy. The kind of culture which they are anxious to transmit through education is a culture which has a democratic political order at its heart. What this suggests, to me at least, is that the movement from a narrative to an entrepreneurial understanding of the self is not merely a movement from the backward-looking to the forward-looking; it is also, and connectedly, a movement from a (broadly) social and religious understanding of culture to a political understanding of culture. As the understanding of culture becomes political rather than social, so the understanding of education in general, and of higher education in particular, also gains a political dimension.

However, before pursuing that point and its implications, I want first to reconsider the case which I raised earlier – namely the wearing of the *chador* in French schools. I noted that there has been widespread incomprehension of the French response to this case and, in Britain at least, many people simply fail to see why it has generated such strong emotions. No doubt, this is partly attributable to the different educational practices and philosophies in the two countries: having an established Church, British education has never been secular in quite the way French education has, nor has there been the same insistence on uniformity of education and the creation of a national identity. What concerns me here, however, is whether the secular tradition appealed to by the respondents to the *Memorandum* can, in the end, permit practices such as the wearing of the *chador*: by emphasising the secular nature of the educational tradition in Europe, and urging the importance of creating an active citizenship, the respondents, as we have seen, implicitly preclude alternative understandings of a human life, and in particular they preclude those understandings which make essential reference to the past or to what is 'given'. To appeal to culture as secular and forward-looking is therefore to marginalise any conception of culture as social and religious.

Put differently, if the respondents to the *Memorandum* invoke an understanding of European culture, or tradition, as essentially secular, and if they see the purpose of education as being to transmit and reinforce culture, then it follows that in a European context, religious commitment will be potentially subversive of educational purposes: insofar as religious belief involves obedience to a higher authority, it runs counter to the conception of a human life invoked by the respondents to the *Memorandum*. Of course, it may well be that manifestations of religious commitment, such as the wearing of the *chador*, will be permitted for pragmatic reasons. But it is difficult to see what the principled reason could be for permitting the practice, especially where the religious commitment is one which presupposes a conception of a human life quite distinct from, and in conflict with, the conception implicit in the ideals of democratic citizenship. In saying this I am not arguing that this is the conclusion envisaged by the respondents to the *Memorandum*: my point is simply that their argument drives in that direction, whether they acknowledge it or not.

The conclusion, then, of this section of the paper is that both the respondents to the *Memorandum* and their opponents (MacIntyre and Eliot, for example) accord an importance to religious belief which is, in my view, undesirable. For MacIntyre, this is done explicitly via the insistence that Enlightenment rationality removed the background against which alone progress in enquiry could be attained. It follows, he claims, that coherence can only be reinstated through the establishment of a variety of universities each of which is a place of constrained disagreement. In short, universities must give up the forlorn attempt to operate without any appeal to background conviction and revert instead to their pre-liberal role of advancing enquiry *from a particular point of view*: 'a rival set of universities would result, each modelled on but improving upon, its own best predecessor, the Thomist perhaps upon Paris in 1272, the genealogist upon Vincennes in 1968' (MacIntyre 1990: p. 234). Here, religion becomes central since in many cases it constitutes the essential background against which higher education can take place.

By contrast, the respondents to the *Memorandum* emphasise the secular and humanist tradition of European higher education but, in so doing, they imply a particular understanding of what a human life is, and that understanding conflicts with other, specifically religious, understandings. Since this is so, they will have difficulty tolerating religious commitment in an educational context: the conception of a human life as active, critical, and entrepreneurial sits ill with the understanding of life as a narrative, lived out in a context already given by society or ordained by God. The desire that education should fit people to lead active lives in a democratic society equally sits ill with the encouragement of any form of religious belief which emphasises obedience to higher authority. Therefore, for both MacIntyre and the respondents to the *Memorandum* the attempt to reconcile the requirements of religion with the requirements of life in a democratic society is ultimately doomed. We must either revert to a pre-liberal conception of the university, or we must marginalise religious commitment in educational contexts.[1]

Democracy and Higher Education

Earlier in the paper I suggested that the move from a backward-looking to a forward-looking understanding of culture was also, and of necessity, a move to a distinctively political understanding of education. The time has now come to say a bit more in defence of that suggestion. Whereas the respondents to the *Memorandum* are clear that education has a political dimension, and that one of its purposes is to encourage the qualities necessary for active citizenship in a democratic society, Oakeshott's account of education (and of higher education in particular) eschews all such reference to purposes or aims. Education, he insists, is not *for* anything: 'There is plenty that might properly be criticized in our universities, but to quarrel with them because they are not clear about their "function" is to make a mistake about their character. A university is not a machine for achieving a particular purpose or producing a particular result; it is a manner of human activity.' (Fuller 1989: p. 96)

Oakeshott's account raises the question of whether there is a middle course between the claim that universities should serve a specific political function (that of fitting students to be active citizens in a democratic society) and the claim that they serve merely as repositories of an accepted tradition. He emphasises the importance of critical reflection, urging that the student who graduates from a university will know that it is not good enough to have a 'point of view', that what we need is *thoughts*. Accordingly, Oakeshott writes: 'He will not go down in possession of an armoury of arguments to prove the truth of what he believes; but he will have acquired something that puts him beyond the reach of the intellectual hooligan' (Fuller 1989: p. 102–103). At the same time, however, he resists vigorously any suggestion that this critical capacity is something which is to be justified by reference to some wider political purpose. The university is what it is and not another thing; it does not exist to serve political ends, and universities themselves should resist being cast in the role of handmaiden to politicians, businessmen, or industrialists.

How, then, does the understanding of culture invoked by the respondents to the *Memorandum* lead to a distinctively political justification for higher education? I have suggested that the thin and forward-looking conception of culture brings with it a specific understanding of what a human life is like, and that that understanding conflicts with others: it gives priority to a conception of human beings as active entrepreneurs at the expense of a conception of human life as, in some sense, 'given'. But it should be emphasised that the *motivation* of such an account is not to exclude; on the contrary, it is to identify a 'common core' which will be compatible with a variety of different understandings of how a human life should be led. In the earlier part of this paper I expressed some reservations about whether that aspiration is attainable. My concern now is with the conditions which prompt it, whether or not it is attainable. In the Introduction to *Political Liberalism* John Rawls writes: 'Now the serious problem is this. A modern democratic society is characterised not simply by a pluralism of comprehensive religious, philosophical and moral doctrines, but by a pluralism of incompatible yet reasonable comprehensive doctrines. No one of these doctrines is affirmed by citizens generally. Nor should one expect that in the foreseeable future one of them, or some other reasonable doctrine, will ever be affirmed by all, or nearly all citizens' (Rawls 1993: p. xvi). In other words, modern democratic societies are ridden with conflict. If this conflict is to be 'tamed', then there is a need to provide a political framework which can be agreed upon by all despite their incompatible comprehensive doctrines. It is important to note that, for Rawls, the fact of conflict is a permanent and ineradicable fact: we should not expect that any one doctrine will, in the foreseeable future, be affirmed by all. Education must, therefore, serve two purposes: it must provide students with a knowledge of their legal and civil rights in a democratic society while at the same time honouring their specific cultural background. And he concedes that it might be difficult to fulfil these two aims simultaneously: 'it may be objected that requiring children to understand the political conception is in effect, though not in intention, to educate them to a comprehensive liberal conception. Doing the one may lead to the other if only because once we know the one, we may of our own accord go on to the other' (Rawls 1993: p. 199). I have suggested that there are indeed reasons for thinking that the one may lead to the other.

What is important here, however, is the emphasis which Rawls places on the fact of conflict as *ineradicable and permanent*. By contrast, the respondents to the *Memorandum* envisage a Europe bound by a common culture. They see the purpose of education as being to create, reinforce, and transmit that culture. Whereas for Rawls the fact of conflict is indeed a fact – a permanent problem standing in need of a solution – for the respondents to the *Memorandum* conflict is to be transcended by invoking and instilling a common culture. This movement is crucial, for even if Rawls's reservations are well-founded, and there is, in the end, no way of halting the move from the political to the more substantial, it is nevertheless central to his ambition that education should, so far as possible, remain thinly political, and that it should do so precisely because conflict is an ineradicable fact. For him, therefore, the attempt to deploy education as a means of transmitting culture is to be resisted.

This distinction between those who perceive conflict as an ineradicable fact and those who perceive conflict as something to be transcended is vital for our understanding of education and also, I would suggest, for our understanding of political philosophy generally. Faced by the facts of conflict in modern Europe, yet unable to adopt MacIntyre's solution of educational separatism, the respondents to the *Memorandum* are forced to look to education as a means of creating solidarities. They cannot deny the facts of conflict, nor can they accept those facts as natural and unavoidable. Therefore, they turn to education to provide the remedy for the disease and require of it that it reinforce and transmit a distinctively European culture. It is this which is implicit in the requirement that education be *for* something, and it is this which Oakeshott objects to in his insistence that education be what it is and not another thing.

Conclusion

I have suggested that the thin and forward-looking understanding of culture may be deceptive and difficult to sustain: even a thin conception of culture carries with it an understanding of what a human life is like, and that understanding rules out other and competing conceptions. However, I have also suggested that this thin conception, allied to a conviction that conflict is an ineradicable fact about the modern world, is a necessary insurance against an objectionably political conception of education. The thin conception may be difficult to sustain, not only because it carries its own baggage with it, but also because, by renouncing historical understandings of culture, it is forced to adopt instead social and political understandings. Culture then becomes something to be created, not something to be acknowledged and received. And the obvious place for the creation of culture is an educational institution. This, I suggest, is the danger encountered by the respondents to the *Memorandum*: their belief that education transmits the secularism of the European tradition is false if taken as a statement of fact, either about European culture itself, or about the inhabitants of modern Europe. Neither the tradition nor the inhabitants are secular in the full sense of that word. However, if they are advocating the pursuit of secularism as an ideal, then they should note that this can very easily become an injunction to educators to serve a political purpose. The purpose is, moreover, a politically contentious one, since it assumes that conflict can indeed be eradicated. The history of modern liberal societies is, however, a history of learning to live with conflict, not a history of replacing conflict by harmony. As Stuart Hampshire has remarked: 'We should look in society not for consensus, but for ineliminable and acceptable conflicts, and for rationally controlled hostilities, as the normal condition of mankind; not only normal, but the best condition of mankind from the moral point of view' (Hampshire 1989: p. 189). To enjoin educators to remove that conflict via the creation of a common culture is to issue an instruction which is both philosophically contentious and politically dangerous.

Note

1. It is worth pointing out at this stage that the difficulty in accommodating religious commitment is more acute regarding some religions than others. Islam is often thought to be particularly problematic because it denies the distinction between church and state and is, or can be, an all-encompassing religion. In the Christian tradition, by contrast, the distinction between church and state is familiar, as is the conception of a human life as active, entrepreneurial, and critically self-reflective. No doubt this convergence encourages the belief that the understanding of culture invoked by the respondents to the *Memorandum* is secular in the sense that it does not require any appeal to religious commitment, rather than secular in the sense of being prejudiced against certain sorts of religious commitment.

Chapter 5

The Value of Multiculturalism in Education

Jorge V. Arregui

It is a fact that we live in multicultural societies and states, and that we will continue to do so for years to come. This is not only because of the existence of the European Union but also because many nation-states of Europe have a variety of cultures within them. If the problems generated as the result of European integration are to a certain extent new, the requirements and the achievements of cultural minorities in educational matters within each state are not. On the one hand, higher education in individual countries has for decades reflected differences deriving from different cultural backgrounds, and so homogeneity has been prevented. On the other, European unity has become a challenge for higher education. Having in the past been located within cultural and socio-political contexts determined by national governments, universities now have to reformulate their objectives. If universities have – above all in their Napoleonic conception – been educating citizens, they now have to be aware of the fact that these citizens will be European as well. With the added demands of multiculturalism within nations, these new requirements cannot be fulfilled exclusively in curricular terms.

These two phenomena, the exigencies of cultural minorities within each state and the new European integration, do not necessarily imply opposing tendencies. Since the new pro-European requirements of the universities are not to be read necessarily in homogenising terms, it may be that the two tendencies can progress in the same direction: clearly the European development of the university has to take into account its place in different cultural traditions. No culture has a monopoly over human nature; every cultural tradition is just *one* among others; there is no centre of the world any longer. The requirements of European unity are not *per se* opposed to the demands of cultural minorities. Indeed, as Ibáñez Martín has reminded us, the assertion of the Maastricht Treaty (Article F, third paragraph) that the European Union will contribute to the development of the cultures of its member-states refers also to the different cultures that there are within each state (Ibáñez Martín 1996: pp. 97–98).

The prospect of dealing at the same time both with the demands of cultural minorities within each state and with pro-European commitments raises questions across the range of political theory and practical politics. It is arguable that the backcloth where the outlines of both Europeanism and nationalisms are drawn is the crisis of the nation-state, the reason indeed why we should not be surprised by the strong pro-European commitment of many nations in recent decades. If the nation-state is in crisis, it is plausible that only greater autonomy in universities can enable them to face the challenges of the new Europe. Such autonomy will lead to differentiation.

Cultural pluralism also raises philosophical problems, however. It is not just that the concepts underlying questions of the aims of the university need to be clarified. It is also that awareness of the existence of different cultural traditions obliges us to reformulate old questions and to revise old assumptions. Is the equality of all before the law sacrosanct? Does the kind of questioning which leads to political and cultural relativism lead to epistemological relativism? Is the existence of an irreducible plurality of cultural traditions a hard fact which we must face, or is it to be regarded as a blessing?

Education and Cultural Traditions

European states are beginning to be aware of two realities: their internal multicultural composition and their insertion in supranational structures which are no less multicultural. But their attitude towards multiculturalism varies considerably according to whether they see it as a mere fact or as a blessing. To be more specific, the ideal of neutrality in classical liberalism, as formulated by Rawls, for example, tallies with acceptance of the existence of multiple cultural traditions and a variety of distinct all-embracing moral views as *facts* or, to be more precise, *as inescapable facts* (Rawls 1993). With regard to the versions of liberalism that have been labelled in

Waltzer's terms 'Liberalism 1', it is no coincidence that multiculturalism should appear only as a fact (Waltzer in Gutman 1994a: pp. 99–103). For to consider it as a good the proponents of this view would have to adopt some such all-embracing view, a particular conception of the good life.

The revised versions of liberalism, Waltzer's 'Liberalism 2' – call these moderate varieties of multiculturalism – have as a correlate the idea that the very existence of a plurality of cultural traditions is *per se* good. Consequently, they consciously adopt conceptions of the good life and particular interpretations of human nature and its plenitude – that is, distinct all-embracing moral views – even when they are aware, as in the case of Taylor, that it is not easy to prove that diversity is of itself a value. Taylor underlines the Christian origin of the idea that diversity as such is good, but he does not demonstrate it: he maintains only that, when attempting to understand other cultures, we need to accept the supposition – until the opposite is proven – that they incorporate something valuable for mankind (Taylor in Gutman 1994b: pp. 67–70). This amounts to something like Davidson's principle of charity.

Insofar as Liberalism 1 keeps as an ideal the strict neutrality of the state with respect to cultural traditions and different moral perspectives, as it is programmatically blindfolded to these differences, it cannot assume as its own any cultural task. The state must ensure fair play between different cultures, but it is indifferent as to whether there are, in fact, different cultures or not. According to Liberalism 2, however, if the state can take responsibility for any particular culture, it can also engage in promoting several of them. In this case the criteria of justice that must govern its actions are independent of the alternative conceptions of goodness represented by the different cultural traditions. This last option is not merely a reformulation on another level of the fair play promoted by a blindness to cultural differences: there is here a positive interest in defending and keeping them.

The different attitudes of the state towards multiculturalism – whether it is considered an inescapable fact or a good – are very relevant to education. On the one hand, where cultural plurality is judged simply as a fact that must be recognised by the neutral state, it is usual to try to establish a public educational system that considers itself capable of ensuring a common base of understanding among those who belong to different cultural traditions although it remains neutral between them. To be more exact: its goal is to provide a civic education that will transmit a common core to all as a natural consequence of their common condition as citizens of the state. On the other hand, where cultural diversity is regarded as an intrinsic good, the neutrality of the state is abandoned. It is then possible to promote a public educational system that firmly accepts the fact that all education is necessarily bound to a cultural tradition and that takes as its starting point the promotion of respect and understanding.

The Ideal of Education

The intention of setting up a neutral educational system with respect to cultural differences can be manifested in two ways. Although they might seem different at first, in the long run they coincide. First, it is claimed sometimes that the best way to ensure the neutrality of the state in educational matters is the maintenance of a plurality of different schools – corresponding to different linguistic communities and informed by different religions, ideologies, cultural traditions, etc. Each person can then choose between these options. Along the same lines it is usual to emphasise the right of the parents to choose the kind of education they consider appropriate for their children until the children can choose for themselves. It has not been uncommon to add to these proposals the substitution of the direct financing of schools and universities by a voucher system designed to widen choice for the consumer. The neutrality of the state in educational matters with respect to diverse cultural traditions implies in this view the dismemberment of a single education system.

Second, the neutrality of the state can also be ensured by drawing a sharp distinction between the public and the private spheres, and then confining education to instruction or professional training within the former. Providing the same education system for all will help people to live together even where they have different beliefs and values belonging to different cultural traditions. As the education system is blind to these differences, it can act as a common denominator in the public sphere, despite all the cultural and moral differences in the numerator. Education will involve, on the one hand, the acquisition of basic technical and intellectual skills and elementary scientific knowledge, and on the other, the teaching of public virtues that are essential for life within a democratic state, such as tolerance or solidarity.

The neutrality of the state towards rival conceptions of goodness and human plenitude, therefore, does not imply for this second interpretation the need to eradicate *all* moral content from public education; rather it requires the drawing of a clear distinction between the moralities of particular groups – which are the only ones, as Rawls reminds us that give sense to life – and public moralities. The aim of this kind of education is the development of the kind of citizenship that will provide every individual with the self-reliance to decide straight away about herself and her future and that will ensure meanwhile the transmission of the public (civic) virtues needed to live together in harmony in a liberal society. In other words, in such a system the initial phases of socialisation, which are left up to the family and the community, would be different for the members of the various cultural groupings, while at the secondary phases the education given would be similar, whoever should be responsible for it. The common denominator among citizens would thus be guaranteed by the universality of reason in its theoretical aspects – that is, in positive science, and in its practical use in the form of civic virtues.

In spite of the apparent disparity, however, these two solutions become one and the same: the first shades into the second. Even if the educational system breaks up into a multiplicity of different schools – liberal, socialist, Jewish, Muslim, Catholic, and so on – and these in turn are combined with their different languages, the fact that positive science, on the one hand, and public virtues, on the other, will be held in common by both these schools and those devised according to Liberalism 1 means that the results will be substantially the same. There will be a public sphere containing science and the virtues necessary for democracy and a private sphere determined by cultural, moral, and religious traditions.

The difficulties which arise out of both models of the neutrality of the state, however, are manifold. How, for example, is the individual affected? Such a conception of education necessarily restricts the realms of truth and rationality to the intersubjective public sphere, the contents of which are positive science and abstract morality; the private sphere, in contrast, is starved of rationality and truth. The kinds of moral perspective that give sense to an individual's life come to seem irrational and arbitrary: rationality is monopolised by public morals. Besides, the worst is not that any comprehensive morality comes to *appear* arbitrary: it is that, insofar as reason loses its critical purchase, such a morality *becomes* so, and is *de facto* withdrawn from reflection and rational discussion. To the extent that people can only plan their lives from concrete, pre-rational points of reference, and can do so only by referring to concrete, non-abstract morality, an irremediable hiatus appears between existence and reason: we end up by constructing perfectly rational societies only to let our lives within them be governed by the crassest irrationality. Furthermore, society thus understood proves too abstract and rationalistic, too technical and inhuman, for people to recognise their place within it: it does not succeed in creating an environment in which one can live out one's own life story.

From the sociological perspective, a society constructed according to this model might be said to have very little social integration; indeed it is likely that a socialisation process of the type described would be unable to function properly. Social integration cannot be left up to something as abstract as rationality. In this sense, Vico maintained the existence of a *sensus communis* as the basis of society. *Sensus communis* here does not mean some individual sensory faculty, but the whole set of convictions which members of a society have in common, their common *topos* or meeting place. This is not available for dispute; rather it is that which makes argument possible. Aristotle is right to associate agreement on what is just and unjust with language. But the common feeling of a society is closer to rhetoric than logic: it is not what is demonstrated, but that by which things can be demonstrated, something that precedes the unfolding of reason and acts as its *humus*.

In this way, social integration and agreement on the basic convictions which serve as a foundation for society prove not to be the fruits of reason; instead, as Vico explains, what does issue forth from the exercise of rationality is discrepancy and cultural disintegration (see Choza 1990: pp. 163–94). Even though reflection can dissect and criticise this common sense (see Geertz 1983: pp. 79–93; Ricoeur 1986), and even if philosophy is born of a mistrust of common sense, they cannot replace it: the attempt to establish reflective thought which is free of assumptions is, from the start, doomed to failure.[1] The subjective correlate of the social *sensus communis* is obviously primary socialisation, while reflection and rational critique correspond to a secondary phase. Just as rational discussion cannot replace the *sensus communis* when it comes to providing a basis for social integration, the secondary phase of socialisation cannot replace the primary one.[2]

Against this exposition it is possible to pile up, as in fact has already been done, objections at all levels. To start with, it is not clear that justice can be dispensed independently of a conception of good or of some conception of what human plenitude is. In Naval's words, 'it is the shared possession of a rationally justifiable conception of human goodness that constitutes a previous and necessary condition for the acquisition by a political community of the moral rules which are common to all, precise and rationally based' (Naval 1995: p. 405). From this perspective, public morals cannot be independent with respect to the content of comprehensive private moralities. Public morality lives and nourishes itself on this private content. In accordance with this, it does not seem possible to set out a civic education based on public morals without putting into question certain conceptions of life and human plenitude. The ideal of neutrality proves to be illusory: in morality there is no *view from nowhere*; nor is there a unique perspective concerning public morals that is not in the end dependent on comprehensive private moralities.

Furthermore, as Taylor has repeatedly argued, the concept of the individual that the doctrine of the neutrality of the state entails is inevitably abstract. Although Rawls presents his conception as a political theory rather than a metaphysical doctrine about what a person is,[3] his exclusive characterisation of the person in terms of rational and free agency is too formal and perhaps lacking in content. Rawls interprets the idea of equal dignity in Kantian terms, emphasising above all the individual's *capacity* or *potentiality* for free moral agency (see Taylor in Gutman 1994b). This effects a kind of atomism in which the person becomes something of an abstraction. It also assumes the fiction of a hard and largely unalterable nucleus to the self. 'Liberalism', Feinberg explains, 'treats the self as basically fixed and essentially ineducable with regard to its own nature … . What an individual wants, however, is essentially unconnected with what that individual is.' (Feinberg 1995: p. 49)

In contrast to these views, however, it seems, as Taylor claims, that man is a self-interpreting animal and that humans build up their own personal identity dialogically: 'We become full human agents, capable of understanding ourselves, and hence of defining our identity, through our acquisition of rich human languages of expression.' (Taylor in Gutman 1994b: p. 32) But as we only learn language in social contexts, our self-understanding is necessarily mediated by society. Our self-interpretation – always carried out through systems of symbolic references, essentially of a social nature – is for us constitutive: we forge our personal identity dialogically. There is no hard nucleus to the self superimposed on by cultural and biographical determinations, with ultimately external results. In consequence, beyond the generic and abstract capacity of self-determination, we need recognition of what we have *de facto* made of ourselves. It is exactly this that makes each of us different.

Education and Cultural Pluralism

The assumption that multiculturalism is a fact does not lead very far. But if, in contrast, pluralism is not a *fact* but an intrinsic good, things appear to be different. It is then no longer a question simply of tolerating but of acknowledging it as a good-in-itself. The challenge is then to abandon the search for something like a hard and fixed nucleus to the self, one which is not subject to cultural modulations and biographical decisions. There is no human nature which acts as the substratum common to all cultural differences, and consequently it is inappropriate to devise some form of education tailored to fit it. No civic education can be based on a supposed common condition of all citizens.

Education cannot be understood as a transaction between atomic individuals; education is necessarily initiation into a specific cultural tradition. As Naval has pointed out, education has to be understood, 'as a social practice accomplished within a social tradition and not simply as a transaction carried out among isolated individuals. A social practice is guided by a way of seeing and doing provided by a tradition.' (Naval 1995: p. 131) And its goal is not (narrowly) the autonomy of the individual but (broadly) becoming a person – a moral agent in a community made up of other moral agents.

For that reason, an education sensitive to multiculturalism is not simply a training which includes in its syllabus the study of other cultures. Yael Tamir has argued that there should be three strata to education: a unified stratum of civic education (which in fact will be similar in all multicultural societies), a particularistic stratum of communal education, and a shared stratum of cross-cultural education which will introduce children to the diversity of their own wider society (Tamir 1995: p. 8); but this misses the point insofar as it is impossible to teach the first and the third of those levels from a neutral point of view. An education that acknowledges the existence of different concrete cultural traditions must be aware of the fact that citizens are always educated from and through a particular culture.[4] As a consequence, the central aim of education cannot be personal autonomy, as if there were a self exempt from any cultural influence that might determine itself and reason about itself *ex novo*.[5] There is no such self: every human self is set in a precise social context, rooted in a singular cultural tradition which opens onto certain possibilities even as it closes off others.

Our freedom – like our own self-consciousness – is located. We do not start from nowhere but from a springboard that generations of our forefathers have made possible. We are, as Dilthey insisted, historical beings: we are links in a chain. For that reason, the authentic aim of education is not an absolute fictitious self-determination in empty space, but a real self-understanding. Moreover, to understand oneself implies, amongst other things, the capacity to see oneself as a member of a cultural tradition, which is always *just one* tradition among many others. Self-understanding involves realising that we do not complete human nature; we are only one of its versions.

Feinberg is exactly right when he says that one of the aims of education is the understanding of ourselves, of our own choices and of our own way of living as cultural beings. The aim of a multicultural education is not simply to acquire familiarity with other cultures or to be able to operate in them. It is rather to understand them, because only by understanding other cultures can we understand our own, that is, can we see it as a culture. Freedom does not consist in a fictitious and absolute self-determination, in believing that one is exempt from restrictions; rather it is based on working within a tradition, knowing where we are and being able to modify our situation. The aim of a multicultural education is to enable the student to understand his behaviour and his norms as culturally bound. 'Ultimately', Feinberg explains, 'knowledge of the other cultures enables the student to see her own position as contingent and subject to reflexive knowledge and change. To be educated in a multicultural way means to understand the nature of this contingency and the possibilities for development and change that it provides' (Feinberg 1995: p. 57).

To the same extent, the public system of education cannot have as its aim a civic education based on the cultivation of a public morality determined exclusively by the virtues required to live together peacefully in a liberal society. This is not due to the lack of public virtues – there are indeed public virtues – nor because of the lack of a genuine distinction between public and private spheres of human life. It is because there is such a distinction and because all public virtues are experienced, acquire sense, and are nourished through a private comprehensive conception of the good. There are, of course, characteristic and necessary virtues for the correct functioning of a liberal and democratic society, a society where not everybody thinks the same and where we maintain ideas of the good and the good life that are clearly discrepant; but these public virtues can only be experienced through particular comprehensive moralities, through concrete vital conceptions. Public and civic morals can only be practised in singular enculturations.[6]

There is no neutral ground in cultural traditions or comprehensive moralities. There is an overlapping consensus, but that coincidence always happens in particular situations. Against the idea of a True Description of Things in ethics we might direct all the diatribes that Putnam has raised within the realm of the theory of knowledge. Even if there is an overlapping consensus we do not have access to it *from nowhere*; we cannot claim, to sustain his metaphor, a God's Eye Point of View. And this in no way commits us to the relativism of Anything Goes (see Putnam 1987). I am not asserting that everything is the same, nor denying that there is an area of confluence among all reasonable private comprehensive morals: I am only saying that the realm of public morality is only approachable from our individual starting points.

For this reason, as McLaughlin has claimed, the idea of educational neutrality has to be substituted by a deep discussion about the cultural norms that are to be taught to the students. Even under the assumptions of Liberalism 1, it is not possible to educate only from liberal principles. A cultural consensus is required to determine where to start: 'The common school has an obligation to "transmit" the basic or non-negotiable forms which articulate the framework of a liberal democratic society. In addition to these, the common school cannot avoid transmitting some norms which are culturally distinctive in the sense that they selectively favor some beliefs, practices and values in ways that go beyond what could be justified from a strictly neutral point of view' (McLaughlin 1995: pp. 88–89). The solution does not rest so much on attempting an impossible neutrality but in foregrounding resolutely discussion of those norms that constitute the starting point for further reflection to open them to criticism. In the same way, schools must not ignore particular moralities, as if they were only a spin-off of the overlapping consensus. Rather they should teach us to reflect rigorously on its contents and assumptions in order to understand them better because 'the view that certain issues are significantly controversial, and that they ultimate require personal assessment by individuals, is importantly distinct from an acceptance of relativism' (McLaughlin 1995: p. 93).

The Value of Cultural Diversity

According to Taylor, the idea that cultural diversity is a good in itself and not simply an inescapable fact has religious origins. Beyond theological considerations, however, the analysis of the interaction between nature and culture can show in what sense cultural diversity as such is a good. With that in mind, it is convenient to review first the 'uniformitarian' conception of human nature. This will lead to the consideration of a teleological conception of nature which will allow us to assert cultural diversity as a good.

The idea of an ineducable core of the self has ramifications for the relation between nature and culture. These correspond to what Clifford Geertz has called 'the "stratigraphic" conception of the relations between the biological, psychological, social, and cultural factors in human life. In this conception, man is a composite of "levels", each superimposed upon those beneath it and underpinning those above it' (Geertz 1973: p. 37). This stratigraphic view fits well with the classic Kantian distinction between the *natural* – what nature has made of man, the object of study of physiological anthropology – and the *cultural* – what man has made of himself, examined by anthropology from a pragmatic point of view. In this approach, nature reappears as what is given to the human being in advance, whether on the biological or the psychological plane, whereas culture is regarded as what the human being makes of himself.

Nature and culture are opposed in this conception. The next step is to think in terms of two separate spheres that are self-sufficient and mutually exclusive. There would seem to be an independent natural order which centres around itself, onto which a similarly autonomous cultural order is superimposed. Constant, unchanging, and eternal, the natural constitutes true human identity, whereas what is cultural and acquired is viewed as inessential, contrived, transient, and accidental. The natural and the given determine the universal essence of humanity, while culture is variable and therefore accidental and transitory. The historical succession of cultures and their plurality then show up as a carnival while natural human identity can only be apprehended by removing masks.

Writers from Lovejoy onwards have termed this interpretation of the relationship between nature and culture 'uniformitarianism'.[7] The uniformitarian thesis is summed up well by Geertz: 'The Enlightenment view of man was, of course, that he was wholly in one piece with nature and shared in the general uniformity of composition which natural science, under Bacon's urging and Newton's guidance, had discovered there. There is, in brief, a human nature as regularly organised, as thoroughly invariant, and as marvelously simple as Newton's universe. Perhaps, some of its laws are different, but there *are* laws; perhaps some of its immutability is obscured by the trappings of local fashions, but it *is* immutable' (Geertz 1973: p. 34). This uniformitarianism corresponds to individualism: the chemically pure 'individuals', these atoms which later form society, are exactly the same as each other. They possess the same uniform human nature, later concealed by different cultural masks. But beneath each mask, behind each cultural *persona*, the person is always essentially the same.

The illustrated conception of nature implies the rise of a new educational paradigm: the ideal, paradoxical though it may sound, of a natural education. An education based directly on human nature would liberate it of cultural prejudices and of all attachment to a singular tradition. But it would include what was already within that very nature: being based on the universality of nature and reason, this would be essentially cosmopolitan. 'The laws of nature', writes Willey, 'are the laws of reason; they are always and everywhere the same, and like the axioms of mathematics, they only have to be presented in order to be recognised as proper and correct by all men' (Willey 1940: pp. 1–2). The uniformitarian concept of nature was thus able to carry out the function previously exercised by concrete cultural traditions in the educational process, with the advantage that this change ensured concord, tolerance, and progress among human beings.

The illustrated uniformitarian conception of human nature – in which the latter appears as an inalterable core, as a constant bio-psychological structure of the human being, or as what is given beforehand – is bound to an empiricist assumption. This is that the nature or essence of a species or genus is determined by the set of characteristics that are common to all the individuals which fall into that particular category: a process of abstraction, a process by which we would forget the individual characteristics concentrating only on the universal features, should be enough to determine the essence of something. Consequently, human nature is seen merely as the set of contingent features common to all members of the human species, that which is in fact common to all human beings.

Since empiricist abstractionism produces uniformitarianism, abandoning the empiricist abstractionist view enables us to rupture the identification of nature or essence with what is in practice common to all, and therefore to leave uniformitarianism behind. For Aristotle human nature is not what is factually common to every man. Rather it is defined teleologically. Human nature is not identified with a supposed uniform common substratum, but takes its identity from what human beings are to become once they have reached their full potential, if they do. As Aristotle writes in the *Politics*, 'that which each thing is when its growth is completed we speak of as being the nature of each thing, for instance of a man, a horse or a household' (p.1). Human nature is not seen as an ingredient of the human being, but as what man is when he attains his maturity. For this reason, nature lies not at the beginning but at the end.

Compared with a view such as the uniformitarian, the Aristotelian concept of nature may seem relativistic. How are we to decide what the best is, or what is meant by man's 'maturity'? There seem to be – perhaps against what Aristotle himself thought – many different interpretations of what exactly this human fullness is. The Aristotelian approach does not provide the bedrock which uniformitarianism purports to offer. Aristotle does not use the concept of nature as something that runs counter to the concept of culture; nor does he seem to have felt a sense of vertigo in the face of cultural relativism. When people do suffer from vertigo, what they want is *terra firma*, and this is just what uniformitarianism seems to offer. When faced with existential vertigo, people seek certainty rather than truth. But the Enlightenment concept of nature, however solid it may seem, cannot even serve the function for which it was introduced: nature as a series of facts, however common and universal they may be, does not rise above the level of the factual, and therefore lacks moral significance. Even if nature is, under this view, as solid and firm as possible, it has no moral value.

Nature is only a criterion for our moral actions when it is understood teleologically, in terms of tendencies, not of pure facts.[8] It offers a guide for action at the price of losing its straightforwardness. As 'nature' and 'plenitude' define each other, there arises in Aristotle an authentic hermeneutic circle because in the second book of his *Physics* Aristotle defines nature in a teleological way. In the first chapter he maintains that those things are natural, or exist naturally, that have in themselves, essentially and not accidentally, a principle of movement (or change) and rest (p. 1). But if the natural is what holds within itself the principle of movement, nature is regarded in a nonfactual way, being understood as something teleological and dynamic. What is natural is not identified with what is merely given; something is natural because it regulates its own operations itself, for which reason these operations can truly be called its own. What is natural is what has an operation of its own, and to this extent it is not so much what is given; rather it is the end of its own natural dynamics.

As it is in the very nature of living beings to attain their fullness through their own activity, it is not possible to have a naturalistic reading of the Aristotelian concept of nature. There is no point in constructing an opposition between what nature has made of men and what they have made of themselves. Insofar as the nature of an animal is revealed not in the original embryo but in the adult individual which that embryo is destined to become, Aristotle can declare roundly that 'nature is the goal for the sake of which the rest exists'; and he can specify that not any kind of termination is a goal, but only the best. Nature, he states in the same chapter, 'which is received through generation, is a route towards nature' (p. 2).

If nature is defined by its end, it includes what man makes of himself, and therefore in Aristotle's view nature embraces culture and art. In the eighth chapter of Book II, he explains without hesitation that 'indeed as a general proposition, the arts, either, on the basis of nature, carry things further than nature can, or they imitate nature' (p. 8). Art, then, sometimes proves to be *mimesis* of nature, but on other occasions it is a genuine *aletheia*, a revelation of what something really is, as it is only through the mediation of art, of culture, that nature can reach its best. In this sense, Gadamer has stated that in the classical view, as opposed to the modern approach, nature and art 'complement' each other positively (Gadamer 1975: p. 74).

There are perhaps two places in Aristotle's works where the teleological concept of nature and, consequently, the way in which nature relates to culture are especially clear. For in the *Politics*, Aristotle maintains that man is by nature both *zoon logistikón* and *zoon politikón*. First, man is by nature a being endowed with language, the only animal capable of speech. Yet however natural man's ability to speak may be, it can only be put into practice within a cultural context, as we can only speak in a particular, concrete language, and every language is cultural. To state that man is by nature endowed with speech is not the same as saying that a natural language once existed which human beings could speak spontaneously, that the human vocal cords once produced propositions as the pancreas secretes bile, but rather that man is the only animal capable of learning a language. The natural ability of learning a language can only be put into practice in cultural terms: nature refers back to culture. In no way can it be said here that nature is the common substratum underlying all languages.

Secondly, the fact that the *polis* is natural does not mean that it is common or spontaneous, but that it is the optimum means of organising the human social community. Furthermore, Higinio Marín has recently stressed that the Aristotelian thesis as to the nature of the *polis* and his teleological concept of nature imply that Aristotle considered culture – a concrete form of culture – to be natural. Aristotle lacks any idea of cultural relativity: the cultural sphere is so natural that Aristotle tends to deal with it as though it were nature. Thus, what for us is *a* culture and *one particular* socialisation process represents for him *the* culture and *the* socialisation process, that is, the specific human nature. The *polis* and its socialisation process, the *paideia*, are so natural that all the other forms of social community and all the other possible socialisation processes are orientated towards them, as if to their natural end. For Aristotle, then, man is Greek, adult, male, and free. Other specimens of the human species – barbarians, slaves, women, and children – are human only up to a point, as though by participation (see Marín 1993).

To the extent that the teleological version of human nature is accepted, as against Enlightenment uniformitarianism, it can be understood that human nature itself refers to the cultural sphere, that man is *by nature* a cultural being, or even that culture *unveils* or may unveil the truth of nature. 'The interpretation of the instinct', as explained by Spaemann, 'does not happen by itself, nature is what we call "rational". Only through reason nature is manifested as nature' (Spaemann 1989: p. 244). Culture is the truth of nature (see Choza 1988: especially pp. 431–40), because if, in the physical world, only through human work can nature become all that it has the potential to be, only through his own activity can man become everything that he can be. This is why Pascal's definition of man as the being who overcomes himself is fair and accurate (Pascal 1960: pp. 80, 82). Man is always more than what he is, because he has to do something with himself, because he has to do something with what he is.

Nature and Culture

Although Aristotle holds that Greek culture is not just one culture among many, but nature itself, it is clear that the cultural order is essentially plural and that the processes of humanisation are, therefore, also many and varied. It is of the essence of man that he has to become *human*, and there is no 'natural' process of humanisation. It is not necessary to subscribe to all Foucault's opinions in order to admit that 'Man' is an invention of the Enlightenment. In fact, only *people* exist, and they must necessarily belong to different races, cultures, traditions, and ways of life. Just as it is not possible to speak in general, but only to speak a particular language, it is impossible to be a man in general; one can only be a Bushman, a European, etc. Man is *by nature* a cultural being: each culture has to provide an interpretation of what a human being is, how human beings behave, and what activities need to be carried out in order to reach fulfilment. If we give the label 'human' to the model that each culture provides of human fullness, of the type of activities it considers to be the 'highest', 'most noble', or 'best', then we have to accept that there are different forms of human being at different periods in history. Different cultures in different historical periods always have their own different models of what is best for the human being, and how this should be achieved (see Marín 1990: p. 4). The archaeologist Graham Clark puts it succinctly:

> By contrast with other animals whose behavioural patterns are determined by their species, are programmed by genetic inheritance and with only local exceptions are homogeneous within breeding populations, it is of the essence of human beings that they conform to the customs and values of the societies to which they belong, societies which being constituted by history are necessarily unique. Men have not attained to human dignity by sharing a generalised culture, nor have they reached their peaks of attainments by achieving the abstract status of being civilised. They have achieved humanity by sharing specific cultures and particular civilisations. (Clark 1983: pp. 150–51)

There is no uniform nature to which a variety of cultural accretions adhere: there is no common substratum. If we try to strip away the cultural layers to find out what human nature is, we shall be left with nothing specifically human at all. But criticism of uniformitarianism need not lead to cultural relativism. The teleological conception of human nature leads rather to pluralism, as opposed to both uniformitarianism and cultural relativism: the fact that there is no single way of being human does not imply that anything goes. The fact that we cannot incorporate into one single matrix all the phenomena and values expressed by different cultures, that no common denominator exists that might enable us to add together all the cultural fractions, that the realms of the human are irremediably multifarious, does not imply relativism.[9] Some things are better than others; some actions are right, others wrong. There are cultural phenomena that carry nature beyond itself in the direction it is heading itself, and others that betray that same nature. Abandoning the supposed bedrock of uniformitarianism does not mean that we are doomed to founder on the shifting sands of relativism: the fact that many cultures exist does not mean that they are sealed monads between which communication is impossible, or that value judgements are out of place.

But it is not just that no Man exists. Rather people exist, and they differ. The truth is that the process of every human life is a process of burgeoning individualisation. 'When seen as a set of symbolic devices', as Geertz summarises, 'for controlling behavior, extrasomatic sources of information, culture provides the link between what men are intrinsically capable of becoming and what they actually, one by one, become. Becoming human is becoming individual, and we become individual under the guidance of cultural patterns, historically created systems of meaning in terms of which we give form, order, point, and direction to our lives. And the cultural patterns involved are not general, but specific' (Geertz 1973: p. 52). What human beings have in common, he concludes, is neither a uniform substratum nor certain empirical cultural universals; it is rather a task, the job of becoming individuals, and it is in the course of this process, in the archetype of human existence, that we should seek man's nature.

There is no one single way of being human. Just as the human being is always male or female, belonging to a sexual type, so each culture produces a modification of nature, a different realisation of human nature's possibilities. The only way to reach the true, unfathomable nature of man is to heed the diversity of its expressions. As the nature of the human being is not a common substratum, it is not to be found behind or beneath cultural diversity.

In Dilthey's foreword to *The Spiritual World: Introduction to a Philosophy of Life*, written in 1911, the year of his death, he expressed this idea poetically in the following words: 'I grew up with an insatiable desire to find in the historical world the expression of our life in its multifarious forms and depth.' (Dilthey 1973–82, Vol. VII: p. 4) For as he tells us repeatedly, we can only penetrate into the depths of human nature by examining the diversity of its expressions: 'What man is cannot be discovered by ruminating about oneself, or by psychological experiments, but through history,' (Dilthey 1973–82, Vol. VII: p. 180) given that 'the entirety of human nature can only be found in history' (Dilthey 1973–82, Vol. VIII: p. 204). When self-consciousness is understood as a solipsistic reflection, we end up by confusing the essence of man with a concrete historical product. In order to reach an awareness of what man is, we must become conscious of his human variety; that is, we need an historical consciousness.

What, then, is the ultimate basis for this pluralism? In the rationalist, uniformitarian vision of the Enlightenment, the differences are always suspect. Lovejoy expresses this clearly: since uniformitarianism regards it as being obvious that reason is the same for all men, rational life admits of no diversity. Boileau had formulated the very same idea: '*La raison pour marcher n'a souvent qu'une voie*' (Boileau *Art Poétique*, Chant Premier, v. 48). Differences of opinion or taste are in themselves signs of error, while their universality is a guarantee of truth. 'Every phenomenon', Lovejoy concludes, 'whose intelligibility, verifiability or real affirmation is restricted to men of a particular time, race, temperament or condition is *eo ipso* lacking in truth and value, or is an occurrence which does not hold the least importance for a reasonable man' (Lovejoy 1948: p. 80).

The basis for pluralism would lie in the negative approach: there is only room for cultural pluralism because man is not perfectly reasonable, or because his knowledge is always imperfect. Were his knowledge perfect, if man were capable of comprehending reality and himself at a glance, there would be no grounds for pluralism. If human existence were not spread out in time, if man could possess himself in one instant, if he could gather together in a single act of reflection all his possibilities, were he but capable of bringing together the whole of himself in one, timeless instant, there would be no place for his extension in time or for the multiplicity of his facets and expressions. The truth would be undivided. Everything would fit perfectly, the truth would be, as Parmenides wanted, round and solid, and human subjectivity would have a single expression that would take all its aspects into account. In this view, pluralism, however inevitable it might be, would arise out of a shortfall or limitation in our constitution.

Nonetheless, the dream of an absolute cultural expression for human subjectivity turns out to be more of a nightmare than a mirage. As man is a historical being, as he is intrinsically temporal, the notion of an absolute culture or spirit is utterly senseless. If man were a spirit simply contained in this world by his bodily machine, perhaps he might be able to dream of a perfect and absolute temporal expression of his spiritual essence; but man is not a spirit in time, or a spirit in the world: he is a certain type of animal whose first act, which Aristotle calls 'soul', is spiritual. Man is not everything that he can be at once because he has to go on as he lives, he has to set about realising his potential little by little. This is why the idea of *one* absolute cultural expression, *one* objectivisation of his subjective spirit, is inappropriate. The notion of culture, or of an absolute historical epoch, is, as Dilthey strives to show to counter Hegel, intrinsically contradictory. Man is a historical being not so much because he has a past as because he has a future. The objective spirit, which is what culture embodies, is, like human existence itself, a constituent *not yet*.

Only man forms his subjectivity through the unending process of cultural objectifications. The plurality of his cultural objectifications, however, proceeds not from the poverty, but from the wealth of what goes into them. It is not that the human intellect is deficient; it is rather that both it and reality are rich. We cannot speak of a plurality of possible perspectives, characteristic of the human intellect, in the knowledge of animals. Because animal consciousness extends only as far as what is known, it does not know of itself as an entity which knows reality, it cannot stand at a remove from its own awareness and relativise it. The wealth of the human consciousness, however, appears not as absolute knowledge but as awareness of man's own finiteness, of which it is only one view. The animal knows things about the world, but it does not know about its own knowledge, and so cannot compare what it knows with what is real. Its knowledge is not reflexive: although it is conscious of the real, it is not aware of its own consciousness; it is not self-conscious, in the proper sense of the word. Man, however, precisely because his knowledge is reflexive, because he knows that he knows, becomes aware that his knowledge does not encompass the entirety of what is real, that new manifestations of reality are always possible that do not tally with what he knew before, that reality can always disconcert us. For this reason, human wisdom, that attribute of the man who is an *expert in humanity*, can never be an absolute knowledge, only a form of knowledge that is always open to new experiences.[10]

As Dilthey remarked, 'the last word in the historical vision of the world is the finiteness of all historical manifestations' (Dilthey

1973–82 Vol. V: p. 9). But consciousness of finiteness does not imply relativism, rather the awareness of the sovereignty, independence, and freedom of the human spirit with regard to all and every one of its manifestations (Dilthey 1973–82, Vol. V: pp. 252, 406). The wealth of human nature is such that it requires multiple forms of expression: there is no place for uniformitarianisms. Cultural pluralism is therefore the expression of superabundance, not poverty.

Notes

1. See, for example, Ricoeur's criticism of Habermas (Ricoeur 1973: pp. 25–61; 1997).
2. Rorty has defended the idea that education implies two different processes which have different aims: socialisation and individualisation. The first must precede the second. While the target of the first is to transmit those beliefs that the society holds as true and without which it is impossible to function as a member of that society, that of the second is to stir up reflective and critical thought. According to Rorty, the processes must not be confused: the first probably applies to schooling and the second to higher education (see Rorty 1989a: pp. 188–204; Rorty 1989b: pp. 28–31; Rorty 1990: pp. 41–44). Naval has pointed out that it is not clear that Rorty has offered enough reasons to consider socialisation and critical thought as two consecutive processes rather than two aspects of the same process that can be pursued simultaneously (Naval 1995: pp. 154–58).
3. See J. Rawls (1993: pp. 29–35). On the impossibility of offering a treatment of justice, or even a political theory of what a person is that is not related to metaphysical conceptions, see J. Haldane (1991: pp. 77–95).
4. The difference between teaching about culture and teaching through culture is underlined by W. Feinberg (1995: pp. 45–58).
5. For questioning of autonomy as the only aim of education, see S. Cuypers (1992: pp. 5–17; and Cuypers in Amilburu, 1996: pp. 119–33).
6. I have argued that ethics must be enculturated in specific cultural traditions in my previous work (1988).
7. See A.O. Lovejoy (1948: pp. 79–82). However, this claim is not as universal as he pretends. Very recently, Rodríguez Lluesma has underlined the fact that Adam Smith breaks with the stratigraphical model since for the Scottish thinker intersubjectivity is constitutive of subjectivity (1994).
8. See R. Spaemann, in Alvira, pp. 49–67. Spaemann has developed the idea of a teleological nature in many of his books (Spaemann 1987; Spaemann 1989; Spaemann 1992). Another very interesting conception of the relation between nature and morality is spelt out by M. Rhonheimer (1987).
9. For an excellent defense of this thesis, see I. Berlin (1991: pp. 70–90); see also H. Putnam (1987) and R.J. Bernstein (1983).
10. The best exposition of this point can be found in the corresponding epigraph of Gadamer's *Truth and Method*.

CHAPTER 6

MULTICULTURAL EUROPE AND THE UNIVERSITY:

A MORAL *AND* EDUCATIONAL CHALLENGE?

Paul Smeyers

In answering the question stated in the title of this chapter it is necessary to be clear about what we understand by the term 'university' and also what we mean by that essentially contested concept *par excellence* – education. In order to answer this question in a clear way, then, I will use as a frame of reference Belgium's university system because I am convinced that so many issues are interconnected here that it is not fruitful to deal with this matter in general terms.[1] It is with this context in mind then that I will try to answer the question whether we have to change university education as a consequence of what has come to be thought of as multicultural multi-ethnic Europe. To put the matter another way, does Europe or the EU confront us with a moral or an educational challenge? I will begin in a fairly broad way by acknowledging the historical background to this question in terms of the kinds of universities which have in fact developed. It is not my intention to go into the detail of historical developments, as, for example, in the chapter by Weijers, but some scene-setting is necessary in order to understand the kinds of changes which have taken place and the situation we now face. In particular, the different expectations people have of the university need to be sketched. Is multiculturalism one such expectation? Two issues will be dealt with: the radical challenge of multiculturalism and the politics of multicultural initiatives in the university. What are the implications of relativism with regard to such questions? Ultimately the chapter seeks to explore the conclusions which can be drawn for educational theory and policy concerning the curriculum of the universities.

Changing Conceptions

According to the *Encyclopedia Britannica* the earliest universities (in the late eleventh and twelfth centuries) were institutions in which the essences or 'universals' were studied. They were corporations of students and masters and they received their charters from popes and emperors. Provided they taught neither atheism nor heresy the early corporations were free to govern themselves. They also financed themselves, this being the price of their independence. So teachers charged fees and had to please their students. Though a lot has changed since the 11th and 12th centuries, the question of who pays has always been a cause of concern. I will return later to this matter but let us consider first what we expect a university to do.

If we exclude its useful social roles, the purposes of the university can generally be understood in terms of education and inquiry. When we think about the aims of education, our primary concern is with how we are to go about nurturing and enhancing the powers of the mind. We are asking what knowledge, beliefs, and values we want cultivated, generally and systematically. We are also concerned with methods of inquiry and with the conceptual and empirical issues that questions of methodology raise. A university does not teach mindlessly; it scrutinises its teachings in order to criticise, re-examine, and reformulate received ideas. It thinks for itself. Ultimately the intrinsic purpose of the university is to understand human life and the nature of reality. Over the centuries this project has taken different forms and has led in diverse directions, but by and large it has remained a place where people have gone on voyages of discovery and returned to tell us what they have found. The university does not trade in everyday knowledge; it tells us how things are outside our immediate locality, beyond the boundaries of the commonplace and of common sense.

The university does not just pass on a tradition but creates a particular story that gives the tradition point and meaning: it provides understanding. Traditional universities have tended to develop in divergent and unsystematic ways. Clearly not everything can be taught and so inevitably a university's curriculum and practices are selective. In the views of some, it is imperative that the university make manifest its criteria for the selection of its curriculum. Then, some critics believe, the overriding influence of the white male-dominated cultures of western Europe and (traditional) North America, with their assumptions of superiority and universality, will become apparent. The issue of multiculturalism is a matter I will return to below.

There is a conflict here. On the one hand, it is accepted that what is taught is simply *a* tradition. In this case the question of how that tradition is to be construed and defined is settled by the assertion of power and control. On the other hand, standards independent of culture are invoked – for example, standards of reason as independent of context and cultural legacy but universal in application. It is assumed that there is a view from 'nowhere' from which one can judge the credibility of statements, the trustworthiness of observations and beliefs, or the excellence or utility of a human performance; and that creates huge epistemological problems.

By analogy, if we take the function of inquiry seriously and assert that the importance of the university's disinterested and unfettered pursuit of truth, then acculturation can never be a primary objective. To that extent the university must, of necessity, stand outside and interpret a culture, deciding what should be emphasised and what ignored. Again, to do this legitimately it must invoke standards that are seen as independent of a particular culture or of a culture that is dominant during a particular period. Of course, the culture and the university are not discrete things. The university forms part of a culture and functions, it is to be hoped, as a centre for criticism of that culture. It goes without saying, therefore, that what is important here is the teaching of these standards rather than simply the uncritical transmission of cultural products. It is not what the university knows but how it finds out that matters particularly. Its real work is to produce useful ways of thinking, to find out what can be done with the powers of reason. In essence this is to construct or invent ways of thinking – habits, techniques, disciplines of reason, and practices of inquiry. But again: matter and content are not independent. The offering of a paradigmatic method together with a particular set of problems and solutions is a way of making clear how research is properly done.

This concept of a university is reminiscent of Von Humboldt's ideal of a university, an ideal which has origins in the philosophies of Kant and Schelling (see Menze 1976; Habermas 1986; Hellemans 1994). Kant reverses the medieval division between higher faculties (theology, law, medicine) and philosophy – the latter enjoying a greater freedom as it is not of interest to the state. Because the faculty of philosophy is the only one which is to operate not under the law of the government but under the law of reason, serving the truth, it now becomes the highest. The traditional higher faculties can only claim to be scientific when led by philosophy. Sciences which aim at being useful are, according to Kant, in contradiction with the concept of science itself. His position is further radicalised by Schelling: the sciences will become a part of a more general philosophical framework. Only insofar as they reach the general (in the particular) are they true sciences. In this idealist picture truth presents itself in an historical, external, objective shape. The particular historical reality is a result of the truth, which can come anew to itself through scientific knowledge of that reality. For Schelling, the sciences become constitutive elements of a more all-embracing philosophical question. And by assigning this task to the sciences and the university, Schelling can combine the task of research with that of development and education (*Bildung*).

In Schelling's university the purposes of inquiry and education become one. The university's inquiry is not aimed at practical knowledge but at the general in diversity: to see the essential through the inessentials in order to achieve absolute and true knowledge. From an individual point of view this opening up of truth coincides with the process of self-realisation. This coming into the openness of truth coincides with the subject accomplishing its essence. Identifying inquiry with education (*Bildung*), Schelling emphasises that university education is never just the transfer of knowledge, that it has to be inquiry and research at the same time. University education must stimulate the productivity of the mind; only thus can one become fully human.

Von Humboldt accepts neither Schelling's notion of the absoluteness of truth nor the role of philosophy to determine what is true. He does not agree that a university education is essentially a study of a philosophical nature. Nevertheless he maintains the identity between inquiry and education. For Von Humboldt, scientific research has no other aim than the production of knowledge and this is how human beings are essentially realised. In this kind of university the higher faculties are those leading towards knowledge for its own sake, the highest disciplines those whose knowledge cannot be used as a means towards something else. Thus, mathematics and the arts are elevated to join philosophy while the empirical sciences find their place at the periphery. Real university education is once again that kind that furthers the development of the individual, and this is the pursuit of truth as an end in itself. Education in essence can never be aimed at usefulness because that would imply a reference to particular individuals and groups; that which most fully realises the human being is that which is universally true.

Developments within the sciences, but also within philosophy, have radically altered this picture of the structure of the university and of knowledge. Sciences are now elevated on a pedestal and general insights are less highly valued. New disciplines have emerged producing high expertise in ever smaller parts of reality. What universities used to teach seems, therefore, out of touch. The evolution they find themselves in has itself been led by an interest in outcomes. It is particularly those (sub-)disciplines concerned with the progressive manipulation of the world that have expanded. The place for the general has gradually been eroded. This moreover makes clear the embeddedness in its time and place of any university education.

Though universities have developed differently within different countries, they are brought together by the tension in the role they now commonly face. The crisis – some speak of the death of the university – has to do with the university's seeming inability to live up to society's expectations. On the one hand, the higher educational system does not deliver the output needed by the economic system, and it struggles against demands that it adapt or disappear. On the other, it is criticised for narrowing its aims to *economic ends* and for the *functional/mechanical* concept it has developed of itself. In this second case, the university is criticised for the position in society which it takes on. The university finds itself captured in *several contradictions*: between a place of learning (where what is learnt is somehow useful) and a place of personal development, between individual and social education (though these need not to be mutually exclusive), and between a technical and an ethical practice (focused on rethinking and applying the fundamentals of how we ought to live together). Within the range of the ethical there are different (sometimes conflicting) 'value-frameworks' for which no solid basis in social consensus can be found. Of one and the same person, the university is expected to make not only both an emancipated autonomously thinking individual and an efficient contributor to the economic system, thus building social cohesion and safeguarding present frames of value reference. To put this more bluntly, there is a rift between the university mission statement and what it in fact does because of all kinds of social and economic pressures. The idea that a university education should be primarily concerned with the individual's *Bildung* has waned. The knowledge (and skills) to be acquired now have to offer the prospect of a well-paid job, or otherwise of contributing to what is socially useful. The ends of higher education have faded from view as it becomes yoked to an instrumentalism geared to the satisfaction of (basic) needs.

Here it must be asked of the university whether a competence-based system can be reconciled with a commitment to personal development. One thing that is involved here is *who* decides the good for the student. Are the decisions of the business community to be overriding when these are governed by the needs of the economic system and their desire to a mass profit (see Blake in this volume)? Another thing is whether an education that is aimed at individual autonomy can be reconciled with society's expectations (see Smith in this volume). If one accepts that such objectives cannot be reconciled, then this is – in light of the educational ideal of the modern age – an important and far-reaching position. Maybe the *contradictions* indicated are the result of the modern concepts of *rationality* and *subjectivity*. Recalling the criticisms of the Frankfurt School, one can refer to the degeneration of rationality into instrumental rationality and one can also point to the disconnection of ethos and technicity (a positivism also amounting to a particular *concept of action)*. As it is quite evidently not possible to deal with these matters within the scope of this paper, suffice it to indicate the contradictions and the tensions these create.

There is yet a further element to be outlined to do with differences between Anglo-Saxon and (Continental) European universities. Where the former, in the social sciences, at least, have first degrees which are generally nonvocational and in general followed by the possibility of subsequent vocational education, most of the latter have systems of earlier vocational specialisation. In Belgium, for example, university degrees in psychology or in educational sciences have a vocationally specialised curriculum from the first year onwards. Though still a place for learning, the focus on a specific area of learning is geared to particular demands from professional interests in society. This professional/vocational education is the very essence of those contemporary European universities. The central commitment, the single activity that gives it clear identity, is to the sustained examination of established doctrine and techniques, to the end of enhancing some form of human practice. This professional education is obviously not just a matter of learning how to apply the 'steps' of a prescribed technique. It is always a subtle, sensitive, and somewhat elusive process. It is a matter of evoking dispositions to perceive and interpret in a certain way. It is learning to judge and to act according to a system of ideals, norms, and standards. It is also always moral education, a process of induction into a normative culture, a way of life, an order whose code is justified as contributing to excellence in the performance of a vital human function. The tantalising questions this raises will have to be left for another occasion. There are, however, two clear strands which can be seen: specialisation and theory, on the one hand, as opposed to specialisation and techniques, on the other.

Is There a Challenge in Multicultural Education?

It is then a rather specialised education that is generally offered by the university nowadays. We have come a considerable distance from the medieval university with its insistence on theology but also from the idealist conception of a university with its emphasis on the general and the individual's education. Can we go on like this, do we want to go on like this, or is change necessary? The EU has again combined forces and offered some 'guidelines'. As others in this volume have dealt with its dominant economic focus, I will take the argument in a different direction and radicalise the question along different lines. I want to focus on the sense in which the EU is multicultural or multi-ethnic. Of course, we need to be clear about these concepts too, as the chapters by McLaughlin and Williams demonstrate. Let us begin by enumerating some key points of difference. First, there are many languages spoken within the EU – at present some eleven just to mention the official languages. Second, although the Catholic religion is the dominant one, there are many differences between Protestantism and Roman Catholicism, which in the past especially (and usually in conjunction with other forces) have occasioned numerous conflicts. Third, though difficult to define, there certainly is a broad distinction between northern and southern European culture. Fourth, perhaps even more important, are the different ways in which the respective societies are organised at a social, economic, judicial, and educational level. Fifth, in universities themselves degrees are awarded in different subjects (university faculties are differently structured) not to mention the differences in entrance regulations or duration for particular subjects. Sixth, different attitudes towards abortion, divorce, soft drugs, taxes are more than superficial. Seventh, on a political level different parties have developed, while in Scotland, the north of Spain, the north of Italy, and parts of Belgium, for example, there are those who press for independence. Against these centrifugal tendencies there are other political forces advocating greater unity so that Europe can speak with one voice in a competitive world. Finally, there are the immigrant communities – especially of Asian, North-African, or Central European origin – in almost all EU countries.

In this debate, at least two different issues can be distinguished. First, there is a level where, without invoking matters of power or injustice, different (sub)cultures can be indicated in the EU. Second, because of economic reasons (poorer and richer regions) or because some countries have more inhabitants than others, issues of power make their entrance. In this sense some languages can be more dominant that others (for example, English, French, and German); some regions can set the standard for others – for example, six countries are endeavouring to join the single currency. This process may also be noticed within a single country (or culture) when a particular group (for example, blacks, Asians) or a particular community (Basques, Flemish, Scots) is considered. Here the matter is political in the sense that it is felt that something ought to be done to deal with injustices.

The different countries of the EU provide in some sense a multicultural and a multi-ethnic context. How far does this provide a challenge to university education? I will pursue this along the two tracks indicated. First, I will consider what a radical multicultural approach could possibly be like. Here the question is in what sense a different culture can, or ought to, challenge our own. Second, I will examine particular multicultural initiatives taken within the context of university education where matters of injustice and power issues are involved. The question I will more generally address is thus something like this: Is there a lesson to be learned from the general multicultural educational debate? Finally, I will draw some conclusions from these explorations and will indicate where I see the focus of university education to be nowadays. Here again I will relate matters particularly to the Belgian context.

Though not completcly without difficulties I find Michael Katz's definition of multicultural education very useful: 'Multicultural education is preparation for the social, political and economic realities that individuals experience in culturally diverse and complex human encounters... Multicultural education could include, but not be limited to, experiences which (i) promote analytical and evaluative abilities to confront issues such as participatory democracy, racism, and sexism, and the parity of power; (ii) develop skills for values clarification including the study of the manifest and latent transmission of values; (iii) examine the dynamics of diverse cultures and the implications for developing teaching strategies; and (iv) examine linguistic variations and diverse learning styles as a basis for the development of appropriate teaching strategies' (as quoted in Modgil 1986: p. 5). What this implies for the day-to-day curriculum will vary, of course, according to its relative emphasis on assimilation, cultural pluralism, or anti-racism, but generally this quotation provides a fairly good indication of what concerns us.

Let me recall some problems which have been raised about multicultural education. There is first of all the issue of how to think about our culture or about any other, for that matter. Is it a fertile jungle of different influences, as Mary Midgley claims, so that the picture of a separate, unmixable culture is quite unreal (mentioned in Zec 1980: p. 82)? Exactly this so-called separateness seems to be one of the basic presuppositions of the multiculturalists, who tend to mount their arguments in support of the defence and maintenance of particular (sub-)cultures. John White also points to this and argues that 'members of ethnic minority communities living in Britain do not live and cannot live completely apart from other communities' (in Haydon 1987: p. 15). A second point is that a paradox is evident concerning the maintenance of any specific ethnic culture: the more it is maintained, the less there will be integration, however much this may be the aim (see Rizvi 1986). Third, the idea of cultural relativism (in the strong sense) cannot support multicultural education because its claim that different cultures are incomparable and incomprehensible renders impossible the mutual understanding which that education seeks. As Patterson has rightly argued, it is not clear how pupils could possibly interfere with one another's culture (see Pratte 1985: p. 105). If the argument is for broad-mindedness (as an educational aim) this could be made for other types of education as well. Fifth, it is not that there is any agreement in the political field about the desirability of multicultural education. From the right it is argued that multiculturalism will bring down the standards of a good educational system and that, raising ethnic consciousness, it will work against integration. From the left people despair at the effects it will have on deep-rooted racism: they do not expect that this will change people with such views. Further, they argue that it depoliticises and weakens the resistance of an ethnic group and adjusts it to the ideology of the present society. Finally, if it is the case that almost any culture is in fact heterogeneous, there is a certain incoherence in arguing for a strong separate (minority) culture. Ironically multiculturalism, as characteristic of the way of life of some groups, itself adds to the range of already existing cultures.

Crucial in this matter, so it seems to me, is the concept of an ethnic group. In delineating the nature of ethnic groups Appleton takes as a starting point the fact that various people within a society recognise differences among themselves and have names for themselves and others based on these recognised differences (Appleton 1983: pp. 40–43). 'These names', so he argues, 'are an important feature of a group's identity and symbolise the group's conception of itself in relation to all other groups' (Appleton 1983: p. 40). The intensity and the meaning of the label may vary among groups and among individuals within a particular group. The content of the differences revolves around three components: cultural content, historical experience, and group image. In the case of an ethnic group it is particularly important, Appleton argues (following Isajiw), that it is involuntary: 'The idea of common ancestral origin (i.e., sharing the same cultural traits or being of the same descent) indicates that a person is born into a group and acquires the traits through socialisation... Persons are identified by others as belonging to one or another ethnic group' (Appleton 1983: p. 41) and it is 'the involuntary nature of the ethnic group, Isajiw believes, that is connected with the affective ties that tend to develop among group members – the feelings of sympathy and loyalty toward members of one's own ethnic group' (Appleton 1983: p. 42). If education and child-rearing deal with this process of participation in a certain group, of participating more and more in a certain culture, then it seems that a collision between two relatively separated groups is unavoidable. Is a search for common values a solution then?

White argues along these lines in 'The quest for common values' but he also points to the fact that 'any acute incoherence among these wider cultural values constitutes a threat to one's sense of one's identity' (in Haydon 1987: p. 16). Though I sympathise with his suggestion that we see the formulation of the value-framework not as a discrete, if revisable, act, but as an on-going and unending collective activity of society as a whole (in Haydon 1987: p. 20), I fail to see the educational implications of his suggestions. First, I would argue that this unending process is in a way always going on. Second, I think it is only very seldom the case that it is the result of a true deliberation about values; it is rather something that happens and on which people later reflect. Finally, I believe that the possible influence of an educational system on society in general is in his argument enormously overstated. White's emphasis on the possible clash between the 'home-culture' and the broader culture, however, foregrounds what is in my opinion the most important issue in this matter. I will return to this later.

The Radical Challenge of Multiculturalism

In the same Bedford Way Papers a similar suggestion is made by Jones in 'Prejudice'. Having explained the difference between those prejudgements that are and those that are not open to criticism, he argues that the only sensible thing to do is to accept that all participants in a discussion must accept as given certain foundational prejudgements which form the bedrock of our various culturally vouched-for ways of understanding our experience. Though not totally inaccessible to revision this could only take place, Jones argues, 'against a background of foundational prejudgements which are not found problematic, which provide the "safe ground" of agreement from which disagreement can be resolved' (in Haydon 1987: p. 43). They are acquired tacitly together with all kinds of habits in the process of socialisation and are usually not accessible to conscious reflection. As the truth of these basic propositions cannot be established, Jones suggests considering them as rationally tenable but contingently undecidable (in Haydon 1987: p. 45). He also points to prejudice as a psychological phenomenon and to the attractiveness of unreflective living to many human beings, to the comfort and pleasure which we can derive from indulgence in what is familiar. At this point Jones brings together the philosophical insights about the bedrock and our psychological sentimental attachment to home, summarising this with 'home is where the heart is'. Again he insists that the only thing we can do is to accept the universality of prejudices. After that, he argues, we can hold a conversation between members of different cultures based on the idea that we are all emotionally tied to culturally vouched-for prejudgements: 'The aim of such a conversation would be that the participants should work towards understanding one another as emotionally committed members of various forms of life, together with some understanding of what it is that each is committed to, what each sees as important social issues, how crucial that importance is and why' (in Haydon 1987: p. 51).

There are serious doubts about the possibility of pursuing all this so consciously and deliberately. It is even more difficult to follow Jones when he speaks about the school as the place where people should be given the understanding and the personal and social skills necessary for participation in such a conversation. I imagine that this would demand a lot of the participants, and a lot more than would ever be possible for most of its pupils. It is one thing to talk about prejudices (and prejudgements), another to accept that we are attached to them, and something different again to change them – if any of this is possible at all just by talking in an educational context. But this does not mean that nothing can be done. Not only is it doubtful whether the impact of the educational system on society is as great as what is assumed, it also seems to me that the wisdom that is needed for all this is beyond that what is attainable for most people.

It is not implausible that one's sense of oneself – what one aspires to, hopes and longs for, the moral and emotional development one goes through – is severely threatened in such an open Babel of values. Here we are confronted with a new paradox: on the one hand, we long for certainty; on the other, we cannot be comforted by what we achieve because of its (necessary) groundlessness. There is the groundlessness of what we believe and what we will live for, but there is also our longing for certainty. Without this certainty it seems we cannot live, but at the same time we realise that certainty can be stifling. Ultimately we cannot take other people's certainties seriously without at the same time being threatened by the groundlessness of our own. In this sense the fear of what is different is at the same time also anguish at the groundlessness of what is one's own. To this the rather incoherent idea of multicultural education can offer little comfort. It may be that the problems on which it focuses are of a different nature, political rather than educational. And however clear it is that our day-to-day experiences demand urgent solutions, it is not clear at all what education could contribute beyond being good education, incidentally the position which is argued for concerning racism by David Cooper (in North 1987).

The poet Edmond Jabès wrote: 'L'étranger te permet d'être toi-même, en faisant, de toi, un étranger' (1989: p. 9). Perhaps being confronted with what is radically different is an opportunity to be released from what is set in one's habits. In the end this may be unsatisfactory – though it is not at all clear how it might be decided whether this is so. That things could be different concerning the society I live in and concerning what I value is by now clear, but this does not imply that I am in the position to re-evaluate all this – certainly not if it presupposes a view from nowhere. Those who are different and that which is different prompt us to reappraise what we stand for, and there does not seem to be a particular kind of education that could teach us exactly how to deal with this difference. Perhaps we need not be angels, though it looks as if being saints is the least that is expected of us if we are to accomplish this.

The Politics of Multicultural Initiatives in the University

So much for our first alternative: a radical confrontation with what is really different is not the kind of thing to be expected within the EU. Our European culture is in general much more shared. And though probably not desirable at the level of child-rearing, even university education could not really aim at trying to shake the student's fundamental beliefs. What would the effect of such an action be, short of creating severe confusion? But surely something worthwhile has already resulted from the idea of being confronted with what is different. This will help us to see more clearly what we already do. What message does this offer for university education? Perhaps only that the community of scholars lives world-wide, so that a good education should guarantee an initiation in the world-wide conversation of mankind. Let us consider now the multicultural initiatives that have been taken at the level of the university.

In their introduction to *Toward the Multicultural University* Bowser, Jones, and Young (1995) start from the following:

> Imagine a middle-aged and middle-class white male professor teaching a required humanities or social science course. The syllabus consists of readings from or about the great thinkers associated with the definitive movements and developments in European and American history, arts, literature and sciences. Imagine also that the students in class range in age and have had some life experiences beyond high school. White students are a minority, and the majority of students have historical and cultural roots outside of Europe in Mexico, Puerto Rico, China, Japan, Africa and Native Indian nations. Standard English is either a second dialect, even for the white students or a second language entirely. Women are a majority in the classroom. The students range widely in their academic preparation, seem difficult to motivate, and are indifferent to the course content. One day some unexpected questions begin to be asked: 'What is the point? Who cares what these rich white men did? Are their ideas responsible for what happened to my people? Isn't this European American (white) studies? Have any women or people outside of Europe contributed anything of significance in the modern world?' (Bowser, Jones, and Young 1995: p. xv)

How will we react, the authors ask us? Will we ignore it, encourage them to go to black studies or women's studies to have their questions answered? There is, however, another possibility. University teachers can learn enough about the cultures, peoples, achievements, histories, and interactions that their students' cultural and historic nationalities have had with one another and Europe, and start to answer the students' questions. In doing so, teachers might find the keys to motivate all of these students and to excite them about learning. Multiculturalism with substance requires experiencing and studying cultural groups and people who live in circumstances different from one's own. To be educated in the liberal arts in the next century will mean having to encounter the human spirit across cultural and historical expanses. These matters are important not just concerning the curriculum, but also in its preferred modes of instruction. And this does not necessarily mean the teaching of a particular canon or the use of a particular teaching method, both of them thought to be unchangeable. Constant re-evaluation is indeed needed because of the changing conditions in which people live and how they conceive the life they want to lead.

Bowser also offers some strategic planning for change. Long-term plans with gradual short-term goals spelling out the specific actions to be taken to achieve each goal. These plans and goals should arise open debate and discussion among students, teachers, administration, and community. The execution will require staff leadership, while all aspects of the planning and execution must be open to revision based on experience. Finally, a culturally more inclusive education for all students throughout their whole education must be provided. A closer look at more detailed suggestions shows a broadening of pedagogy. For example, instead of selective introductory courses here the advice is offered to accept students for what they are when admitted to a college or university. Find out what their strengths and weaknesses are, then show them how to improve their weaknesses – not necessarily conceived exclusively in terms of skills. This rather than large introductory lecture classes is real education, so it is claimed.

The process that is proposed by Bowser involves a transformation from an essentially Eurocentric institution to one that is multicultural. It is in the opinion of the authors of that collection possible for well-run, effective educational institutions with quality programmes to exist and to make major contributions to the human community without European studies as the central and core curriculum. Here teachers and scholars from many different backgrounds come together as a community of teachers, scientists, and scholars. While each may come from a different place and social context, they will be united not only around their discipline but by their cross-cultural and cross-community training and experiences. The search for the development of the human spirit, as for ways to improve society and the quality of life, will not be fruitful within one culture, one regional history, or one social class, the authors argue. Instead working in collaboration across disciplines and cultures will be essential to address common problems that affect everyone. It will be realised that what people have produced as culture, as ways of surviving and of bringing quality to their lives, is not theirs alone but there for all to see, study, and appreciate for its strengths and for its weaknesses.

Others (as Giroux in Goldberg 1994, for instance) will reassert the importance of making the pedagogical more political. He attempts to define the pedagogical meaning of what he calls an insurgent multiculturalism. This is a kind of multiculturalism that is not limited to a fascination with the construction of identities, communicative competence, and the celebration of tolerance but instead shifts the discussion to a pedagogical terrain in which relations of power and radicalised identities become paramount as part of a language of critique and possibility. It seeks to challenge the narratives of national identity, culture, and ethnicity as part of a pedagogical effort to provide dominant groups with the knowledge to examine, acknowledge, and unlearn their own privilege. In treating cultural narrative and national history in fixed and narrow terms, conservatives relinquish one of the most important defining principles of any democracy: they ignore the necessity of a democratic society to rejuvenate itself by constantly re-examining the strengths and limits of its traditions. When a critical encounter with the past and a recognition of the importance of cultural diversity is absent, multiculturalism works out in practice as a reverence for and transmission of the cultural products of different and separate groups, rather than a pedagogical practice that puts people in dialogue with each other as part of a broader attempt to fashion a renewed interest in cultural democracy and the creation of engaged and critical citizens.

So again it is not clear what if anything follows from this for my own university confronted with the European dimension – or do I miss the point? At present in Belgium, one does not find mixed groups of students studying at a university, and, given the language that is used, it is very unlikely that this will change. Must university education become more political? Perhaps it should, but would that address what is at stake here? Are we willing to accept that all culture is nothing but a function of power? Though they do interconnect in numerous ways, 'culture' and 'power' do not coincide, or do they? And does anything follow at all from the Eurocentric critique concerning our own areas of scholarship, anything different from what is implied by the discipline itself?

Educational Sciences and the University

If it is correct (and how can it not be correct) that the picture of a separate, non-mixable culture is quite unreal, we all nowadays in the EU (the fifteen countries) live in somewhat the same culture. Though there are regional differences (to a large extent linked with different languages), at a more general level post-Second World War Europe does not confront education (and certainly not university education) with a radically different task. Though universities might need to broaden some of their curricula to meet the 'new' European situation, they still have an unchanged first responsibility: to initiate (at an advanced level) students into the ongoing conversation of mankind so that students are able to continue this for themselves. Perhaps being confronted with what is to some extent different is an opportunity to be released from what is set in one's thinking and what in the end is unsatisfactory, even if it is not clear at all how the unsatisfactoriness might be decided. But there seems to be no need either to strengthen at this level one's cultural identity or to look more deliberately for pluralistic identities – that is if it even makes sense to think of the relationship between education and culture (and culture itself) in such a way. Perhaps it is more important now to stress more than before the primordial aim of all universities (what they stand for and what is worth keeping and cherishing here) and to look for the necessary means for them to continue in this aim, especially given the dominance of economic rationality and the generally anti-intellectual climate. To argue in this sense, is, however, different from trying to set up another kind of university, a more pure and elite institution which could conceive itself more removed from society. It is realistic to accept that certain degrees will be in high demand by society. This need not suppress the university's commitment to this aim (see Weijers in this volume).

It seems indeed to me neither desirable nor possible to put society between brackets, and to try to conceive university education *de novo*. The university graduate will have to find a job within a society dominated by market forces. Offering a university education completely separated from the requirements for particular jobs flies in the face of reality. It would generate a strange university within an even more strange society, where the problems that preoccupy society would be of no interest to academia.

All the university can teach then derives from what has been learnt so far: the ideas that seem to work in practice. We teach the ideas we think best correspond to the workings of the world, of the human mind and spirit, and the practical methods that seem to work best. Though admittedly this touches but a partial reality, an aspect of reality, maybe even a distorted reality, it is the best we can do at the moment. The core educational aim of the university then is to teach those ways of thinking, those habits of mind, that it can show work well in comprehending the world and deciding what to do in it. This includes making as explicit as possible the presuppositions of enquiry.

Rather more than in the past, it should now be demanded of the universities that they make clear what they stand for. As all rationality starts somewhere, it is important to make clear where one starts from and what reasons were decisive – though explanation, of course, must somewhere come to an end. University educators have to address the questions society nowadays is confronted with. Refraining from simple ready-made answers (with their seductive force), they will have to address the crucial issues and indicate the reason-why for preferring certain options; above all they must make the alternatives clear. University education will have to equip students with the questions that need to be raised, questions that have to be put again and again – those deep questions that recur throughout human history. It has to make explicit what is worth cherishing and keeping in mind for the future. It is not just an education for a particular job; it also brings into the openness of being what within the scope of a discipline has impressed us most as valuable. Within this scope questions about what is going wrong in society have to be asked. It is this confrontation that will prove crucial in the personal education of each student: it is indeed her *Bildung*, her education.

Let me recall Rorty who argues for an encounter with great thinkers who solved the problems of their time by creating new languages, new disciplines, and new societies. He wants to encourage students to fall in love with their intellectual tradition and emulate the achievements of their heroes by solving new problems of their own. General study, he says, is basically 'erotic' and should be more like 'seduction' than instruction. And for that matter it does not matter who the students' heroes are, as long as everybody has more than one and is able to appreciate and respect those who have different ones; and overlap between the courses should ensure that interesting conversations can take place. Finally, he states that the best way of fixing the content of the core is the way it always has been done, that is by the most influential faculty members' choice of books that have given them pleasure, university libraries being the place in which students can find practically any book and then find somebody 'around there' to talk with about it (see Rorty 1983).

Coming back to those students of eighteen years of age registered for educational sciences, the implication is perhaps that the curriculum has to be attuned to the discipline they are going to study (rather than to purely vocational considerations). Here certain practical problems will be addressed but there will also be ample opportunity to study the theory for its own sake. Education and knowledge in the university do not serve the particular interests of certain individuals or groups. Such educational institutions contribute to the development of 'human resources' and 'human capital' and aim to realise excellence. Though these institutions are part of a learning society in which adaptation and flexibility are highly ranked, they are not only instruments of their own preservation and development, or of securing their own future, and reinforcing their own identity. Their identity and development are not completely dependent upon their position in competition with others neither upon their success in the economic market. Instead the development that is followed is directed by a search for the variety of multiple truths that originate from human existence.

Multicultural education and the challenge of multiculturalism can mean different things. I argued that the school is neither the place for deliberate radical confrontation nor the instrument of a grand plan to change society. Obviously things are different for a primary and secondary education, on the one hand, and for higher education, on the other. The more a society develops into a multicultural society, the more multiculturalism needs to be evident in the curriculum of schools. But higher education is in that respect quite different and it is for this reason that the position argued for is not reactionary: higher education operates in a different frame. I argued that it is the logic and content of the discipline that ought to guide criteria for the content of courses. For university subjects there already is an international forum, irrespective of the boundaries of language and culture in which research is generated. Of course, universities should not be afraid to discuss content and method; of course, university education should continue to be offered in the language of the region (if the community is large enough to be able to support this); and, of course, the more Europe becomes united at different levels, the more there may be a need for extra courses where, within a particular subject, something about other countries (or language areas) is learnt – though the appropriateness of this will vary from subject to subject. There is room here for some specialisation in the field of European studies. But again, besides this a university ought to be a good university; this in my view must still be a place which fosters independent judgement and creativity rather than one which is measured on its success in market terms and subjected to the imperatives of profit. But this is not to say that university education has to be as general or universal as it once was. The university cannot ignore the different professional fields in society (see Blake in this volume). The position argued for retains a balance between society's market forces and academia. No one has the right to predetermine the course of the discussion: it is for this reason that we expect so much of the conversation. There is room for pluralism here provided that universities take up their autonomy.

Still, in a subtle way the university will want to be an island. It aims to generate within its students a way of thinking which puts them in a position (and moreover encourages them) to be pragmatic in a philosophical sense (see Standish in this volume). To care with all their heart for what is human and to accept the contingencies not as a curse but as a blessing, they might aim to acquire what recently has been called, and was already present long ago in Habermas's work: the attitude of the researcher.

Note

1. After secondary school, students have the right to proceed to university provided they have gained a high school diploma. A sustained majority achieves this. They are not required to satisfy further entry requirements. The pass level, however, of the first year is around 40 percent (not norm referenced). Students are normally successful once they have passed this stage. From the start the curriculum is varied. For example, if someone enrols for educational sciences in her first two years (the candidate years) she will study philosophy, psychology, sociology, and a number of courses more directed towards education. The licentiate years (years 3, 4, and sometimes 5) are specialised along vocational lines. For educational sciences the student opts for teacher training, special education or adult education (continuous education). For psychology the student 'specialises' in clinical psychology, organisational psychology or counselling and guidance.

Part III

The Response to the Economic Demands

CHAPTER 7

BILDUNG VERSUS BENEFIT?

EDUCATING THE RESPONSIBLE EXPERT

Ido Weijers

At the end of the 1950s C.P. Snow alerted the western intellectual world to the danger of a growing gap between two cultures for both of which he cared. He believed the intellectual life of the whole of western society was increasingly split into two polar groups: 'at one pole we have the literary intellectuals, who incidentally while no one was looking took to referring to themselves as "intellectuals" as though there were no others … at the other scientists, and as the most representative, the physical scientists. Between the two a gulf of mutual incomprehension – sometimes (particularly among the young) hostility and dislike, but most of all lack of understanding… The feelings of the one pole become the anti-feelings of the other. If the scientists have the future in their bones, then the traditional culture responds by wishing the future did not exist' (Snow 1974: pp. 4, 11).

More than thirty years later this gap has grown even wider. We have become accustomed to the idea that the scientists indeed have the future in their bones, and that the literary intellectuals respond by wishing that the scientists' future will never come, at least not everywhere. But since the beginning of the eighties this gulf in the intellectual life of the western world has been almost completely overshadowed by a new gap which manifests itself in academic life. For more than a decade two completely separate vocabularies have been functioning within academe. In one vocabulary the educational goals of university training are central; the other concentrates on the economic benefits of higher education.

Both vocabularies are operating in separate circuits, circuits which scarcely meet. The first is clearly inspired by the tradition of the literary intellectuals, but it is not restricted to their culture. It is, however, the other vocabulary that has definitely become dominant in many policy documents on the future of higher education. The 1991 *Memorandum on Higher Education* fits comfortably into the discourse of benefit, in spite of its references to cultural, human, and social issues. Sometimes this vocabulary is identified with the tradition of the scientists, since many science departments and research institutions have developed close ties with industry. Nevertheless, thinking in terms of economic benefit as such is *not* typical for the culture of the scientists: it is the vocabulary of managers and administrators. When it comes to their vision of the future of higher education, however, and in spite of their getting used to what John Ziman has called the 'steady state', many scientists, like most scholars, have problems with this vocabulary (Ziman 1987).

In Europe we now see a radical conflict between these two vocabularies. This has nothing to do with the 'uniform development' of the modern university: within Europe there are still far-reaching structural differences in national higher education systems (Teichler 1988; Teichler 1993). Like Snow, who recognised that the phenomenon of the two cultures had different forms in different countries, I also acknowledge that the conflict between *Bildung* and benefit takes a different shape and has a different weight within the variety of national European contexts. In the last decade, however, this has been a hot dispute in British and Dutch higher education in particular, and also in the Scandinavian world. In the French higher education system with its strong professional tradition, the gulf seems less deep, and in the German and Italian systems *Bildung* still has substantial authority. Yet, everywhere in Europe the tension between *Bildung* and benefit is increasing (Neave and Van Vught 1991; Gellert 1993).

Benefit

Benefit, return, and efficiency, these are the keywords in the present debate on higher education. Terms such as liberal, general, or intellectual education are functioning only in the margins of this debate. This is clearly illustrated by the current popularity of the notion of 'quality'. In 1982, a leading article in the *Times Higher Education Supplement* predicted that 'quality' would become an organising principle for higher education in the 1980s. A decade later the notion of 'quality' is the benchmark for every policy maker and university manager in western Europe. 'Quality' has become of clear interest across the private and public sectors, a 'quality industry' has grown up almost overnight whose initiates know the subtle distinctions between 'quality assurance', 'quality control', and 'quality assessment', and between 'total quality management' and 'strategic quality management'. The quality vocabulary is the one that must be learned by any aspiring academic who wishes to escape from the increasingly arduous daily chore of actually teaching more and more students. As the *Higher Education Quarterly* stated in its special on 'Quality and the Management of Quality' in 1992, 'what is worrying about the current developments is that an extremely complex and problematic issue is treated as if it were susceptible to simple one-dimensional solutions' (1992: p. 2).

Here the preference for performance indicators is typical. Everywhere we see the same pattern: the academic community favours peer review, but the policy makers favour numerical performance indicators (while some champions of the 'free' market-led university favour consumer preferences). Numerical performance indicators meet the requirements of the policy makers, but, as Ronald Barnett and others have noted, the sureness, the stability, and even the objectivity that numerical performance indicators seem to offer is illusory (Barnett 1992: p. 12). Certainly performance indicators can be useful: they may prompt critical questions about the quality of the educational process. But to believe that we can say something of real insight about the quality of an educational process by describing it in numerical terms is an illusion (Pollit 1987; Weusthof 1994). Qualities and quantities are different things. Running them together is a category mistake. In the innumerable memoranda and research reports on the quality of higher education this category mistake is constantly made. The current language of quality is lacking in educational insight; conversely, it is saturated with ideas derived from management and economics.

This way of perceiving higher education is of relatively recent date. It dates, to be precise, from the end of the 1970s. Around 1980 the 'human capital' approach to (higher) education, which started two decades earlier with the well-known address of Theodore W. Schulz, became established. On this view the financing of education is conceived on the basis of, and motivated by, the same considerations as investment in buildings and machines: 'Although it is obvious that people acquire useful skills and knowledge, it is not obvious that these skills and knowledge are a form of capital, that this capital is in substantial part a product of deliberate investment, that it has grown in western societies at a much faster rate than conventional (nonhuman) capital, and that its growth may well be the most distinctive feature of the economic system' (Schultz 1971: p. 13). With these observations Schultz opened the eyes of the economists to the possibilities in the planning of education. The human capital approach points at the significance of educational effects for the dissemination of skills, for the improvement of operating procedures and manufacturing processes, for technological innovation, and for the necessary flexibility and mobility of the labour force. The implications of this approach, however, are much more far-reaching. It has supported and even brought forward policies that have direct consequences for the organisation of education. The study preferences of the students and the possibility of influencing their choice have become central elements of policies inspired by so-called 'rational choice' theory (Becker 1968). Schultz emphasises the incentive for government investment in education on the grounds of public interest. Economists such as Becker, in contrast, stress the motivation of individual self-interest. Here the leading idea is that, in their choice of course of study, individuals weigh systematically how much, on the one hand, they will probably earn in the future as a result of their education and how much, on the other, their college expenses will be. Investing in your education makes good financial sense – that is the core of this way of thinking. The reason that people spend money on education and are prepared to postpone the time when they will have a direct income is not that they appreciate the intrinsic worth of education, as the classical view would like to suppose. Rational choice theory holds that people do not go to university primarily because they are interested in mathematics, engineering, law, or philosophy, but because they expect to be better off in the future by doing so.

This line of reasoning has been challenged from various sides and with various arguments. It has been made plausible that the contribution of higher education to economic growth applies particularly in the case of fundamental research. The economic benefit of education without the acquisition of research experience, however, cannot be demonstrated (Walters and Rubinson 1983; Sanders 1992). It has been argued that education is productive because people get accustomed to the existing hierarchy in the division of labour (Bowles and Gintis 1976). Has higher education always been merely the plaything of the labour market? At crucial moments and in crucial fields it appears to create new professions, institutes, and functions (Van Vucht Tijssen 1990). Rational choice theory presupposes that changes in the labour market will generate changes in the training people attend, but it has also been established that changes in the labour market contribute little to the expansion of education (Van der Ploeg 1992). Rational choice theory presupposes also that prospective students or their parents have a clear idea of their future incomes. But labour is much too heterogeneous and the structure of the labour market much too complex to allow such assumptions (Borghans, de Grip and Heijke 1989). In any case it is clear that wage levels are not determined exclusively by the education received (Hartog 1986).

Although these objections against defining higher education in terms of benefit are serious, there is another kind of critique which is more relevant to my argument. I am referring to the sociological finding that higher education is not productive primarily because of its transfer of qualifications, but rather because it functions as a filter, selecting and sorting students (Arrow 1973). The economic value of higher education is not primarily that it raises the productivity of students, thanks to their specific training. Its economic value has to do first of all with its social sorting function. That means that the extent of the skills which students acquire through their education is less important than their relative capability (van Hoof and Dronkers 1980). This approach seems to accord with the observation that when government and other employers are seeking to recruit graduate academics they do not in most cases pay detailed attention to what those students have studied. First and foremost employers value flexible ability to solve problems of a high level of complexity, a trained intelligence for these kinds of issues (WRR 1995). So-called absolute skills and capabilities belong to the classical research university. But considering the demand for trained academics with a high degree of flexibility, the average student seems to be better off with a broad training that enables him or her to formulate and analyse complex problems.

In consequence of the competition between departments and between disciplines, our universities have shown a tendency for over-specialisation in the last two decades. This development has not only failed to increase job opportunities for the average student; it has also seemed counterproductive in (at least areas of) the production of knowledge – that is, at the borders of our knowledge where those who are most talented are most needed. In recent years, many scientists have come to the conclusion that their potential for solving complex problems is not (sufficiently) increased by more specialisation; rather what they need is broadening and lateral association. It has become clear that many complex problems, to do for instance with the environment, health, communications, and procreation, need research teams of varied composition; ideally these will include specialists with a trained intelligence who can offer flexibility and a broad perspective.

My argument is that we need a shift from a preponderant emphasis, even fixation, on very specific diplomas and absolute skills to a concern with relative aptitude for academic work – or 'trainability', as Thurow has called it (Thurow 1979). In most cases the knowledge and capabilities that are directly relevant for a function have, in fact, to be acquired 'on the job'. Given that this is so, it would seem that higher education ought to be training the majority of students to acquire a high level of 'trainability'. It should be offering them a sound basis for lifelong learning, with the provision of feedback courses, and other forms of continuing education. I will argue that this shift vis-à-vis the more restricted 'choose your success / acquire your skills' orientation of the rational choice approach opens up new possibilities for a dialogue between the advocates of benefit and the advocates of *Bildung*. But if such a dialogue is to be realised there has to be a similar shift in the conception of higher education which is held, and fostered, by university teachers.

Bildung

From various sides the criticism can be heard: the university is neglecting its original mission. The university is held responsible for the supposed disappearance of the intellectual from our social world. The academic professional communities have closed in on themselves in an indulgent self-referentiality. The ramparts around the academy have never been higher (Bender 1993). We live in an 'age of academe', as Russell Jacoby pointedly puts it. By the 1960s the universities virtually monopolised intellectual work, Jacoby says, and this monopoly involved a fundamental change in the character of higher education – from classical, liberal, and general education of the intellect to narrow, vocational, and professional training. According to Jacoby, this change has led to a cultural impoverishment and particularly to the disappearance of the classical intellectual *habitus* (Jacoby 1987). Many similar criticisms have been launched lately, some conservative, some radical. Some critics mourn for the 'orphaned' university; others warn against the erosion of academe; some even proclaim its death, the death of the 'original idea' of the university.

What kind of university do these critics have in mind, however, when they refer to the 'historical mission' or the 'original idea' of the university? What kind of university should be reclaimed? Usually these critics refer loosely to Von Humboldt's notion of *Bildung*, or to the resolute statement of Mill about what a university is not: 'It is not a place of professional education... Their object is not to make skilful lawyers, or physicians, or engineers, but capable and cultivated human beings' (Mill 1984: p. 218). Alternatively they refer to Newman, who stated that 'if a practical end must be assigned to a university course, I say it is that of training good members of society. Its art is the art of social life, and its end is fitness for the world' (Newman 1960: p.134). In the eyes of Newman useful knowledge was a 'deal of trash'. He favoured a university training aiming at raising the intellectual tone of society, at cultivating the public mind, and at purifying the national taste.

The general premise of these critics is that we have a kind of clear historical and in fact typically European standard which can be used to calibrate the modern university: and this is the notion of *Bildung*. First, however, there is in my view no such standard. There are different national histories of higher education and profoundly different historical phases. Second, the history of the European university does not lend itself to such a standard. Keywords in this history have different meanings in various historical and national contexts. For instance, when nowadays the phrase, typical of *Bildung*, 'unity of education and research' is used, something completely different is meant from what Von Humboldt had in mind with his proclamation of *Einheit von Forschung und Lehre*. Briefly, Von Humboldt's neo-humanist notion of *Forschung* did not refer to empirical research but to philosophical reflection.

Let me dwell a little bit on the vicissitudes of the notions of *Bildung* and of liberal education. The ideal of *Bildung* started its career at the end of the eighteenth century. In order to understand the success of the new concept it is necessary to realise the way it accorded with traditional German ideas about the life of the individual person reflecting the historical development of mankind. A *gebildeter Mann*, that is to say, a man who manifested *Bildung*, epitomised the full realisation of human nature. The emphasis on historical development, however, introduced a new element. *Bildung* came to signify a process (or the result of a process); it implied the tacit cooperation and commitment of the student in learning. The role of the teacher was never to impose knowledge but rather to draw out those talents and dispositions that were regarded as most fully human. Therefore, in this context the process of learning meant self-realisation. The student who became *gebildet* learned to actualise something he or she already potentially had (Liedman 1993).

As Fritz Ringer has shown, at the end of the nineteenth century, *Bildung* became the single most important tenet of what he calls the 'mandarin' tradition. University educated people, and most of all the professors, defended their position and privileges with the help of this concept. Especially after World War One, this defensive struggle was fierce and embittered. The allegedly unique *Bildung*, accessible only at the universities, came to be used as a cultural weapon by the conservative defenders of the university (Ringer 1969). What typified *Bildung* and made it fundamental for higher education was philosophy. Philosophy, the professors claimed, featured the basic principles behind all knowledge; it provided a fundamental and comprehensive perspective. The rise of specialisation and professionalism, however, had already as a matter of fact 'decentralised' philosophy in the university. Philosophy itself had dispersed into a set of disciplines instead of functioning as the foundation for all specialist knowledge. Since the mid-nineteenth century German universities had changed in practice into empirical research institutes with their laboratories and experimental testing (McClelland 1980; Stichweh 1984). In fact, at the end of that century *Bildung* started a second career, this time as an ideological umbrella for a completely changed academic reality.

A comparable difference between ideas and reality can be found in Britain. The emergence of the modern university in late nineteenth-century Britain runs parallel with a revived emphasis on the importance of a liberal education: education should be free from narrow considerations of utility and vocational interests – a stand supported by the much quoted statements of John Henry Newman and John Stuart Mill. But these re-articulations of age-old opinions about the primary task of British universities – to form the characters and minds of their young students – happened to become intimately linked with the formation of the political and administrative elite of the British Empire. Actually, there is a close tie between British elite higher education, on the one hand, and the growing political and administrative demands of the British polity, on the other. The British universities largely succeeded in creating a homogeneous governing class, because they organised liberal education, in all its social, intellectual, and moral aspects, within the college. In the latter part of the nineteenth century the universities became places of intensive training for those who would later be employed in the governance of the outside world (Soffer 1987).

Moreover, in the same period there was a renewed emphasis on the role of universities in preparing students for a professional career. This process, which Sheldon Rothblatt has identified as the 'revolution of the dons', entailed a deep-seated restructuring of British universities. This development became visible at Cambridge, for instance, when new schools for medicine and engineering were established (Rothblatt 1993). Other consequences were the material manifestations of a new scientific professionalism, in particular the new and crucial role of the laboratories (Wachelder 1992).

Historical research has made at least two things clear. First, the ancestors of today's universities are certainly not their medieval precursors, as is often supposed (Scott 1984). Second, the emergence of the modern university is not a product of the late eighteenth or early nineteenth century; it is, by and large, a phenomenon of the late nineteenth century (Wittrock 1993). The type of university we are familiar with in modern Europe emerged about one century ago, at the time that *Bildung* and liberal education were beginning to function as ideological (counter-)conceptualisations of the new realities of university life. The coincidence of these ideas with the emergence of the modern university at the end of the last century has led them to become not clear historical standards but highly ideological notions.

The modern university is primarily a knowledge-producing institution, concerning itself with the production and reproduction of expertise. And it is only at the end of the last century that universities have developed in that direction, as institutions for empirical research and for the education of experts and professionals in such fields as law, medicine, psychology, physics, and history. This development of the modern western university is intimately linked with the rise of the modern European nation-state, whether in newly formed polities, such as Italy or Germany, or through the reform of older states, such as in France, Britain, and the Netherlands (McClelland 1980; Wagner 1990; Wagner et al. 1991; Baggen and Weijers 1995). Björn Wittrock comes to the conclusion that our universities, far from being detached from the basic social and political transformations of the modern era, form part and parcel of the very same process which manifests itself in the emergence of an industrial economic order and the nation-state. This conclusion implies, I think, that *Bildung* and liberal education cannot be the denominators any more for higher education nowadays. Put differently, accepting ideas of self-fulfilment and character-development derived from Von Humboldt and Newman as denominators for the university draws us into a purely ideological position; it renders us helpless when dealing with the present problems of our universities as knowledge-producing institutions.

Richard Smith in his contribution to this volume rightly points out the tendency to see higher education in individualistic terms, characterised as this tends to be by a thin conception of the person. One strength of Von Humboldt's *Bildungsideal* was precisely its thick conception. But if this was its strength, its weakness, it should be conceded, was its thin conception of professional expertise. In contrast, the strength of the Weberian ideal was its thick conception of professional expertise, its weakness its thin conception of the person, as Jaspers makes clear. I do not consider that it is our task to thicken both weak dimensions, although that is indeed what Jaspers seriously tried to do. To do this would be to dazzle ourselves with grand historical ideas and to blind ourselves to today's real problems.

Educating the Responsible Expert

Almost a century ago, Max Weber (1972), who maintained a careful balance between two different cultures, described this pivotal point as the struggle between the old Man of Culture (*das Kulturmenschentum*) and the new Expert (*der Fachmenschen-Typus*). It was the latter that he favoured, and in doing this he was in opposition to the old elite institution of the university mandarins. Those who want to turn back and still opt for the Man of Culture need to be aware that they are choosing in favour of an elite institution. Given the widespread consensus over, and the force of, the meritocratic ideology in western culture, this option would now be much harder to realise than in the time of Weber. At the end of the twentieth century, university education has come within the reach of many people. Within one century we all have come to live in a culture of the masses; we now work and study in universities characterised by mass access. The solutions for the problems we meet in this new situation cannot come from a return to the elite institutions of the past. In any case, from an educational point of view it is highly undesirable to aim for an elite institution, as the critical discussion of Allan Bloom's objections to mass higher education in Paul Standish's chapter helps to demonstrate.

On the other hand, there is little to be said for returning to the pure knowledge-producing institutions of the first half of this century. Two points are important here. First, as from the beginning of this century European universities generally became centres of research and professional training. The rapidly increasing role of knowledge in our economies, politics, and culture has been an important stimulus to this change. The stratum of experts, counsellors, and advisers is not only the fastest growing element in the workforce of advanced societies; it is also functionally indispensable in the political and economic administration of these societies. Expertise has become a productive force in industrial society, and in the latter part of our century its impact is ever more clear. We live in a 'knowledge society', it might be said, in which there is a permanent scientisation of most spheres of social action (Stehr 1994). The dynamics of modern western society require the mass production of academically trained professionals. In contrast to Weber's view, this implies that dedication to pure research (*Wissenschaft als Beruf*) is no longer appropriate to the university as a whole: here the dominance of the research dimension is presupposed, as is learning as an end in itself. Nowadays, however, research is, and can only be, relevant to a part of the mass institution.

Weber was concerned, moreover, with the political disinterestedness of the pursuit of knowledge. The purification of science and scholarship of all traces of ideology was, in his eyes, the constant responsibility of the expert. The degree of confidence in scientific and scholarly knowledge which this presupposes is something we no longer possess. Our modern concept of specialisation and expertise requires a concept of knowledge that incorporates our disenchantment with pure research. We need 'responsible experts' because we fear freaks and blinkered specialists, who are blind to the broader picture. This means that we need experts who realise that their expertise is pre-eminently, as Ulrich Beck puts it, that of societal risk producers (Beck 1992).

Here the notion of reflectivity is especially significant. The responsible expert has to reflect on her knowledge. She considers what her expertise involves, both in its cognitive and in its social aspects. This social and cognitive reflectivity needs to become part of the intellectual habitus of the specialist. And to develop this broad-mindedness she has to be purposely educated in that direction. That does not mean that her education has to be inspired again by the past ideals of *Bildung*, self-realisation, or character-development. On the contrary, her training has to be orientated towards a deepening assessment of her own expertise – to apply critical thinking in her field of specialist practice, to learn and to consider problem-solving strategies that are relevant for the kind of problems in her field, to reflect continuously on learned strategies, to reconsider her know-how. From the beginning the student has to gain the capability to apply her knowledge and skills with confidence within varied and changing situations. And this does not mean that her education must incorporate something 'general' alongside specialist study. It does require a deepening and broadening of specialised education itself. It means constantly raising the capability of the student to reflect on the practice, to bring it to the theoretical surface, and to articulate the principles embedded in it. Crucial here is the ability to subsume experience within a growing and more inclusive theoretical framework. In order to do this it would be inappropriate to fragment studies in numerous subspecialisations. The argument is rather that we have to adjust or change the character of those specialist studies themselves; to make them more reflective will indeed be to make *them* more 'philosophical' and more 'historical'.

It is not the task of our universities to develop character. We are not concerned with producing people of good character, but responsible experts. But it is the task of higher education to educate experts who have learned to consider their specialist knowledge in a wider, historical, and social context, and to reflect collectively on its philosophical and ethical implications. So-called 'integrated curricula', involving the interplay of different perspectives, may be helpful here as long as they are incorporated into 'problem-solving' educational strategies. Gerald Graff's idea of integrated and jointly taught courses to help, as he puts it, in 'turning conflict into community' may be useful as long as we clearly see that we are trying to form a community of professionals (Graff 1992). We do not need a group of blinkered specialists but a community of reflective experts. The educational aim of creating the reflective expert may offer a vital alternative to the individualistic and functional vocational training which characterises current trends.

To assign a central place to reflectivity in higher education, with its professional doubts, with its passion for reconsidering what has been learnt, will not only stem the tide of academic functionalism. It also offers the best defence against the tendency to gear the university directly to the labour market. This does not mean that we need to reject altogether economic approaches for higher education. Rather it is a shift of attention that is needed from the dominant human capital approach to the so-called filter theory. This means, as was propounded in the first part of this chapter, that the economic benefit of higher education is looked for not so much in terms of the increased productivity of people – that is, in their specific professional training – as in the social sorting function of their education. This implies that the accent shifts from bodies of knowledge, skills, and know-how, which students have to acquire, to relative suitability or 'trainability'. The *Memorandum* emphasises higher education's vital role in 'equipping all members of the labour force and young people with the new skills needed to meet the rapidly changing demands of European enterprises' (Commission of the European Communities 1991: p. 5). The education of reflective experts implies that the main task of higher education becomes the development in students of a readiness for further specialist and professional training. The concept of trainability compels a shift from the training of 'ready-made' researchers and professionals, with emphasis on the assessment of fixed, subject-related skills, to the training of relative capabilities and 'unfinished' suitability.

As Paul Smeyers points out in this volume, the university finds itself captured in several areas of tension. I am fully aware that my plea for the education of reflective specialists stands in a delicate relation between competing vocabularies. On the one hand, policymakers and managers may be inclined to cling to their belief in very specific diplomas and skills because they cannot see how to manage 'trainability' and 'reflectivity', especially within current resources. Perhaps also they cannot see how to sell these goals to their students: are these really attractive ideas in today's education market? On the other hand, in the eyes of many teachers, 'trainability' may seem a rather dubious concept. First, they may think, it fits too neatly into retrenchments in higher education budgets: no long and expensive specialist studies but short and cut-price general studies. Second, it inclines us to think in terms of a single uniform labour market, whereas in Europe we find, in fact, a variety of labour market policies. But against the teachers it might be pointed out here that the more, in general, that an active labour market policy is pursued, the more significant the meaning of the notion of trainability can become for a nation's higher education system. Third, some might think that 'trainability' superimposes the alien logic of the labour market onto the logic of higher education, thus reducing the prospects of dialogue between social and educational approaches to academic training.

These concepts, it must be conceded, need to be further worked out in these and many other respects. Given the absence of any real dialogue, however, between the vocabularies of benefit and *Bildung*, and given the gulf of mutual incomprehension, I take the view that the development of a kind of 'bridging' vocabulary is urgent. Trainability and reflectivity may become the keywords in that new vocabulary. The combination of these two notions may create the opportunity to reconsider the idea of higher education from a socially germane educational point of view.

Chapter 8

Industrial Innovation, Local Identity, and Higher Education:

A Democratic Response to Globalisation

Nigel Blake

From the very start, the original architects of the European Community envisaged political union as their long-term goal. They must have been openminded as to the probable or desirable consequences of union for culture. Indeed, in the postwar world, it must surely have seemed frivolous to posit political union as a threat to culture; on the contrary, the most drastic and vivid threats were quite clearly totalitarian nationalism and war. By contrast, the loosening and democratisation of the constraints of the state on society, if not the dissolution of nations, seemed an imperative, for the protection of society itself and *a fortiori* for culture and for cultures.

If their long-term aim was political union, then the projected path to that goal was through economic cooperation, developing into economic union and eventually political union. The priority accorded to economic development in Europe should not be seen cynically. The cultural and social history of Europe is tightly intertwined with a form of economic development grounded not just on accumulation but on technological and managerial innovation. Since the eighteenth century, the alleviation of poverty through economic growth has fostered political emancipation; and furthermore, the forms of social innovation required in the economic sphere and fostered by an innovative economy – urbanisation, democratisation, systematic training, and vocational education – have often made possible both social emancipation and the sustenance, elaboration, and widening dissemination of European culture at every level (this notwithstanding the oppression of early industrialisation and the social disasters that currently flow from managerial reform). Economic growth does not in itself constitute a threat to culture or to cultures – it is often their ally; and by no means was it an ethically inappropriate project for postwar Europe.

So Europe began the task of unification by pursuing the goal of a modern growth economy; and the economic organisation best suited to that end is some form (or mixture of forms) of advanced capitalism. But the consequences of this project begin now to seem paradoxical. On the one hand, technologically innovatory capitalism, with its internal drive to ever enlarging markets, is wonderfully effective at dissolving the hegemony of the nation-state. As Barry Smart puts it, 'global diffusion of economic activity and trade, and communications media and cultural production, coupled with higher levels of international travel, and a significant increase in supranational political and economic organisations and forums have precipitated an erosion of the political sovereignty and cultural specificity ascribed to the "national state"' (Smart 1993: p. 57). As nations progressively relinquish sovereignty, so too they align less exclusively to particular cultures. So far, so bad for European nation-states and so good for the European Community.

But as Smart goes on to say, this constellation of developments 'in turn renders problematic the principle of unity formerly considered to be constitutive of "society"' (Smart 1993: p. 57). Many sociologists, including for instance Anthony Giddens and Alain Touraine (see Smart 1993), have noted that traditionally, societies were differentiated and identified as the societies of particular nation-states; and that as the nature and priority of the state changes and diminishes so also does the concept of society. Societies are not merely fragmenting, as is so often claimed, but perhaps too eroding, dissolving, or reconstituting themselves in other and as yet unsettled and tendentious forms.

What does this imply for cultures themselves and the identities they subtend? It is fair to insist that there is no one-to-one correlation between societies and cultures (though I would resist the suggestion that the idea of a national culture is senseless); and fair to add that identities are determined or negotiated as much within cultures as by societies. Nonetheless, culture and society are not mutually autonomous realms. While there are indeed cultures that find representation in many different societies (think of Judaism and Islam within Europe) and indeed more and more cultures tend to do so, a culture is nonetheless worthless to a group if it cannot provide resources for its members to negotiate a way of life within the particular society they live in. And I do want to insist on the stronger thesis here: not just that a culture is of reduced value if it fails in this task, but that it is then of no value at all. The function of a culture is to sustain ways of life that make some kind of sense of human existence for its members. But any way of life is necessarily grounded in material practices and bounded by economic exigencies, which in turn have social and political aspects and implications. A culture can only sustain ways of life within specific societies and their respective economies; and there has to be some kind of accommodation between any culture and the society within which it is being sustained. It follows, I suggest, that the dissolution or protean transformation of society itself necessarily strains the resources of any culture within it and, further, will promote confusion and uncertainty within any such culture. (One response to this is, of course, cultural dogmatism and fundamentalism.)

Ultimately, then, the very forces of the modern growth economy on which we have relied to knit Europe together have both weakened the nation-state and, as Smart notes, eroded its cultural specificity (apparently a good thing), but furthermore arguably strained, eroded, and befuddled Europe's very constituent cultures. (The British Conservative Party does its conscious best to make electoral capital out of our own cultural unease within Europe.) But the cultural confusion, in turn, so far from prompting any compensatory European unity at the cultural level, promotes a crisis for the very concept of culture and cultures.

And what does all this seem to mean for higher education? Traditionally, European universities have performed important roles in sustaining at least some forms of culture within their societies, primarily high forms of national culture or religious forms (as formerly the case of the Catholic universities). And less obviously, the different disciplines represented within them have also sustained connections and involvements with a wide range of subcultures within their societies: political, social and aesthetic, technical, and professional. But this cultural role is now doubly in question. On the one hand, the very confusion and erosion of subcultures and cultures themselves provides an increasingly unclear and uncertain context for the universities to work within – and the increasing salience of identity politics within the modern university further exacerbates the problems (see Blake 1995). On the other, the demands of the growth economy impinge ever more urgently on higher education, and increasingly seem to pre-empt its cultural role. For these demands seem to entail a managerialist reform of higher education in terms quite inimical to the humanist heritage of European universities.

In looking at such pressures from a European perspective, one is bound to see these pressures as part of the phenomenon of globalisation – in particular, the globalisation of culture riding on the back of the globalisation of the new post-industrial economic order. Globalisation is readily considered the very hammer of cultural identity. It seemingly bids to erase whatever is most distinctive in local communities and undercut their claims on popular loyalty, all the more readily where communities have previously been rooted in specific industrial traditions. Similarly, it threatens to detach universities from cultures if not culture itself and subordinate them within a global economic nexus. In this context, the search for a European identity comes to look like a last ditch resistance to globalisation.

Now while I accept that there may be much that is important and valuable in its own terms in the search for a European identity and its promotion, it would be a mistake to assume that only this can offer hope for the retention or redefinition of identity for the peoples of Europe, or that it can offer any such hope on its own. I want to explore new ideas arising from economic research that suggest that a relation between industry and higher education need not be inimical to the sustenance of local identities, but can still be (as it has often been in the past) a positive support for their development and a democratic influence on their evolution. My own intuition is that a sense of European identity would in turn flourish better where local identities are also strong (whether national identities are strong or not). Without roots in such identities, and without a local context in which a European identity can be 'cashed' and understood, that identity is surely likely to prove dangerously abstract and thin. What is needed is not for Spanish, Scottish, Flemish, or Lower Saxon communities to swap their own identities for that of Europe, but for them to find the distinctively Scottish and Spanish ways, Flemish or Saxon ways of being European.

But first let us consider more carefully how the globalisation of the modern growth economy can come to seem inimical to local industrial identities and communities. We may subsequently come to see how our philosophical ideas about the relation between higher education and the economy can be distorted by assumptions related to neo-classical economic doctrines, assumptions that are now vigorously questioned by economists on the centre-left.

Economic Growth and Knowledge: The Neoclassical View

A capitalist economy grows through profit-making, generated and increased through competition. The sources of profitability are generally recognised on all sides as twofold: on the one hand, the reduction of costs and the extension of markets, on the other, technological innovation. But neo-classical theorists, whilst recognising the latter, emphasise the primary importance of the former. In a global economy these processes impinge negatively on local communities and their sense of identity in two ways. On the one hand, workers in different locales are in competition with each other, and must try to provide the lowest common denominator of labour skills for the cheapest price. Local talents and specialities and their traditions are not at a premium, expensive (and 'untransferable') as they tend to be. On the other hand, the extension of global markets entails 'MacDonaldisation' – growing uniformity in provision of products, services, and outlets from region to region. The impacts of both processes on cultures is obvious: 'Coke is it!'

Thinking of the functioning of the global economy in these terms encourages a conception of technological knowledge as a commodity, as something generated by a specialised process in a specialised place, but readily transferable from one place to another. Knowledge is thought of either as pure information or as theory in the form most abstracted from the practical context (scientific or technological) in which it may have been generated. As John Cantwell puts it, 'The knowledge element of technology has [been thought of as having] the characteristics of a latent public good: it is costly to create but may be transferred to other people for next to nothing' (Cantwell 1995: p. 67). Precisely because it is expensive to produce but so easily transferred, firms themselves have small interest in producing it. To do so is to subsidise one's competitors, at high expense. The research function very readily comes to be (in authoritarian market societies) a service demanded of the university. And the more that is demanded of the university in this way, the more its economic and thus social 'duties' pre-empt its responsibilities to the culture.

It's important to grasp that this dangerous requirement on the universities is predicated on a 'linear model' (Cantwell 1995: p. 68) of the relation between technological knowledge and successful production. In this model, R&D antedates product innovation; and the two spheres of activity are the concern of different professional communities, potentially and often actually in different institutions. Both antedate production and diffusion, which constitute a third institutional sphere. Each sphere forms an autonomous community of specialists (though practically the third is usually linked to the second within the same firm). The only links required are for the transfer of knowledge, finance, resources, or goods.

As we have seen, this kind of industrial organisation is antagonistic to the sustenance of local cultures and identities insofar as it responds principally to an emphasis on cost reduction and expanding markets. It also has comparable corrosive effects on academic research communities and their values in turn. While some sense of academic or research community and of shared intellectual and ethical commitments is intrinsic to the production of knowledge, these values and commitments are external to the value that knowledge is supposed to have for industry. Industry, it may seem, wants just the information and the theory. Worse, from the managerial point of view, the research priorities that academic or intellectual commitments and values dictate are unlikely to be those of the client industry. Research leads in one direction if one seeks to verify, modify, correct, or create a theory; in quite another to supply the knowledge requirements of some practical project.

When one adds the sheer expense of academic research to the externality of academic values and the apparent hidden cost of the alien priorities they dictate, it is hardly surprising that external sponsors of research should disregard the validity or necessity of academic values or undervalue the democratic communities they seem to presuppose; nor is it surprising that they should attack the seemingly inefficient practices these communities support. If research is simply a production process, whose product just happens to be intellectual rather than material, why cannot this form of production be rationalised on the same managerial lines that govern industrial production? What is wrong in academic research with clear line management, contracting-out by tender, top-down task definition, unambiguous objectives, simple performance indicators, quality audit, and the maximal deployment of transferable skills? Do we really need an egalitarian community of scholars, argument, imagination and reconceptualisation, tenured talent, peer review, academic freedom and autonomy, or deep immersion in specialised intellectual traditions?

If research relates to industry on the linear model, then almost inevitably economic pressure will steadily erode any sense of tradition, community, and identity in the research sphere. And insofar as it is difficult to isolate this sphere from that of teaching in higher education and its curricular concerns – which anyway are now subject to the same managerial reforms – it must become far harder to transmit academic traditions and identities to students or to induct them into academic communities. In turn, any role of universities in culture and in sustaining local identity must also be put in jeopardy.

Innovation and Tacit Capability

It seems the linear model has much to answer for. But as I argued earlier, economic growth is not a good to be lightly jettisoned. So any perspective that offers us economic growth without the linear model is clearly worth our attention. Just such a model has emerged in recent years in empirical economic research on innovation, industrial districts, and R&D. This research is related to the current of centre-left dissent in economics from the neoclassical orthodoxy of the last two decades. It shifts attention away from cost reduction and market power as engines of profit. Let John Cantwell again describe it: '[This] school of thought, associated with Schumpeter but with strong roots in Adam Smith and Karl Marx, says profit is derived from innovation in terms of the creation of new products and processes. Innovation consists primarily of the accumulation of *tacit capability* – sometimes termed "technological accumulation". Tacit capability is *embodied in social organisations*, mainly in firms, and so tends to be tied to production *by a specific set of firms in a particular location*' (Cantwell 1995: p. 66; author's italics). Here Cantwell posits a connection between a different conception of technological knowledge (as 'tacit capability'), its embodiment in institutional communities, and its geographically specific location. If, as Cantwell further writes, 'profit through innovation has become even more important' with globalisation (Cantwell 1995: p. 67), then it seems to follow that globalisation need not be destructive of local identity if it is intelligently understood and managed. Indeed, when discussing the specificity of national systems for innovation in science and technology, Cantwell explicitly claims that 'Contrary to what is sometimes alleged, globalisation and national specialisation are complementary parts of a common process, and not conflicting trends' (Cantwell 1995: p. 70). I want to investigate the educational implications of such a model; and to indicate that, on this understanding, technological innovation can be a force that interacts with proper academic values to give positive support to local community and identity.

I shall first consider the role of tacit capability and some of its educational implications, then deepen the discussion by trying to analyse its epistemological character. The purpose of the epistemological characterisation that I shall offer in the third section is not to supplant or guess at any empirical economic account of the kinds of activity that generate tacit capability or the ways it is embodied in firms – such as , respectively, problem solving or organisational routines (as cited in Cantwell 1995: pp. 67–68). Rather it is to supplement it with another layer of analysis: to show what it might mean to say that individual actors have tacit knowledge that is nonetheless shared with others in their organisations and that can be effectual in processes of technological learning and change, problem solving, and organisational development. Some such account is necessary if we are to say anything clear and useful from the educational side about the desirable interconnections between industry and higher education. But I also dare to hope that it might contribute to a theorisation of a variety of richly resonant empirical findings concerning innovatory firms and their institutional characteristics.

So let us turn to the role of tacit capability. Cantwell writes:

> Public technological knowledge has a tacit component, understood only by individual practitioners trained and experienced in the activity in question. Similarly, tacit capability is acquired through a *collective* learning process within the firm, and thus becomes embodied in a form of social organisation.
>
> [According to this view,] knowledge and tacit capability are strictly complementary. The one cannot be used to produce anything without the other. Thus, technological knowledge and skills that are potentially public [and thus globally transferable] can only be effectively exploited by firms that accumulate the requisite tacit capability. (Cantwell 1995: p. 68; author's italics)

Cantwell draws an important policy implication from this idea. Firms and more generally regional and national economies that want to reap the benefits of economic growth cannot hitch a free ride by neglecting their own R&D efforts and just cannibalising research done elsewhere. The innovative use of R&D presupposes that degree of tacit capability that can only be acquired through involvement in innovative R&D of one's own – not necessarily on precisely the same projects, though clearly they must be related. He notes that 'The most innovative firms are also generally the best imitators.' For firms 'need their own R&D facility to tailor [acquired] knowledge to their own needs and to monitor and understand what knowledge is useful to their needs' (Cantwell 1995: p. 68).

But while there is no free ride, small to medium firms and local economies cannot reasonably pay their tickets on their own. This is why they also need the involvement of higher education. For while there are inevitable returns to firms from their own R&D, returns that corporations can easily capture, for small or specialised firms the returns can be too small if the firm has to foot the whole cost. 'Therein', writes Cantwell, 'lies the role for public policy. By supporting education and training, governments help lower the costs and facilitate the creation of tacit capability. That is, government can address what is at root an institutional failing rather than a malfunctioning of the markets... Public research is not replacing some "missing" private endeavour but acting as a catalyst for the widening of private research.' (Cantwell 1995: p. 69) That, at least, is how it should be – not, as it seems increasingly in Britain, a matter of the private sector 'contracting out' its own work to the universities: 'What *innovative* companies expect from local universities is not research with immediate commercial application in their own sector, but rather a wider base of knowledge creation and skills with which their own facilities can interact' (Cantwell 1995: p. 69; author's italics). And what is 'in it' for the universities themselves? Once firms are drawing on the output of higher education to form and strengthen their tacit capability, then 'In practice, there is continual interaction between learning in production (innovation) and research and science, but on the whole there tend to be more links that run from technology in production to research and to science than the other way round… An illustration is the impact of computer technology on scientific enquiry' (Cantwell 1995: p. 68).

On this optimistic account, then, it may seem that the universities need not fear erosion of their academic functions if their relation with industry is the one that is best for industry itself; and they can in fact gain from the process in their own academic terms. So if the involvement of higher education in the generation of industrial tacit capability is potentially benign if properly appreciated, it seems a proper concern for philosophy of education to analyse its epistemological character and its implications for the healthy functioning of firms, of universities, and of the links between them.

Conceptualising Tacit Capability

How then shall we analyse a technological tacit capability? It might seem that inasmuch as it is indeed tacit, appeal to the mechanisms of language would be inappropriate. Indeed, we might be tempted to look rather to the ideas of Polanyi, for instance, with their emphasis on mind-body interaction. But a key characteristic of *technological* tacit knowledge is that it is shared. The appropriate forms of learning are ultimately forms of collective learning. As Cantwell says, tacit capability 'becomes embodied in a form of social organisation'. It is impossible, I suggest, to conceive of shared learning and capability other than as at least potentially linguistic or mediated by interactions that themselves are explicit and hence linguistic. Language is intrinsically involved in any sharing of knowledge. Knowledge that is shared cannot be explained solely by reference to something as personal and (in some senses) private as the body.[1] The theory of communicative action of Jürgen Habermas addresses the social structure of linguistic interaction and provides resources more promising for the analysis of tacit capability.

Philosophers of education tend to think of Habermas primarily as the heir of the Enlightenment and the apostle of transparency, however guarded his rationalism. But this may mislead us into overlooking the important role of the tacit dimension in his thinking. Habermas follows speech act theorists, pre-eminently J.L. Austin, in conceiving speech as a sequence of interknit social acts of a particular kind. Austin was at pains to emphasise how little of what we say is geared primarily to the exchange of information or the description of facts. Speech is a stream of 'doings', such as greetings, enquiries, expostulations, attitudinisings, assurances, and commitments. In such acts, what we do is often, if not always, constituted by what we say. Paradigmatically, to make a promise is to say the words 'I promise'. Austin's contribution emphasised the disparity of these different speech acts; but others since, notably J.R. Searle, have redressed the balance by trying to tease out a common logical (or more properly praxiological) form for speech acts (see Searle 1969). They have sought to emphasise the structure of presuppositions underlying speech acts generally; and Habermas has contributed to this project.

Habermas argues that all speech acts rest on three different presuppositions of different kinds – presuppositions that, of their very nature, typically remain unspoken. Habermas calls these presuppositions – which may or may not be correct – 'validity claims' (see Habermas 1984: pp. 302–309). First, any utterance raises a validity claim that some factual state of affairs obtains: a claim to truth. Second (as I explain below), it raises a claim to the normative validity of the relationship between speaker and hearer. Third, it raises a sincerity claim, a claim that the attitudes and feelings appropriate to the speaker who makes the utterance are indeed truly her own attitudes or feelings.

The thesis of three validity claims is not an empirical generalisation nor is it an hypothesis. Rather, it is intrinsic to the very nature of a speech act that it must have each of these three kinds of presuppositions.[2] Performing a speech act is a pointless activity unless the act is in some way consequential for the hearer, unless the hearer's disposition to action, emotion, or will is somehow modified (if only reinforced) by receiving the speech act. This has certain quite general implications.

First, there must be at least some minimal overlap between the 'life worlds' of speaker and hearer. Unless speaker and hearer at least make reference to *some* of the same states of affairs, then the speech act can have no importance or consequence for the hearer. The validity claim to truth is the specification of this overlap or shared reference to reality.

Second, since a speech act is intrinsically a social act, it can only be effective between speakers who can specify some relation between themselves, however tenuous and abstract (for instance, the relationship of strangers, which has its own structure and norms). If there is no relationship, then the hearer cannot know 'how to take' the speech act, what to do about it or with it (ignore it or take it seriously, treat it with scepticism or respect, decide to respond or simply to conform, and so on). Moreover, for any social act to be effective, not as it were to misfire, the actors must actually agree (by and large) as to the nature of the relationship. Since any social relationship is defined by certain norms (manager and worker, director and fellow director, shareholder and accountant), any speech act necessarily raises a claim that the general relationship of speaker and hearer is governed by particular norms enacted in a particular way and agreed by speaker and hearer.

Third, inasmuch as any social act is governed by particular purposes or perceptions (if the act is more or less a rational one) one may reasonably impute more or less specific attitudes or feelings to the speaker. If these feelings or attitudes are found not to be actual, then the character of the whole act is called in question. Thus, any speech act necessarily raises a validity claim as to the sincerity of the implicit feelings or attitudes.

Speakers and hearers understand what each other is saying only inasmuch as they share the same interpretation of the validity claims a speech act raises and, moreover, share an acceptance of those claims. If in fact they do not share the same interpretation, it may be expected that they will eventually come to find themselves 'at cross purposes'. If they do share the interpretation but do not agree as to the correctness of some validity claim, then normally we may expect one party to raise and question the claim explicitly – 'But it's not really like that!' / 'Who do you think you're talking to?' / 'You're not being honest with me'. On the other hand, if there seems nothing amiss with sharing these presuppositions, they will not be voiced explicitly and will constitute a tacit dimension of the dialogue. Insofar as the validity claims are generally accepted, they specify the content of the tacit knowledge.

This apparatus can be used to demystify tacit capability inasmuch as it shows how it can be thought of as substantive and effectual in the real world of technological activity. It also shows that necessarily tacit capability *can* be made overt and explicit, when need be. On the other hand, it also shows that and why so much is necessarily actually tacit at any given time in any shared discourse – the discourse of the laboratory or factory floor no less than any other. The very act of making any validity claims explicit and discussing them constitutes in its turn another dialogue with its own tacit dimension. It is not just unnecessary but impossible to make everything explicit all the time. Tacit capability, on this account, is like a machine part.

It can be left in place and not thought about as long as it functions properly, and is better left alone; but it can be and has to be taken out and examined whenever something goes wrong with it, in other words, when it ceases to be unproblematically shared.

To point to the substantive content of tacit capability is to explain how it can be used. But to conceptualise it as the agglomerated background of a multitude of speech acts (or interactions) is to show that it cannot but be diffuse: an attribute of the group rather than the individual and fostered and elaborated by group learning (or by the individual sharing her learning with the group). Indeed, even when there are no disputes over background assumptions, it need not be that any two members of the same group will have exactly the same shared knowledge as any other pair. We are talking here about overlaps, and overlaps between overlaps, and so on.

At one level, shared experience is clearly a precondition of this group knowledge, as Cantwell says (witness the pervasive importance of uncontested validity claims to truth – a multitude of overlaps in the 'life worlds' of the individuals involved). But perhaps more interestingly, at a deeper level social interaction, either actually or potentially linguistic (actually voiced or possible to voice), is the precondition of there being any shared experience at all. For people to share experience, it is not enough for them to be at the same place at the same time or even, in some simple sense, to observe the same events. To say that they have the same experience is to say that they make the same sense of what they observe. It is to say that by and large they not only explain but would actually describe it in compatible and overlapping, if not identical ways.

However, they cannot know that they do so unless they can somehow communicate their agreement to each other. The direct way to do this is to talk about their experience; and in talking about it, they will almost inevitably come to negotiate any differing perceptions or beliefs, modifying their own in the light of their partner's accounts. Shared experience is not simply discovered; it is constructed in communicative interaction, which is potentially and often actually linguistic. Through interaction, we come to *create* shared experiences.[3] But the knowledge of them that we share may remain in large part tacit. The evidence that it exists is (necessarily) indirect. It is given in the generally untroubled consensus of the group. And sometimes this consensus is not voiced at all. It can be evinced in the simple fact that co-workers carry on with the task together without problems. The very ability to do so without difficulty indicates agreement, which can be made explicit if need be. Thus even the tacit interaction that may characterise social trial-and-error learning has an implicit conversational structure.[4]

The rhetoric of shared experience points strongly towards a preference for intense and local interaction as a precondition of the creation and maintenance of tacit capability. But need this be so? In the age of the instantaneous computer link, surely the connection between tacit capability and geographical (and hence social) closeness must be coming loose – and with it, social and cultural links between industry and the local university? Apparently not: '[A] good deal of recent empirical work has shown that the intensity of the links between science and technology still tends to decline with geographical distance. The links between science, research and technology have remained essentially localised, owing to the importance of face-to-face contacts in communicating the results of complex learning processes that embody a tacit element.' (Cantwell 1995: pp. 68–69) This is readily understood if tacit knowledge is seen as the construct of a multitude of speech acts in a complex and many-voiced conversation. Interchange would need to be rapid – more rapid for instance than e-mail, at its snappiest – for participants to monitor and modify the flow and accumulation of validity claims, contested and uncontested. (Think, for instance, of testing out new apparatus on a factory floor.) However helpful remote communications may be, they cannot substitute for the sheer density and detail of face-to-face conversation.

This conversational account of tacit capability also goes to explain some important conditions for the success of small firm webs, which has accounted for some of the happiest successes in regional economies within the EU in recent years: '[B]esides geographic proximity, the firms must also be tied to one another at some point in the production process, or have other interconnections – through their personnel or firm histories, professional associations, trade shows or common customers. Writers on industrial districts assert that these interconnections *create a "culture" that shapes firms' organisation and function*.' (Miller and Sugden 1995: p. 86; author's italics) So we also glimpse here the important connection between tacit capability, local community, and local culture. Inasmuch as universities have an important role to play in webs of firms, we can begin to see their potential importance for helping to secure cultures and identities within the dynamic of globalisation.

Implications for Management

Tacit capability, then, not only relies on but in large measure consists in a conversationally constituted shared experience. So a well-managed institution should attend with care to the conditions under which the construction of shared experience is best fostered. Habermas recognises a debased form of linguistic interaction, which he characterises as 'strategic interaction', that is inimical to the construction of shared experience. In interactions of this kind, the speaker aims to influence the hearer in nontransparent ways. That is to say, he aims to deceive the hearer with regard to the presuppositions that actually inform his part in their conversation or at least to conceal them from her. In a sense, the success of his speech acts relies not on their being understood but on their being misunderstood, in a kind of conversational poker game, as it were. (In Kantian terms, he treats his hearer as a means to an end.)

This form of interaction is grounded in inequalities and nonmutualities of knowledge and understanding. And it is a typical mode of the form of top-down authoritarian line management characteristic of economies operating with the linear model of technological knowledge.[5] But strategic interaction positively aims at fragmenting the mutual 'life world' rather than sealing and enlarging it. It might do this by deconstituting the experience supposedly shared by managers and the managed – 'We know something you don't know'. In that situation, the combined talents of the group who are not 'in the know' are necessarily not focused on achieving the firm's objectives because these must effectively be suppressed. Similarly, sheer insincerity on the part of managers is also symptomatic of a failure to commit to the same aims as the rest of the firm, or to commit with comparable intensity, so that potentially fruitful developments of tacit capability will go undervalued and wither. Further, insincerity once unmasked must imperil the cooperative relationships essential to the building of shared tacit capability. The same can obviously be said for any discovery that managers do not actually share the workforce's view of the ethical norms governing their relationships. And even if kept covert, any such disjunction must involve a discrepancy in the views of managed and managers as to the mission of the firm, a discrepancy that must, in the long term, make for a mismatch between the supposedly shared tacit capability and its actually covert purpose.

Miller and Sugden claim empirical confirmation for the importance of nonstrategic interaction at the level of relationships not within but between firms in small firm webs: 'Trust is another important factor in webs. It reduces transaction costs and establishes a foundation for cooperative relationships. In well-established groups, trust seems to have developed through members' shared experience, common training, and adherence to the same normative structures. Trust has provided a vital glue among firms and a building-block for innovation' (Miller and Sugden 1995: pp. 86–87).

Here, indeed, we glimpse how transparency in terms of any one kind of validity dimension (truth, normative acceptability, and sincerity) can support, and the lack of it undermine, transparency in the others. Insincerity, for instance, can erode the shared cognitive 'life world'. Miller and Sugden address relations between firms; but it is surely impossible to doubt that the same considerations apply to relations within firms. The point that needs to be underscored is not just that strategic forms of management are immoral (which of course they are) but that they are actually, in the long term, ineffectual and destructive of the very knowledge capital, the tacit capability, a healthy growth economy requires.

Education has an important role to play here, and higher education in particular. Miller and Sugden go on to consider how relationships between firms, and we may assume within them, are created and maintained: '[These relations] are partly defined by institutions – the rules and norms governing behaviour. Institutions in their turn are taught, monitored and evolved by *organisations that are commonly public*... An important type of institution that determines the rules and norms for a given group is the educational process' (Miller and Sugden 1995: p. 87; author's italics). They go on to consider, as a case study, the Italian packaging machine industry of 'Packaging Valley' near Bologna. This is a very successful industrial area[6], and one of the key organisations in that success is its local vocational school, the Aldini-Valeriani Institute, established in the nineteenth century by academics, rather tellingly, from the University of Bologna, specifically with the mission of re-industrialising the area (after the collapse of the silk industry). It is unsurprising that education helps but worthwhile to be clear how and why it helps: 'The common schooling provided by the institute has been important to innovation, in part because it provides high quality technical training in designing and making machines work. But the common training is also crucial to learning the "rules of the game" of the local packaging machine sector. Technical knowledge obviously helps innovation. Less obvious but no less important is that shared knowledge, experiences and normative structure help create a community that is centred on the making of packing machines' (Miller and Sugden 1995: p. 88).

It seems clear that in considering relations between firms, Miller and Sugden are dealing principally with relations between middle and top management and technical staff. And for them, it is easy to see that *higher* education is of particular importance (though not, apparently, for graduate-averse British industry – a local complaint of some bitterness). If we can assume that similar considerations apply to the internal culture of individual firms, then we have to have regard also to the role of secondary schooling in initiating students destined for the shop floor into the local culture. But important as this may also be, higher education retains, I shall argue, a further and particular role *vis-à-vis* the support of innovation.

Miller and Sugden consider the desirable shape of small firm webs and in doing so reveal a startling lack of perspicacity among economic agencies as to the epistemic requirements of innovation. Miller and Sugden find it necessary to point out that 'To achieve the innovation necessary for a successful economy, it is not enough to link small firms via a central hub' (Miller and Sugden 1995: p. 87), as for instance the British government has tried to do with 'one-stop shops' giving services to business and as some multinationals, such as Benetton, have done by creating hierarchical links to a range of smaller firms. The problem is, of course, that such structures confine the flow of discourses to a collection of two-way channels between hub and periphery, but not around the periphery, constricting the rich interchange necessary for the evolution of tacit capability. As Miller and Sugden say, 'something closer to a three-dimensional spider's web is needed... In this kind of structure, it is possible to see more clearly the idea of innovation as a flexible activity that is dynamic and continual over time, rather than as separate parts fitted together, each doing a defined job' (Miller and Sugden 1995: p. 87). But surely, to anyone used to university research, in the humanities at least, this blind spot is incredible. What else could innovation be like? How can a structure of carefully separated roles, tightly interknit and with pre-defined jobs, produce innovation? Surely in innovation these are amongst the very things that may have to change? Industrial innovation may be managerial or technological or both combined. Managerial innovation involves intrinsically changes of working relationships or work-related attitudes. Technological changes involve changes in empirical (technical, economic, etc.) assumptions. And, of course, new technologies can often necessitate managerial change in turn. A social structure of predefined and closely interknit roles is the least appropriate to sustain such changes.

To make any such changes, one must, in Habermas's terms, query implicit and commonly accepted validity claims, cognitive, normative, or affective. But if such change is to be successful, it must also be rational; and as Habermas points out, such rationality requires undistorted communication. We saw, when discussing strategic action, what might constitute such distortions and how they will eventually prove dysfunctional. But non-distortion is not enough to secure rationality in innovative contexts. A kind of radical openness is also essential, and it is the characteristic form of openness of research communities in higher education.

Most conversations, however undistorted, take place within certain limits or constraints. They involve only particular participants, and only occasionally might it be desirable or to the point to involve any others, if possible. The smooth conduct of conversation relies in part, as well, on shared notions of relevance and pertinence. There are ranges of things one does not say or expect to hear. And we do not typically expect to have to explain or defend our own attitudes, feelings, or needs in relation to the conversations we participate in. We expect these things to be tacitly accepted as unproblematic and decorum weighs against their exposure.

But in the conversation of academic research, any of these limits or constraints may need to be broken. One cannot tell *a priori* from which quarter a necessary or pertinent suggestion may come. In that sense, conversation is open to all comers, at least within the community of the discourse. And fundamentally, of course, any attempt at academic innovation or pushing back the frontiers of knowledge will necessarily involve the proposition of claims whose relevance or pertinence has not already been foreseen. By the same token, we cannot construct any acceptable prior limitations on academic conversation that will screen out irrelevance and filter through only that which, unknown to us, will eventually prove necessary to us. Lastly, academic matters can rarely be insulated from ethical or affective concerns. An academic debate about medical matters of life and death, the proper appreciation of the arts, the technological exploitation of a science – or indeed the economics of growth and the role of higher education – may not *require* the examination of attitudes, needs, or feelings; but it surely cannot reasonably exclude it. Indeed, to do so might effectively silence those who feel that the conversation cannot make progress or the community secure intellectual innovations unless some such attitudes are taken into account.

Thus academic conversation approximates better than any other form to what Habermas calls 'ideal speech conditions', conditions in which extraneous constraints discourse are minimised, and rational debate given its freest rein. And these, surely, are the ideal conditions for innovative thinking that industry seems to require. But is there any way that industry can credibly relate to them?

Industry is not higher education itself. Conversations within firms are necessarily constrained in ways in which academic conversations are not and should not be. Firms exist for particular purposes and are governed by financial considerations that may be extraneous to their productive functions. These in turn impose limitations of relevance, participation, and attitude. And however liberal the management of a firm, it is never likely to be as well adapted as the university to the egalitarian demands of non-strategic academic interaction. Industry cannot furnish ideal speech conditions to its personnel without, strictly speaking, ceasing to be industry. As with most ordinary conversations, one positively *does not want them* to function under ideal speech conditions. For the same kind of reason, we can see why those organisations that define rules and norms are, as Miller and Sugden note, commonly public. For it is public organisations that, by definition, preclude the dominance of private interests and that are themselves most open to scrutiny to ensure their impartial functioning. To put it another way, those organisations that centrally define rules and norms for the private sector need to stand outside it for the rules and norms to have the independent status they require.

Yet it does seem that industry needs access to knowledge acquired and defined under ideal speech conditions if it is to innovate and grow; to say this is to explain what is taken for granted in the best practice, their need to enjoy relationships with higher education. As we noted earlier, small firms have to innovate no less than large corporations. They must participate in some form of R&D if they are to build the tacit capability that will help them expand further by taking on board the innovatory knowledge of others. The best innovators, remember, make the best imitators. But the costs of R&D are high, and for small firms R&D is only sustainable within a wider research community. As we saw, this in itself argues for links to higher education. But for firms of any size, there is the fundamental difficulty of providing ideal (or more nearly ideal) conditions of discourse for research. Inasmuch as R&D itself is to be truly innovative, it must approximate to the academic model. On this model, research has to retain all the academic virtues of community, close cooperation, and openness. But these need to be put in abeyance for the pursuance of particular industrial projects.

How is such an institutional conundrum solved? It has been noted already – and it used to be a truism – that innovative firms look to higher education not for the provision of specific knowledge but for a wider base of knowledge creation and skills. What has been overlooked, I feel, is the central role played in this base by the understanding graduates may acquire at university of the (not quite but approximately) ideal conditions of discourse and their point and purpose, which used to typify higher education and still should. Unless graduates have come to understand these things, they will be ill-prepared for fundamental innovations in knowledge and probably less welcoming of them; so slower to seize their implications and potential. They will understand only badly the provisional nature of research findings, and thus may ill-recognise forms of dogmatism in their work that may hinder innovation. They will be unrehearsed in the practice of imagination in research. They may lack the institutional adaptability in terms of teamwork that academic research at its best can foster.

But firms not only need graduates who display these qualities within the firm. They also need people who can maintain contact with university research and appreciate its potential. Such bridging people need to understand and to be able to operate in both of the different institutional settings and under the different kinds of constraint of discourse. They must be able, in fact, to switch between the two. And arguably, an appreciation of the practices and purposes of community and openness is also important where firms interact with other innovative firms, even if conditions for discourse are necessarily circumscribed *within* each firm. In other words, academically intelligent graduates might be expected to facilitate the growth of webs of firms, even where universities are not directly involved.

Another virtue of the traditional university needs to be mentioned as a reason for fostering industry/university links: not its support of specialisation so much as its inherent openness to diversity in research. Consider these words of Keith Pavitt: 'Too much selectivity and concentration in basic research is dangerous. Products are underpinned by many technologies and each technology is underpinned by many sciences. As a consequence, advanced countries are more specialised in their exports than in their technological competence; and in most countries, scientific specialisation is decreasing not increasing' (Pavitt 1995: p. 73). But the 'command' model of industry and higher education fits ill with this picture. For industry to be explicit and specific in the demands it makes on higher education will in the long run militate against the diversity of university research that industry itself eventually needs.

Industry, Universities, and Culture

The background concern that this paper addresses is the fear that Europe's deep commitment to economic growth in a globalised world will so pressurise higher education as to pre-empt its role in sustaining European culture and Europe's constituent cultures. The first pressure point seemed likely to be the organisation (and indeed disorganisation) of scientific research within the academic community. But I have tried to show that a really innovative industrial community requires universities that succeed very much in their own terms. Even at the level of scientific research, truly innovative work requires the openness that can only be realised in a reasonably egalitarian community. Openness and the trust that it presupposes can only flourish in specific and defined (if porous) communities. And the identity of any community is bound up tightly with its own local traditions. Thus industry, where healthy, requires the very commitment to community, identity, and tradition in scientific research that the university traditionally cultivates in other branches of its activity. And it is hard to see how industry would undermine these academic functions more generally if it did not do so in its own particular area of interest.

Yet even so, is there not still a danger of subordinating universities to a global culture, as islands of intellectual freedom in a sea of cultural uniformity? Surely not – or not necessarily. As we have seen, on the 'post-neo-classical' model, economic growth positively requires strong localities. Tacit capability is best built in conditions of face-to-face interaction and, short of this, of geographical proximity between institutions. Universities have a central and definable role to play in tying such localities together, and an appropriate sized locality is perhaps that of a region. Consider this finding, from the supposedly non-regional United Kingdom: 'two thirds of all new high-tech [small and medium-sized firms] were established in the three southern regions [of the UK]. This north-south divide in the innovative activity of [such firms] cannot be explained by differences in industrial structure. It reflects the impact on locally founded small firms of south east England's concentration of research and development establishments (*including universities*), highly qualified scientists, engineers and professionals and information intensive business services and consultancies.' (Hughes, Keeble, and Wood 1995: p. 96; author's italics). Seemingly a 'Europe of the Regions' could be healthy for the universities. Miller and Sugden also note, significantly for us, that 'A concern with institutions is in line with the European Commission's recent use of the concept of "institution building"' (Miller and Sugden 1995: p. 88). But more profoundly, we may be able to see here the possibility of reconstituting the polity on such a scale and in such a fashion as to provide a new principle for the differentiation and identification of societies, which, as Smart, Giddens, and Touraine, amongst others, have noted is disappearing with the nation-state. Such an organisation provides possible focuses towards which cultures might orient themselves. And universities would play a vital constitutive role within them.

We also noticed that locally defined and accepted rules and norms are as important in tying together innovative industrial communities as any other kind of community. Yet it is inconceivable that the norms of such networks could be insulated from or fail to impinge on those other norms that bind a local or regional community together. Universities undoubtedly have a major role to play in developing, mediating, and negotiating between local norms, and can do so within larger and more open cultural perspectives, both metropolitan and cosmopolitan. Inasmuch as universities can do this, their cultural role should also be functional for the local or regional economy.

A democratic polity has a further reason for promoting the involvement of universities in local economies. Miller and Sugden remind us of a problem:

> Strategic decisions are the prime determinant of the nature, form and extent of productive activity. Today, these decisions are made by large transnational corporations, which consider their own interests rather than the interests of society as a whole. The results of their choices are efficient from the point of view of the corporations, but not necessarily so from society's viewpoint. The types of innovations firms tend to pursue tend to be chosen to suit the elite who make the decisions. Companies may, for example, resist new forms of work organisation that might undermine the position of the people making the strategic decisions. Firms have been known to withhold innovation that would disrupt their monopoly positions.
>
> How is this inefficiency to be tackled? … [S]trategic decision-making is still concentrated in a few hands at the pinnacle of hierarchical corporations. What is needed is greater involvement of communities in making the key decisions. In short, we need more diffuse, democratic economies characterised by more balanced involvement in strategic planning. (Miller and Sugden 1995: p. 86)

It is hard to doubt that universities could and should play a major role in such a polity, providing they were returned to their more traditional form from the current managerialist nightmare. And a major force and reason for such a restoration would be the pursuit of a postneoclassical economics, which emphasised the fundamental role of industrial innovation. So here we can see, vividly I think, how assumptions about economics can impinge significantly on our philosophy of education.

Philosophers are familiar with what makes a community; politicians know that education is important for the economy. What has not been clear is how intimately these concerns should be linked. The link is required by the very epistemology of technological innovation.

Notes

1. Of course, the body is not private in every sense; and I would not want to preclude the likelihood that there is much to say about the public role of the body in the construction of shared tacit knowledge.

2. Whether there might be others is of secondary interest here. Of course, the standard of comprehensibility is often mentioned by Habermas's commentators alongside those of truth, rightness and sincerity. But while comprehensibility is clearly a criterion for success in speech acts, it is not right to construe it as a validity claim raised by them.
3. This insight is one that Habermas shares, of course, with Gadamer and with hermeneutics in general. What hermeneutics seems not to provide so well is any account of the construction of shared experience in innovative, non-traditional, and critical conversations. It seems also to imply an inappropriately conservative politics of knowledge for such conversations.
4. I am grateful to Professor Cantwell, in correspondence, for drawing my attention to the importance of this kind of social trial-and-error learning in industry.
5. It is, of course, a favoured contemporary mode of such kinds of management to advertise a spurious openness in their dealings with employees, the better to manipulate them.
6. Miller and Sugden describe Packaging Valley as an area 'where a vast web of companies work together to produce packaging machines: the product is a complex, relatively high-tech capital good; the industry is demand-led, which requires flexibility in order to respond to varied and changing customer demands; there is a highly developed division of labour among specialised firms; various phases are involved in producing a particular machine, including design, parts manufacture, assembly, sale and customer care; and for every machine, each phase involves more than one, often several, firms' (Miller and Sugden 1995: p. 85). They later add, 'Italian packaging machine firms are very successful. They have high rates of employment, especially compared to national employment, and often export 80–90 per cent of their products. Italy ranks fourth behind Germany, the USA and Japan as the biggest producers of packaging machines' (Miller and Sugden 1995: p. 88).

CHAPTER 9

CULTURE, CITIZENSHIP, AND THE GLOBAL MARKET:

CHALLENGES TO EDUCATION IN THE 'NEW EUROPE'

Joseph Dunne

This paper, like Gaul, is divided into three parts. In the first part, I try to establish a critical context, by clarifying a number of themes bound up with the notions of 'cultural identity', 'political union', and 'economic integration'. Within this context, I go on in the second part to formulate central challenges to the contemporary European Union that are now both unavoidable and historically unprecedented. When I then address these challenges in the third part of the paper it is not my intention to offer prescriptions as to how they should be met; rather, drawing on some recent work in European philosophy, I develop a perspective without which, as I argue, they cannot be met at all.

Part One – Critical Clarifications: Culture, Politics, and Economics

Cultural Identity and Wars of the Canon

An attempt to define and defend a European cultural identity has been made within an influential philosophical discourse (quite different from the one on which I shall draw in the final part of the paper). This is a severely polarising discourse which, on the one hand, pours scorn on contemporary Europe but does so, on the other hand, from a lofty perspective which, it claims, represents the real 'soul' or 'form' of Europe. Thus, Nietzsche (the leading figure here) can speak of 'cloudy, damp, melancholy Old Europe', in which 'a shrunken almost ludicrous species, a herd animal, something full of good-will, sickly and mediocre has been born, the European of today'; and at the same time can go beyond this critique to a 'yea-saying' founded on a retrieval of Dionysiac elements of the European 'will to power' and a 'return of the Greek spirit'. Similarly Husserl, oppressed by a flattening naturalism, can look beyond 'the ashes of the great weariness' to 'a rebirth of Europe from the spirit of philosophy', or a recovery of the 'spiritual form of Europe' in a 'universal and pure science of spirit' (whatever that might be). And Heidegger, who sees under Nietzsche's shadow that 'in the history of western man something is coming to an end', can still look beyond this end to 'a land of dawn, an Orient' – and can look all the better because, as he supposes, the German language gives him privileged access to the original Greek spirit that will reappear in this dawn (see Delanty 1995).

There are clearly strong elements of disenchantment, nostalgia and reaction in this philosophical discourse on Europe – to the point where Nietzsche can be seen as a progenitor of (and Heidegger as complicit in) Fascism, with the war and Holocaust which defaced Europe only a half century ago. There is of course an alternative, non-Nietzschean conception of Europe, which invokes precisely the element within European cultural history which Nietzsche repudiated, viz. Christianity. T.S. Eliot, for instance, or Pope John Paul II, can also deplore the direction which Europe has recently been taking; but the return from this path of decline to its ownmost self is to come through some reconstituted version of Christendom. However, if in this century its high philosophy has not saved Europe from barbarism – but has in some respects even contributed to it – the same can be said about its religion in some earlier centuries: in the aftermath of the Reformation, for instance, it was between Christians of rival allegiances that the bitterest wars were waged and the most terrible persecutions inflicted. Nor were earlier enormities confined to its own territory. There is also Europe's shameful history of colonisation, with the depredations it has visited on other continents (especially South America and Africa) in the name of its own superior culture.

As well as invading and subduing other continents, Europeans have projected images of them as external 'others' over against which they have all the better been able to affirm an exclusivist notion of 'Europeanness'; and not only enthusiasts for Greek or Christian revivalism but representatives of the most advanced movements of European thought have engaged in this projective process. Thus, for instance, Thomas Mann (in *The Magic Mountain*) evokes a relentless struggle between the liberalism and cosmopolitan deriving from the French Revolution and 'The Asiatic principle' which threatens *Mitteleuropa* at its heart in Vienna. Or Karl Jaspers, stressing another aspect of the Enlightenment, i.e., the universal thrust of science and technology (what Weber calls 'Occidental rationalism') (see Weber 1979), as the will to history that accompanies it, speaks of 'the radical difference between Europe and China and India'. Or, in a somewhat different register, Ortega Y. Gasset argues in *The Revolt of the Masses* that a demoralised Europe must unite against 'the Slavonic code' (i.e., communism, which in fact was itself a European construct). And this polarising strategy can also of course be deployed in a way that turns it *against* Europe. Long before it became a *fin de siècle* motif, William Blake had already prophetically evoked a tired old Europe, fettered by a degenerate morality and religion, and set against it the youthfulness and vigour not of ancient Greece but rather of the new America. And this theme was to be taken up from the other direction a century later by American writers (e.g., Henry James) for whom Europe as the enfeebled, decadent Old World, torn by divisions of class and nationality, had itself become the 'other' of an America which represented the pioneering spirit and an open future.

Apart from the sharply exclusionary judgements entailed in the above approaches to Europe, perhaps there is a different – a more ecumenical and in a sense more 'empirical' – approach to the question of European cultural identity. The following, then, might be proposed as ingredients of European culture: Greek philosophy, Christian religion, Roman law, Latin language, modern science, and an amalgam of Enlightenment ideals (with some significant Greek and Christian roots) such as the interiority, autonomy and equality of individual persons and a rights-based, democratic form of politics. Or, a representative, though not exhaustive, list of texts might be invoked – by, let us say, Homer, Thucydides, Sophocles, Plato, Aristotle, Marcus Aurelius, Virgil, Augustine, Dante, Aquinas, Machiavelli, Erasmus, Cervantes, Luther, Shakespeare, Galileo, Hobbes, St John of the Cross, Descartes, Newton, Pallestrina, Rousseau, Mozart, Kant, Goethe, Beethoven, Hegel, Kierkegaard, Marx, Darwin, Nietzsche, Dostoevsky, Ibsen, Freud, Joyce, Wittgenstein, Einstein, Schoenberg, Heidegger. In ascribing canonical status to these texts and authors, one need not try to abstract some unifying essence from them, or to assign some order of priority among them. Rather, one might affirm the existence of an historical, multitextured conversation in which they have been signal participants – where 'conversation' here implies not unanimity or agreement but only shared reference points, exchange, influence, response, contestation. This conversation might then be claimed to form the ongoing tradition (of thoughts, beliefs, sensibilitities, and practices) which is picked out by the term 'European culture'. Thus a writer becomes European, not by ceasing to be English or Italian or German, but simply by being read and responded to in other countries of Europe. And thus an interplay of 'identity' and 'alterity' is included in one's conception of Europe so that, it might be claimed, the destructively totalising effects of 'essentialism' are avoided.

If the notion of conversation (incorporating internal disagreement and therefore a play of not only different but conflicting voices) is intended to preclude unequivocal celebration or condemnation, the very notion of a canon with which it is complicit may itself, however, be seen as problematic. Is it not a typically donnish conceit to construe European culture to such an extent as the reading (itself invariably a private act) of high-brow texts which even now – and certainly in past centuries – could only be the preserve of a privileged few? How glaring, moreover, that the canon I have offered (not I think a particularly eccentric one) contains not a single woman! And is this exclusion not simply the now most obvious of many repressions or erasures that haunt the European mind? I raise these questions without even attempting to answer them here, not because I am out of sympathy with the specific notion of a canon, but rather because I believe that they point to a salutary truth: the impossibility of dealing adequately with cultural matters in general, without reference to political and economic ones. And so I turn now to the political.

Political Union: Nationalism and Republicanism Uncoupled?

A striking feature of the debates on cultural identity adverted to above is their almost complete eschewal of politics: the predominant stances are often not only apolitical but even anti-political. For this reason, they never get to grips with the most basic problems facing Europe. The greatest problem in this as in previous centuries – which must provide a kind of baseline for whatever perhaps now unimaginable developments the new millennium may hold – is the problem of avoiding war. And this problem, clearly, cannot be addressed without reference to the constellation of states (mainly nation-states) that comprise Europe. Nation-states – as distinct from, say, kingdoms, city-states (singly or in loose federations) and empires – are specifically modern formations. 'State', as an irreducibly political concept, connotes (in crude terms) a more or less concentrated system of power over a defined territory, the borders of which it can secure and the inhabitants of which it can rule.

'Nation', by contrast, might be taken to be primarily a cultural – and therefore pre-political – concept, connoting a social grouping held together by an amalgam of factors such as shared descent, historical experience and memory, language, custom, and belief. If capitalism was the engine of modernisation through the unleashing of great new productive resources and the expansion and unfettering of trade, then the early modern state was the political instrument which facilitated the development of capitalism by providing an infrastructure of rational administration and a legal frame for free individual and group action. Within this perspective, nations might be seen as somewhat amorphous precipitates of earlier historical processes, whose givenness in the modern era provided the prime matter, as it were, for the formation of states.

This assertion of givenness, however, must not make the process of formation seem too natural; for in fact it involved a complex dialectic. 'Nations' after all were not just facts of geography and history; they were also constructs of the specifically modern ideology of national*ism*. As a new form of cultural integration, nationalism emerged in response precisely to the dislocation, mobility, and isolation of individuals under conditions of early capitalism; and, at the same time, it gave a reflexive – and thus specifically modern – character to national consciousness, by mediating the latter through a newly self-conscious historiography which itself bore the impress of Romantic ideas. This artificial aspect of nations – the fact that building them was a *task* – meant that they did not simply supply already defined masses – of land and people – on which state apparatuses could supervene. For their very definition had to be negotiated: a process in which state apparatuses themselves played a substantial role, not least through their newly developed 'national' systems of education. To every nation, then, a state – for self-expression and self-assertion; but, conversely, to every state a nation – for internal coherence and legitimacy. And of course this whole process (in which coveted natural resources as well as cultural privileges were at stake) involved a great deal of forcible homogenisation, as nation-states often succeeded only by suppressing ethnic, linguistic, or religious minorities (and surviving internal agitation and insurrection) or by appropriating neighbouring rivals (through diplomacy or war). Thus the volatility and apparently endemic violence which characterises the modern history of Europe – from which (as we in Ireland have cause to realise only too well) not even those blessed by geography with island status have been exempt.

If modernity were the era only of capitalism and nationalism, our prospects in Europe might seem gloomy indeed. But there is another strand in the development of modern Europe, closely interwoven with these other two: democracy, and in particular the republican idea of citizenship which re-emerged with it in the new era of nationalism (see Pocock 1975; Skinner 1979). For, if the nation-state was a vehicle for capitalist consolidation and expansion, it was also the ground in which modern democracy grew up. Some aspects of the democratic idea were clearly serviceable to nationalist aspiration – the idea, for example, of self-determination through popular sovereignty, classically propounded by Rousseau. In other respects, however, democracy, as a political form, can be seen to make normative claims which do not depend on – and may indeed conflict with – the prior existence of a 'people' whose collective identity has already been secured ethnically, culturally, or linguistically. For a people must now *constitute* itself – and not by appeal to blood or soil but, rather, by engaging in procedures and fulfilling requirements that have an irreducibly ethical basis. Liberty, equality and mutual recognition are now principles which must be embodied in the political practices which mediate relations between 'the people' (as state) and individual persons; through these practices, then, the former acquires legitimacy at the same time that the latter become 'citizens' (see Habermas 1992).

One definition of citizenship (what might be called the 'liberal' one, with its roots in Locke) sees these relations as external and instrumental; citizens are indeed endowed with 'rights', but these are primarily legal, having to do with benefits with respect to their private preferences which individuals can secure from the state in exchange for their meeting defined obligations of allegiance. There is another conception of citizenship, however (what might be called the republican one, with its roots in Aristotle), which, while also enshrining basic rights in law, looks beyond these rights to modes of active civic engagement. Through these modes of engagement, citizens participate in the deliberative conduct of affairs in the polity. Since this is a *praxis* which cannot be legally enforced, citizenship is less an assigned status than an always precarious achievement. It requires the cultivation of civic virtues, primarily the virtue of patriotism. And these virtues can take root only in a political culture which defines freedom not only in terms of individual liberties but also as a joint practice of self-rule. Self-rule entails an ability and willingness to adopt a 'we' perspective which relativises – or to an extent indeed replaces – the 'I' perspective of each virtuous citizen. The difficult question which arises then, of course, is how the identity of this 'we' is to be constituted, and whether it can be constituted at all without a shared allegiance to a set of goods which is more than – though it must indeed include – the good which is self-rule itself. We touch here on the fundamental issue of *solidarity* and the motivational resources which it must muster. And it is here, of course, that democracy is tempted – if it does not simply succumb to administering a system for efficient production and fair competition between self-interested consumers – to fall back on already charged ethnic or national identities, with the passions and allegiances that they can all too easily harness.

Is this temptation resistible? In other words, has the undeniable conjunction in the modern period of nationalism and democracy been necessary or only contingent: necessary, because the formal nature of the latter always leaves a void which can be filled with substance only by the former; or contingent, because this formality can be seen not as empty but rather as bearing universalist seeds which contain the promise of a post-nationalist version of citizenship? But perhaps this is not quite the right question to ask. In construing a symbiotic relation with the nation as a 'temptation', it presupposes that the latter must have a corrupting effect, which a properly pure democracy *ought* to resist. But should we not, instead, envisage the possibility of a genuine complementarity between nationality and democracy, such that the nation provides sources of solidarity which anchor the democratic process, while the latter provides a universalist thrust which protects these sources from closure on internal difference and dissent or on external cooperation and exchange? To make this formula seem more than a fudge or glib dialectical synthesis would require entry into the ongoing debate between liberals and communitarians – something which I cannot attempt here (see Mulhall and Swift 1996). I will simply register my belief that finding a way beyond the impasses of this debate is an urgent need if a viable notion of solidarity is to be articulated, and that it is only in the context of such a notion that we can sort out what it is from the legacy of nationalism that deserves still to be appropriated. To make progress here, though, we need to look not only at the normative foundations of politics (which themselves raise deep issues of philosophical anthropology; see Taylor 1995). We also need to take account of more empirical matters, and in particular the implications for culture and politics of major economic developments in the contemporary world.

Economic Integration: The Global Market and Postmodern Life

It is now commonplace to see the fall in 1989 of the Iron Curtain (including, most dramatically, the Berlin Wall), and the unravelling of the Soviet Union, as stemming from a huge recrudescence of nationalism; and recent trauma and turmoil in the Balkans clearly give colour to this view. A resurgence of nationalism may be more an effect than a cause, however. And it may even be that the real cause (though it has indeed facilitated the emergence of several new nation-states in Europe) has, as a more long-term effect, precisely the fragility, if not obsolescence, of the nation-state: a result temporarily occluded in the eastern bloc countries, which are only now making the transition to capitalism, but already long apparent in the more developed countries of western Europe.

What brought about the fall of the Iron Curtain was the long-deferred but ultimately unavoidable acknowledgement by the leadership of the Soviet bloc of the futility of trying to maintain political control of the economy by erecting barriers to the exchange of goods, money, and people. Steady seepage had already been occurring through tourism, with its associated black market, through the need to sell Russian oil and gas on western markets or to buy grain in times of shortage or (notably in the case of Poland) to borrow from western lending agencies and, not least, through the penetration of electronic and telecommunications media (especially computers) – a sector of accelerated technical innovation which revealed to the eastern European economies the extent to which they lagged behind in technical advances at the same time that it created products whose very nature made protectionism impossible. The startling suddenness of the events of 1989 easily conceals the significance of this seepage. But, with even limited hindsight, we can now surely grasp the point well made recently by a perceptive analyst: 'The rising tide of information, as of ever more freely flowing capital, was washing at the subsoil on which the iron fence was founded, and in 1989 the sandcastles crumbled away into the global market' (Boyle 1995: p. 112). And we may, of course, see a peculiar irony in the fact that the collapse of communism is thus to be attributed less to the superiority of western ideology (liberalism, pluralism, democracy, etc.), as western apologists and cold war veterans tend to claim, than to the stubborn priority of economic reality, which Marx's own theory affirms (even if it also misconstrues it).

This global market puts in place a vast network of connections, linking the economic activities and fates of human beings across the whole inhabited world. It is most apparent in the ubiquity of the same commodities, from Walkmans to sneakers, with the same images in the advertisements promoting them. It is obvious, too, at the institutional level, in the growth of multinational corporations as well as supranational agencies such as the IMF, the OECD, and the World Bank. But it also has a more deep-seated logic, the full and seemingly inexorable implications of which, for our political, cultural, and personal lives, we are only slowly coming to realise. This is a logic of relentlessly uniform quantification. Not only does every good or service become a commodity with a price, but every activity tends to be viewed as contributory to some good or service and hence to require costing; indeed, in the total market, even activities that do *not* contribute to economic performance are still to be costed as defaults: 'More or less gradually, every non-quantifiable, every contractually non-definable, element is leached out of the system of exchange – the value of solidarity, for example, represented by a shared day of rest – is redefined as a free lunch, paid for further down the line by somebody else.' (Boyle 1995: p. 115) What is sought here is a unit of commensuration which will allow conversion and comparison between otherwise irreducibly disparate activities. The ultimate ideal is a continuous and completely transparent environment, in which everything – things, activities and even people – can be made mobile and interchangeable.

If the nation-state, with its centralising organs, could be seen (as I intimated earlier) as a functional element in the rise of capitalism, it seems to have become markedly dysfunctional in the new era of 'late capitalism'.

> The development of the world market saps the foundations of nations. From the point of view of the market, any act of a national government is a restrictive practice, an unwelcome act of protectionism, and national central government itself, the raiser of taxes, the spender of other people's money, the originator of regulations, the fixer of bank rates and would-be fixer of exchange rates, is just another vested interest, another unjustified obstacle to the free flow of capital. (Boyle 1995: p. 114)

Perhaps nowhere has this antimony been more blatantly demonstrated than in Britain, where Margaret Thatcher embraced the extremes of both market *and* nation – thus impaling her party on a fundamental contradiction which cannot but divide it and may yet tear it apart. It is not just the nation-state itself, however, which is a casualty of the global market. Other intermediate institutions of civil society also come under threat, together with the practices which they have helped to sustain: local education authorities, universities, and trade unions in Britain provide good examples. Here we touch again on the issue of solidarity, to which our reflections on nationhood must always remain significantly tied. For, with the decline of intermediate institutions and associations, which had their own substantial life and traditions, individuals become more isolated as well as more nakedly exposed to market imperatives. And so the issue of personal identity also arises here – or, rather, the lack of it; for it is no longer clear just what remains to give a person identity – other than his or her performance on the market.

'All that is solid melts into air'; the famous phrase from the *Communist Manifesto* comes back to haunt us in the throes of this second industrial revolution. Where now is that living continuity with the past which enabled one to make sense of one's life within some overarching narrative? Where are the practices which had their own standards of excellence, and hence their own markers of achievement and desert, in terms of which one could recognise oneself? What now is to be made of the idea of vocation? For how much longer will it be possible for a person to identify herself as a teacher – rather than as a holder of a two-year teaching contract? Could it be that, outside an increasingly vulnerable private life, a person's identity will contract to the series of consumer choices he has made or the series of jobs from which he has been made redundant – where, indeed, it will scarcely matter that it is the same person, with just one name, who fills earlier and later slots in the series? Perhaps nothing is more symptomatic of this postmodern world (to give it its fashionable soubriquet) than the semantic transformation undergone by two words – traditionally associated with formation of identity and engagement in practices – when they are assimilated into the new lexicon of the market. '*Accountability*' used to mean responsibility, i.e., being answerable to someone (or perhaps just to one's own conscience or judgement) for a task or action whose own intrinsic demands dictated the kind of discourse in which an account might properly be rendered – whereas now accounting is what is done by accountants, and in the end is a matter only of counting. Similarly, '*performance*' used to mean an activity, the meaning or value of which was realised in the very activity itself (so that it was the precise opposite of a commodity) and which was to be judged strictly in accordance with criteria proper to the genre to which it belonged – whereas now all such qualitative differences are dissolved, and performance has to do with 'performance indicators', i.e., 'input-output ratios' which can be applied equally and indifferently to all manner of activities (as those of us in higher education are now learning to our cost).

Part Two – Challenges to 'The New Europe'

The deconstructive turn of the analysis in the three previous subsections will be apparent. First, the notion of a European cultural identity was shown to be deeply problematic. When the focus was then shifted to politics, a basis for the kind of extension of solidarity required by any appreciable transfer of sovereignty from nation-states to federal institutions also proved elusive. Finally, an economic force which is certainly more powerful than the nation-state was brought into focus; but, quite apart from the anomic effects which have just been attributed to it, there seems little reason to suppose that this force (the global market), when fully flexed, will be any less corrosive of an intermediate entity such as 'Europe' than it has already been of the national atoms which compose it. But if we turn now from the relatively abstract level at which the analysis has so far been pitched and ask about the kind of entity this 'Europe' actually is and how it is to deal with some quite new realities which now confront it, the aporias only become deeper. The idealism of early federalists – spurred on above all by determination that the catastrophe of the last war should never be repeated – was given early institutional expression through the Schumann Plan and the Treaty of Rome; and the ingenious quadripartite structure (of Council, Commission, Parliament, and Court) which gradually evolved has been able since then to bring about a good deal of policy coordination in which diverse and often conflicting interests of member states have on the whole been successfully reconciled. Now, however, the European Union is faced with two challenges – one self-created and the other confronting it *ab extris* – which are on a scale not met since the war itself, and which are all the more difficult to meet because the imperatives of each are in quite fundamental respects at odds with each other.

The first challenge is that set by the Treaty of Maastricht: the achievement of a single European currency. This will severely restrict the power of national governments to determine macro-economic policy. The ultimate lever of such policy in adverse circumstances – devaluation – will of course no longer be an option; and each country will be subject to severe fiscal discipline, with 'convergence criteria' and a 'stability pact' setting very tight limits to what it will be allowed with respect to public deficits, interest rates, and levels of inflation. Sound money will be the one overriding priority across the Union (or at least for those countries which manage to meet the criteria) and – with traditional protective mechanisms for social regulation of the economy forfeited by governments – wage reductions, unemployment (or enforced cross-migration) seem set to acquire a kind of inevitability which was alien to the post-Keynesian consensus of both the Christian Democratic and Social Democratic parties which built the EEC. It is ironic that the driving force behind this movement should be Jacques Delors, a life-long socialist in the traditions of the French Catholic Left and so no friend of neoliberal economics; but in Delors's vision a common currency seemed the indispensable step towards the ultimate goal of political union. The latter, however, still seems very far off; nor is it clear how it could ever come to pass without a supranational parliament that was not only democratic but also endowed with real powers – unlike the present parliament which can neither raise taxes nor initiate legislation (but only amend or veto proposals from the Commission or Council). The deeper issue, of course, is not the institutional mechanisms that might give effect to 'political union' but rather whether there is anything like a transnational 'public opinion' or a sense of shared destiny or of common allegiance wide and deep enough to constitute a single European electorate. And my point here is that, while political union may still be only a distant prospect, the problems raised by monetary union, which is now an imminent reality, are hardly less formidable. For it presupposes a very high degree of convergence in economic performance across the EU – or else a willingness on the part of national populations, or of particular constituencies or interest groups within them, to accept the social costs of common fiscal restraints even when such convergence does *not* obtain. It might be argued of course (with a nod at the previous section of this paper) that the rigours of a common currency will be no worse than the ruthlessness that is already implicit in the global market. But while there is certainly truth in this claim, the *political* task of containing popular resistance to the discipline of a common currency will still be an urgent challenge to national governments – even as their hands are tied in attempting to meet it. (Quite how a supranational executive agency could meet it – if political union were really consummated – remains even more obscure.)

The second great contemporary challenge to the EU stems from the fall of the Soviet empire. This event was bound to have a serious effect, given that in its origins the Union was a response not only to the Second World War, which had just ended, but also to the Cold War, which had just begun. (It should not be forgotten how enthusiastic the US administration was for European integration: without Marshall Aid there could have been no Schumann Plan, Monnet was more favourably regarded in Washington than in many European capitals (see Duchene 1995) and, with his gaze fixed on the communist threat, Eisenhower had gone so far as to declare that the signing of the Treaty of Rome would be 'one of the finest days in the history of the free world, perhaps even more so than winning the war' [see Anderson 1996: p. 16]). The Iron Curtain had solved at a stroke what might seem the most basic of problems: determination of the eastern borders of an area which, unabashed by the synecdoche involved, called itself *the* European Community. If this problem is basic, however, it is by no means simple. Herodotus had long ago noted that 'the boundaries of Europe are quite unknown, and no man can say where they end'. And even if our modern geographical knowledge is more complete, still geography does not furnish the required demarcation: as J.G.A. Pocock has piquantly remarked, Europe 'is not a continent but an enclosed sub-continent on a continuous land-mass stretching to the Bering Straits'(see Anderson 1996: p. 16). It was a singular convenience of the Cold War that, beyond the ramshackle and often haphazard delineations and alignments thrown up by cultural and political history, it saw the crystallisation of two ideologies so irreconcilably opposed and mutually exclusive that the dividing line between their respective territories could have been no less ambiguous had it been marked by the starkest of geographical features. In the immediate aftermath of the Cold War it was a conceit of neoliberal apologists to announce the 'end of history'; but in fact what the former Warsaw Pact countries were about to experience was precisely the *return* of history. And, with the stirring of so much in these countries that had been in cold storage between 1945 and 1989, its eastern frontier could not but become, for the first time, a major issue for what was now the European Community.

The pleas for membership from fifteen or so former communist states present extraordinary difficulties to the EU: the economic implications, alone, of even modest and gradual integration of these states are extreme. Of existing members, the poorer countries (Ireland being a prime case) have already for many years benefited from 'cohesion' and 'structural' transfers which have helped to bring their economies to the point where they are at least viable candidates for entry to the EMU – however chastening, as I have just intimated, actual membership of it may yet prove to be. But so great are the baseline disparities between the economies of existing member-states and those of the countries of the former Soviet bloc now aspiring to membership that there is no chance of the latter being able to meet the stringent conditions for EMU. But nor, given established domestic expectations in existing member-states, and the fact that the raising of living standards has been one of the primary motivations of European federalism from its beginnings in the Coal and Steel Community (see Milward 1994), can there be much prospect of creating the political will or the popular mandate in the 'west' to effect the kind of transfers to the 'east' that would be required by any proper integration of the latter. And so the Union seems to be faced with a fundamental dilemma: *either* stick with the projected course towards EMU – and abandon any hope of real assimilation of countries to the east (that would not simply grant them some kind of second-class, associate status and thereby renege on a fundamental principle of European federalism since its beginnings); *or* proceed with enlargement to the east as an overriding historical imperative – and abandon (at least for the foreseeable future) the whole apparatus of EMU.

The *political* problems posed by the 'eastern question' are no less acute – for they, too, go to the deepest springs of the federalist impulse. From its beginnings in the Schumann Plan (1950) and the Treaty of Rome (1957), and at all stages of its subsequent evolution, one consideration has been central to institutional design and policy formation: the absolute need not just for military but for economic and political containment of Germany. (The EMU itself could be seen as responding to this need, and was indeed advocated on this basis by both Giscard and Mitterrand in the Referendum to ratify French acceptance of Maastricht: that Germany's *de facto* economic hegemony – reflected in the magnetic power of the D-mark and the imperious authority of the Bundesbank – would at least be modified if juridical regulation were assigned to a European monetary agency.) With a divided Germany, clearly, this need was more easily met. With the disintegration of the Soviet satellite bloc, however, German reunification itself was not the only new strain on the always delicate dynamics of containment. For when exchange began to open across the previously impenetrable borders it was towards Germany that the eastern countries inevitably gravitated and it was German prestige that was thereby enhanced. And an ominous sign that this new sphere of influence would have not just economic but political implications came early on when, dropping its carefully acquired diffidence in the diplomatic realm, Germany unilaterally recognised Croatia and Slovenia – a pre-emptive move which scuppered all hopes of a concerted EU policy on the Balkans, with the humiliating consequence that it was the US and not the EU (on whose doorstep it erupted) that ultimately brokered an attempted settlement of the conflict in the former Yugoslavia.

It might be, of course, that a resolution of the German question *requires* not just expansion to the east but precisely the most *extensive* such expansion. For if this question can be nicely formulated as 'a Europeanised Germany or a German Europe?' the former outcome may be made more likely if the EU opens not just to Germany's immediate neighbours and traditional allies but also to countries further to the east whose historically justified fears of a resurgent Germany make their strategic interests symmetrical with those of Germany's western partners. And this calculation would seem indeed to be implicit in Britain's preference for the most inclusive enlargement, embracing even Russia (and thus realising de Gaulle's famous vision of a 'Europe from the Atlantic to the Urals'). But the fact of British support for this option is enough in itself, perhaps, to suggest the deep political difficulty with which it confronts the EU. For it is hard to avoid the inference that extension can be purchased only at the cost of a loss in cohesive intensity – which Britain of course would reckon not as a cost but a benefit. At the very least, a major overhaul of existing federal institutions would seem inevitable. For, if the carefully calibrated checks and balances in terms of national representation were to be maintained, it is hard to see how the central agencies (the Council and Commission) would not become so unwieldy and suffer such overload as to preclude effective decision making. But administrative problems would only reflect deeper difficulties. For the political reality is that the ceding of sovereignty by nation-states to federal institutions (whatever the economic momentum towards a single market or huge free trade area) is a slow, piecemeal, painstaking process, in which the concerns of each partner have to be finely accommodated with those of every other partner. Calls for rapid enlargement, then, are easiest made by those least willing to concede on national sovereignty. And so the materials are there for another – political – dilemma: *either* enlarge the 'union' – while at the same time diluting its federalist import; *or* maintain the momentum towards closer federation – while relinquishing any ambitions for quick or meaningful enlargement.

I mentioned at the beginning of this section the aporetic nature of my analysis – which has only been reinforced, of course, by the dilemmas that have since been spelled out. Still, this analysis is not to be taken as evidence *against* the whole idea of the 'European project' nor as a confession of hopelessness about its prospects of success. For I see no *alternative* scenario that is in the least bit desirable (as distinct from all too possible). And so it is in a sympathetic spirit – and only against the welter of fatuously utopian propaganda on its behalf – that I have sought to take full measure of the challenges that face it. The question remains, of course, as to what can be salvaged from the apparently discouraging direction of the analysis, or what basis for hope can be gleaned beyond it. Here I shall not try to offer an answer that is any sense architectonic. For surely there can be nothing like a blueprint for the shape of the Europe to come. If there were, it would be no business of a philosopher to provide it; and in any case the more deliberately constructed it might be the more surely would it be thwarted by unintended consequences and undone by actual events. What seems more worthwhile, then, is to reflect on the difficulties that have already been met and to see what they point to by way of a needed response.

Most of the difficulty, clearly, gathers around the peculiarly modern entity of the nation-state. On the one hand, its very impotence, in the context of economic globalisation, would seem to indicate a logic in the movement towards European federalism. On the other hand, however, the *anomie* brought about by the global market might seem to generate a more acute need than ever for just that kind of rootedness and belonging which nations have provided. Could the contrary pulls here be reconciled by reconfiguring the relation between state and nation? If important functions previously vested in states could be divested to European institutions, might not nations, loosened from state power, play a more benign part in offering some of the resources through which people could find/forge their identities? Indeed, thus loosened, might nations not become more relaxed (within and across themselves) about those regional and local differences which they felt compelled to suppress in their heyday as nation-states?

Here we return to the question of culture – but no longer posed at the level of grand generality introduced in Part One above. If 'Europe' were anchored politically in shared institutions, then perhaps European culture could be what we most need it to be in face of the global market – plural, polyglot, and diverse. Insofar as the federal institutions had a cultural role, then, it would not primarily be one of stoking up the conversation between minds great enough to have earned European status. Rather, it would consist in, firstly, supporting regions and provinces (and cities and towns) in developing what is distinctive to them and, secondly, facilitating encounter, exchange, and cooperation between these culturally diverse areas. In one respect, the second of these functions is parasitic on the first; for only if there is real difference – of customs, language (including accent, dialect and gesture), dress, cuisine, music, dance, even philosophy – is there anything significant to encounter. (The last thing I should hope to find in Burgundy or Tuscany or Catalonia, surely, is a plate of Irish stew or a pint of Guinness – not to speak of MacDonald's or Kentucky Fry.) Still, with respect to the role of the federal institutions, the second function is more significant. For there may only be a modest amount that any central administration can do genuinely to encourage a local culture – if it is not simply to embalm it, or invest it with ersatz charm as a commodity on the tourist market. There may be many types of initiative, however, that the more widely-based institutions could undertake to facilitate exchange across dispersed, heterogeneous cultures. (Students exchanges – as, e.g., under the Erasmus or Socrates programmes – networking of, e.g., women's groups or trainee workers in different industries, or town twinning, are small but potentially significant examples here).

Perhaps it will be objected that this picture of cultural diversity and exchange, superficially attractive though it may be, evades the real difficulty. For it is premised on a dissociation of nation from state that will allow devolution of state functions to federal institutions. And does this not imply a naive notion of culture and of nation – as if these could be confined to language, music, cuisine, etc. (all of which can be shared by interested non-nationals) and not include a sense of identity that has evolved through conflict with others and is still charged with potential for further conflict? Moreover, the conflict-potential resides not only in senses of threat to the integrity of the nation as a cultural achievement (where the biggest threat in any case comes not from other cultures but from the levelling effect on *all* cultures of the global market); it resides also in the fact that this identity, constituting 'us' and not 'them', becomes the basis on which *material* interests are pursued – 'ours' and not 'theirs'. And it is here of course that 'we' as the nation are reluctant to let go of 'our' state; for the latter is the instrument of our protection – if not militarily then certainly of the security of our living standards. This may seem to be the point at which politics runs up nakedly against something in human nature itself: a primordial instinct of self-preservation and exclusiveness proper to ancestral groups no less than to individual egos. And is it not an educated sense of the incorrigibility of this instinct that gives such an air of futility – of windy moralism – to any attempted appeal to altruism in the political domain? This question raises the stakes for any political theory. Hobbesians are the ones most comfortable with it, since it is in a sense their question: one which stumps all other theories and thereby justifies the cynicism of their own. But there are of course other responses to the question. Kantians can acknowledge selfishness and group bias as brute facts, but then posit morality as an imperative order that simply transcends the empirical domain, an order, moreover, whose imperious autonomy can animate the pursuit – as ultimately attainable political goals – of universal brotherhood, world government and perpetual peace (see Kant 1991). And Marxists can entertain a not dissimilar political *telos*, though their route to it is to be guided by an altogether different logic: one that reads national identifications as ideological distortions that must give way to the real interests of class; and that finds in one class, when properly mobilised and conscious of itself, the potential for the realisation – albeit through the dialectic of class war – of harmony and equality in a classless society.

This question, which confronts the narrowness and short-sightedness as well as the rivalry and hostility of nations in pursuit of their own self-interest, is inescapable. It is a virtue of Hobbesians that their reading of the political scene is sufficiently disillusioned to recognise it. And even if their response is singularly unheroic its realism nonetheless saves it from the greater scale of destructiveness and terror that may in the end be inseparable from the unrestrained utopianism of Marxists and even of Kantians. But what Hobbesians, Marxists, and Kantians may all have in common is a refusal to meet this question at the properly *ethical* level which it demands.

Hobbesians of course will be unembarrassed by this charge, though it may seem an unfair one to bring against Kantians and even perhaps against some Marxists. I bring it, nonetheless, because appeals to the unifying power of 'class interest' (by Marxists) or of 'reason' (by Kantians) fail to take full measure of the intransigent passions which drive self- and group- assertion. Or, as this point might be otherwise put, they both take premature flight into the universal, without having felt the proper pull of the particulars from which they depart. It is in acknowledging, and attempting to deal with, the reality of passions and particulars (both terms being a kind of philosophical shorthand) that the irreducibly ethical challenge arises; and, in pursuit of a federal or united Europe, this is a challenge which governments and peoples simply cannot evade.

I take it, then, looking to Europe neither as a super-state nor as a uniform cultural bloc, that the crucial issue is the kind of relations that are to obtain between its constituent members and peoples. But entailed in this issue is a prior one about the kind of political and cultural entities these members construe themselves as – and thus the kind of allegiance they expect or exact from their own citizens. And at the heart of this issue, I believe, must be the search for a kind of citizenship and patriotism that is vitiated neither by the sense of 'blood and belonging' that, at the limit, can lead to drives for 'ethnic cleansing' *nor* by an insouciant cosmopolitanism which may fail to meet people's needs for identity (and, by this failure, help open the door to the very xenophobic nationalism that it wishes to repudiate – see Smith 1991; Taylor 1994a; Miller 1995). But what more can be said about such a notion of citizenship or about the two issues with which it is bound up: what a country amounts to and what kind of relation its people might have to it; and what kind of relations might different European countries have to each other, and what – through these relations – might Europe itself amount to? Any realised answer to these large questions will have to take shape in a (no doubt highly complex) set of institutions, the construction of which presents a huge challenge to the political imagination – and the lines of which I shall not even attempt to anticipate. I shall conclude, rather, with some reflections on the properly ethical dimension of what is involved in meeting this challenge. And in doing so I shall draw on ideas of two French philosophers, one writing at the lowest ebb of this century when a European community of nations could only have seemed the most quixotic dream, and the other writing very recently with some hope that this dream could become a reality.

Part Three – Ethical Dimensions of Citizenship: A Horizon for Education

Simone Weil suggests that a country be thought of as a vital medium, a kind of culture bed that nourishes distinctive, irreplaceable modes of sensibility, speech, and action. Thus, 'one avoids the contradictions and lies which corrode the idea of patriotism. There is one's own particular vital medium; but there are others besides. It has been produced by a network of causes in which good and evil, justice and injustice have been mixed up together, and so it cannot be the best possible one' (Weil 1978: p. 154). In the case of France itself, Weil is acutely aware of the suppression of local identities that accompanied the birth of the modern nation-state. And while this does not lead her to countenance any attempt radically to reverse the historical process it does moderate the kind of sovereignty she is prepared grant to the nation-state: 'It is only possible partially to repair the past ... through a recognised local and regional life receiving the unreserved encouragement of the authorities within the setting of the French nation' (Weil 1978: p. 155). Moreover, this openness to diverse elements within is to be matched by a comparable openness to elements from without:

> If one's native land is regarded as a vital medium, there is no need for it to be protected from foreign influences, save only in so far as that may be necessary for it to be able to remain such, that is to say, not in any rigorous fashion. The State could cease to be the absolute ruler ... over the territories under its control; and a reasonable and limited authority over these territories exercised by international organisations dealing with essential problems whose scope is an international one would cease to wear the appearance of a crime of *lèse-majesté*. Nuclei could also be established ... connecting certain bits of French territory with certain bits of non-French territory. For instance, wouldn't it be a natural thing for Brittany, Wales, Cornwall and Ireland to feel themselves, in regard to certain things, to be parts of the same environment? (Weil 1978: pp. 155–56)

These sentiments of a young French thinker, an émigré in London during the darkest days of the last war who was to die within a year of writing them, seem remarkably prophetic. For of course they anticipate both the limited devolution of national sovereignty and the linking of families of subnational or transnational cultural areas that have come to be attempted under the rubrics, respectively, of 'subsidiarity' and a 'Europe of the Regions'. It is not only in the sense of being prescient, however, that Weil's thought is prophetic: it also cuts through layers of arrogance and evasion to lay bare the ethical requirements of any genuine European community. Referring to '[t]he idea of Europe, of European unity', she writes: 'We cannot do too much to encourage, nourish such sentiments as these. It would be disastrous to create any opposition between them and patriotic sentiments.' (Weil 1978: pp. 158–59) But, as she makes clear, the only kind of patriotism that can count here is a severely chastened one, 'incompatible with present-day views about the country's history, its national grandeur, and above all with the way in which one talks at present about the Empire' (Weil 1978: p. 160). Its essential sentiment is not pride in one's country but rather compassion for it, as for some 'precious, fragile and perishable object':

> Whereas pride in national glory is by its nature exclusive, non-transferable, compassion is by its nature universal; it is only more potential where distant and unfamiliar things are concerned, more real, more physical, more charged with blood, tears and effective energy where things close at hand are concerned. (Weil 1978: p. 166)

This is the kind of universality required, I believe, by the European project: one that does not suppress particularity but rather embraces it, while at the same time remaining capable of transcending it. I have introduced it through the uniquely piercing thought of Simone Weil, but it can be amplified by reference to another French thinker who represents a wider movement in twentieth century European philosophy. In a recent article, 'Reflections on a new ethos for Europe', Paul Ricoeur broaches the question of 'how to get beyond the form of the nation-state at the institutional level, without repeating its well-known structures at a higher level of "supranationality" … the question of … what new institutions can respond to a political situation which is itself without precedent' (Ricoeur 1996: p. 3). But he goes on to suggest that the crafting of such institutions will prove futile unless it is informed by a corresponding ethical orientation:

> it would be a mistake to believe that transfers of sovereignty in support of a political entity which is entirely unrealised can be successful at the formal level of political and juridical institutions without the will to implement these transfers deriving its initiative from changes of attitude in the ethos of individuals, groups and peoples. (Ricoeur 1996: p. 3)

Ricoeur is touching here on the crucial problem of how the basis of solidarity can be enlarged, how, in Weil's terms, the 'effective energy' which is so forthcoming in relation to what is 'close at hand' can be extended to what is relatively 'distant and unfamiliar' – or how, in the now received phrase, the 'democratic deficit' in relation to EU structures and policies can be made good. And he goes on to respond to this ethico-political problem by offering three models of imaginative exchange drawn from the insights of philosophical hermeneutics.

The first model is that of *translation*. The fact that there is not just one language means that translation is necessary; the fact that all the many languages are not self-enclosed or other-excluding makes it possible. There may indeed be an ultimate incommensurability between any one language and another; but short of this limit there is the perpetual challenge of rendering in the one what is said in the other. In carrying through this process, there is no 'master' Language – supplying a kind of neutral template on which correspondences between the two languages might be registered – to which the translator can have recourse. Rather, as bilingual, the latter must live into the distinctiveness (at many levels – phonological, lexical, syntactical, stylistic, etc.) of the other language and try to bring this over, without semantic loss, into her own language. Any attempt to subdue the otherness of what is to be translated or to impose on it the frame of the home language as 'dominant' is entirely foreign to the spirit of translation. This spirit is essentially one of courtesy or hospitality, of endless readiness on the part of the receiving language to put itself out so that the content in the other is made at home in it. It is on this account – that rigour here is a form of generosity that is constitutive and in no way supererogatory – that translation offers such a significant model (and that the learning of another language can be such an educative experience). But in fact its full significance is realised only when the encounter extends beyond language to the other culture in all its density of meaning, custom and belief – when, in Ricoeur's words, it takes on an '*ethos* whose goal would be to repeat at the cultural and spiritual level the gesture of linguistic hospitality' (Ricoeur 1996: p. 5), implicit in the act of translation.

This extension brings us to the second model, that of *the exchange of memories*. For Ricoeur, memory is not just the psychological faculty through which we recall the past; more profoundly, by structuring our whole way of being in time, it constitutes our very identity. The primary work of memory – the genre through which this structuring happens and identity is created – is narrative. A story gathers actions and events that are otherwise dispersed by the ineluctable passage of time; but in telling her story a person also configures *herself* and achieves a more or less stable identity. The 'more or less' here is important; for, as construed narratively, identity is neither fixed nor self-enclosed. It is not self-enclosed because my story is always entangled with the stories of significant others (such as my parents, neighbours, friends, and enemies) – which are themselves, of course, similarly entangled with mine as well as with each other (see Dunne 1996). And it is not fixed because the formative actions and events that are configured in a story can always be *re*configured: through account being taken of other hitherto excluded events or through a shift in 'point of view', an established narrative can be displaced by one of perhaps several alternative 'readings'. It is most particularly through confrontation with the stories of others that a space is opened for such a recounting of my own story. And it is the spirit in which these confrontations occur that Ricoeur is concerned with when he introduces his model of 'the exchange of memories'. In the context of Europe, of course, this whole theme must be transposed from the level of individual persons to that of nations and cultures – on the assumption that one can speak meaningfully of 'collective memory' and that 'the identity of a group, culture, people, or nation, is not that of an immutable substance, nor that of a fixed structure, but that, rather, of a recounted story'. In the case of a nation, the story will profile 'founding events' which, because they are primordial and have been much commemorated and celebrated, tend to hold the story in a fixed mould, to the point even of generating an 'identity which is not only immutable but also deliberately and systematically incommunicable' (Ricoeur 1996: p. 7). In relation to such generative moments in the life of a nation, Ricoeur calls neither for abandonment or amnesia but rather for 'an effort of plural readings'. This effort, then, is not to be conducted against tradition (but only against the kind of fixation required by tradition*alism*): 'Tradition represents the aspect of debt which concerns the past and reminds us that nothing comes from nothing. A tradition remains living, however, only if it continues to be held in an unbroken process of reinterpretation.' And this reinterpretation brings liberation not from the past but *of* the past, or rather of the frustrated potential of the past. For 'the past is not only what is bygone – that which has taken place and can no longer be changed – it also lives in the memory thanks to arrows of futurity which have not been fired or whose trajectory has been interrupted. The unfulfilled future of the past forms perhaps the richest part of a tradition' (Ricoeur 1996: p. 8).

The project of 'reinterpretation', with the debates between 'plural readings' that it gives rise to, can of course be undertaken within a single nation – as it has been recently, for example, by French historians responding to the bicentenary of the French Revolution, or by German historians in relation to criminal episodes of the Second World War, or indeed by Irish historians in relation to the physical force movement and the constitutional nationalism which it eclipsed in the events leading up to the foundation of the Irish Free State (see Brady 1994; O'Day and Boyce 1996). When

Ricoeur speaks of 'exchange of memories', however, he has in mind an attempt by people of one nation to enter imaginatively and sympathetically into the story or stories of *another* people – while at the same time allowing *their own* story or stories to be reconfigured through the impact of this recognition of the other. This attempt would have to reproduce at the level of memory and identity the ethics of empathy and hospitality already operative at the linguistic level in the art of translation. But so fraught are the materials that arise at this level – so marked are they by past conflicts which are still charged with lethal possibilities of further conflict – that they require an even more demanding ethical response: what Ricoeur invokes with his third 'model', that of *forgiveness*.

The kind of 'revision' which can bring about a release from the irreversibility of the past (and thus a real shift in identity) runs up against a limit in the ungainsayable reality of past suffering: what has been endured by one side and inflicted by the other. Not only at the level of *realpolitik* but even at the level of a political morality incorporating principles of reciprocity and justice, past suffering calls for retribution – all the more so indeed when a faithful memory has kept it alive and no mere narrative strategy has been able to efface it or to remove the burden of guilt which it imposes on those who have inflicted it. The drive for retribution, and the justification to which it can lay claim, can be overcome only at a level where the logic of reciprocity gives way to the 'surplus' logic of *gift* (see Mauss 1990). Short of the latter, both perpetrator and victim remain bound to a cycle of reaction – even if, in cases where the oppressing force is overwhelming, retaliation must be deferred and take the form of an as-yet-unreleased potential. It is an act of for*giving* that most conspicuously brings release from the 'relentless automatism' of this cycle (see Arendt 1958; Dunne 1993: ch. 3). Some important clarifications remain to be made, however (which Ricoeur, I believe, does not sufficiently provide), if forgiveness is not to be thrust as an undue burden of expectation on the victim and if, in particular, it is to lead to *reconciliation*. There must be no attempt on either side to 'forget' the terribleness of what has been done; and while forgiveness exceeds justice it cannot be turned into a substitute for it. Beyond remembrance, then, the perpetrator must both acknowledge responsibility and show contrition for his deed – which will entail an intention not to reoffend and, where appropriate, a reasonable attempt to make restitution. It is only when these conditions are fulfilled that the perpetrator can *receive* forgiveness (as distinct from *taking* it, which in fact he can never do) and that, in forgiving, the victim can be released from emotions not only of resentment and revenge but also of righteous anger (see Lennon

1997). Even with these requirements, forgiveness remains a gratuitous act – and one, moreover, for which the perpetrator remains dependent on the victim. For, of its nature, forgiveness is something that an individual can never give to himself; in that respect it subverts the very idea of sovereignty and reflects the character of identity as always already entangled. Moreover, in this entanglement the role of perpetrator or of victim can seldom be assigned exclusively to either side; even if one side be innocent when first attacked, in its reaction thereafter it is unlikely to have remained entirely guiltless. And all this carries over to the political sphere where, in the relations between peoples and nations, forgiveness is as relevant and even as necessary as it is between persons (and where exemplary initiatives by, e.g., Presidents Mandela and Havel can be pointed to).

Returning now from this philosophical excursus in the company of Weil and Ricoeur, I shall try to relate their insights more directly to our earlier discussion. The essential problem of European union, as I have construed it, is one of getting member countries to devolve some substantial political functions to federal institutions and thereby to forfeit some of their prerogatives as states – without, however, losing their distinctive identities as nations. On this construal, since member countries are not to be sublated into a monolith, the *relations* between them become crucial; and, since these relations are to be established at a level where sovereignty is modified in the interests of solidarity, their *ethical* substance becomes an unavoidable concern. In some important respects, of course, solidarity may nowadays appear not as an ethical aspiration but as a practical necessity: so great are the interdependencies between countries in matters of, say, environmental protection or defence against crime or regulation of standards and procedures for new media of the 'information age' that the requirements of self-interest and of policy coordination with others may simply converge. Still it would be naive to believe that the momentum of self-interest will always be centripetal; while it is more easily so at times when a growth trajectory is available to all (as it so conspicuously was for western European countries during the first three decades of postwar reconstruction), at times of recession, large-scale unemployment, or political upheaval (as over the past decade) the tensions and centrifugal tendencies are more nakedly exposed. These latter are charged with the energy of historic loyalties and affiliations; and it is in the face of them that the task of establishing a wider solidarity remains an irreducibly ethical task. The attraction of Weil's and Ricoeur's analyses lies precisely in their articulation of a kind of universality which is commensurate with the nature of this task.

One approach to European citizenship is to found it on principles of liberty, equality, and reciprocal recognition enshrined in a continental constitution (and retrievable by the European Court); this is to see it as a *civic* bond which is to be separated out from *cultural* or *ethnic* attachments. I do not at all reject a constitutional or legal codification of the 'rights' (or obligations) of 'European citizens'. It is just that I do not believe that such rights can in the end be vindicated unless the primary cultural and ethnic attachments have in some way been worked through – rather than simply avoided or ignored. And it is in bringing out what is involved in this 'working through' (see Freud 1968) that the insights of our two philosophers are helpful. As translation pushes back the limits of a language through the friendly contest it opens up with other languages – without thereby hankering for a single language – so the exchange of memories goes beyond uses of history which reinforce chauvinist sentiment and nourish old grievances or enmities – without thereby succumbing to the illusion of a sterilised vantage for the construction, free of all prejudice or partisan encumbrance, of the one definitive, 'objective' account (see Gadamer 1975). This refusal of an apparently attractive – but ultimately repressive – universalism, and the corresponding acceptance of plurality ('difference', 'otherness'), is not a refusal of the idea of European unity; to the contrary, it is a necessary condition for any real movement towards it (see Derrida 1992). This movement can take place only as the different peoples of Europe open to each other – and to the refocusing of their own identities brought about through this opening; and of course it requires more than symbolic gestures by political leaders, however edifying these may be. But how is this opening – at the level where it is informed by the spirit of translation and involves a genuine exchange of memories and, where needed, a healing reconciliation – to be achieved among the dispersed peoples of Europe? It is very difficult between neighbouring nations whose histories have been tortuously intertwined; and perhaps it will be asked whether it is even *possible* between nations which, in distance or historical experience, are remote from each other.

It is pointless to deny the difficulty – and even the suggestion of impossibility – that arises here. Still, it is perhaps too easy to forget what extraordinary feats of reconciliation have already been achieved in the aftermath of the last war – perhaps especially between French and Germans (it was the first President of the European Commission who declared: 'Anyone who does not believe in miracles in European affairs is not a realist' [Davies 1996: p. 1085]). In any case, I believe that the 'models' elaborated by Ricoeur provide a basis for intercultural encounters that would transcend mere cultural tourism and hence would escape the charges of superficiality or sentimentality levelled at such exchanges in the previous section of this paper. But it is in the broader area of *education* that both Weil's notion of patriotism and Ricoeur's notions of dialogue could prove especially fruitful. I shall not attempt to spell out here what they would entail for the teaching of 'foreign languages' and of History as well as for civic and political education. But it should at least be clear that they would have such entailments – ones, moreover, that would set any practice of education informed by them as much at odds with a chauvinistically inspired 'national curriculum' as with bureaucratically conceived modules on 'European citizenship'. Indeed such a practice would be at odds with the whole technicist approach that reduces 'education' to the delivery of prepared packages and measured learning outcomes. And while it would certainly be demanding, it would not, however, be 'academic' in the pejorative sense in which this word is now all too often used. For it would bring languages and history to life for students in ways that would confront them with basic issues about their relations with others and about the formation of their own identities (see Dunne 1995b). And while it is right to be suspicious of any programme of education that is designed too deliberately to further political ends, the practice I am envisaging here is the only kind I can think of that would consort well with the ideal of a united Europe *and* be defensible on properly educational grounds.

I have been suggesting that a citizenship which does not remain rooted in a particular culture – which provides a base for openings to other cultures – is too thin to support the extension of solidarity demanded by federalist aspirations. But it is not only for the sake of the kind of cultural exchange that I see as essential to this extension of solidarity that the adherence to particularity is important; it matters also in relation to citizenship itself – or at least to the robust notion of the latter that we have inherited from the republican tradition. For there is much in this tradition to argue that citizenship is robust only insofar as its focus is local and its radius is small. The European project implies an extraordinarily ambitious broadening of radius – with what may seem an inevitable blurring of focus. The question then is whether such a broadening does not explode this notion of citizenship altogether. And I believe that it *does* – and leaves nothing viable in its place – *unless* a civic base is preserved in the nation and indeed in its subsidiary units.

It is here that a case can be made for decentralisation and devolution downwards within individual countries: a movement which, though it may appear to be the opposite of the federalist one, is in fact its necessary corollary. And this two-way movement is of course implicit in the cardinal principle of the early European federalists, i.e., that of subsidiarity. For if this principle implies (in

Weil's words) the ceding of 'a reasonable and limited authority ... [to] international organisations ... [for] essential problems whose scope is an international one', it implies no less that authority for problems whose scope is local should be based at the local level. And perhaps the real point here is that almost all problems nowadays have a scope that is *both* local and larger; and that laws and regulations made at the federal level need local structures for their effective mediation. 'Effective' here implies more than smooth administration: it cannot be divorced from a sense of 'legitimisation' which comes only through democratic participation. The federalist movement can all too easily conspire with the bureaucratisation and atomisation that are given almost irresistible momentum by the global market – and that were already anticipated a century and a half ago in de Tocqueville's fears of a 'soft despotism' exercised by 'an immense tutelary power' (see de Tocqueville 1982). It is in face of this prospect that the republican tradition of citizenship remains exemplary. For this tradition enshrines an essential political value that can be ensured neither by markets nor by bureaucratic planning – nor even by the kind of 'rights' insisted on by the 'proceduralist liberalism of neutrality' (see Taylor 1991) which is perhaps now the dominant political philosophy in so-called 'advanced' societies. This is the value of participation with fellow members of a political community in deliberation and decision making on matters of common concern. This participation will often be conflictual and for the most part it will be mediated through representative institutions. However, it is only if consensus can be reached in and beyond the conflicts through a real process of 'will formation', in which individuals are genuinely involved, that the latter are *citizens* – and not just functionaries, or consumers, or members of one or another interest group, or (in the case of those significantly disadvantaged economically or culturally) members of an 'underclass' who can perhaps experience not only their own disadvantage but the general alienation which others, because of their relative advantage, can numb or disguise.

I do not believe that 'European citizenship' can ever amount to anything real unless it arises from and remains significantly tied to this local, decentralised, civic involvement. If the latter is retained, and if at the same time it remains embedded within cultures which remain open to the kind of exchanges already articulated under the rubrics of 'translation', 'exchange of memories', and 'forgiveness', then perhaps 'Europe' can indeed become a civic reality. It will be apparent from all that has gone before that the 'if' here remains a large one. And I hope it will also be clear – though I have done nothing to make it explicit – that the kind of spirit which such a

Europe must rely on from its subsidiary parts is the same spirit which, in the end, it must bring to its relations with the rest of the world. (Here, the impossibility of determining the boundaries of Europe may be seen as benign.) To be sure, in articulating this spirit, and defending the integrity of particular cultures, I have quarrelled with a certain kind of universalism. But in doing so, I have appealed to notions which have their own universalist thrust: and which for this reason open not only to Europe, but beyond.

Part IV

Situating the Individual and Society

CHAPTER 10

DEMOCRATIC EDUCATION AND THE LEARNING SOCIETY

Richard Smith

> The most valuable lesson that a democratic regrouping of European nations can offer the world is perhaps the experience of learning, in our daily practice, that the values each of us holds to be universal may be more particularistic than we believe. (EEC Study Group on Education and Training 1996)

David Jones's poem *The Tribune's Visitation* is set in the Roman garrison in Palestine some time in the early decades of the first century AD and depicts a military tribune arriving unannounced to inspect troops of his command. The soldiers are of mixed recruitment, coming from all parts of Europe. The tribune finds them celebrating a saturnalian festival, each according to the rites of his own region or village. Discipline has collapsed; equipment has been neglected or even cannibalised for the festivities. The tribune begins by caustically recalling his men to their duty:

> Is this a hut on Apennine, where valley-gossips munch the chestnuts and croak Saturnian spells? Is this how guard-details stand by for duties who guard the world-utilities?
>
> ... Suchlike bumpkin sacraments / are for the young time / for the dream-watches / now we serve contemporary fact. / It's the world-bounds / we're detailed to beat / to discipline the world-floor / to a common level / till everything presuming difference / and all the sweet remembered demarcations / wither / to the touch of us / and know the fact of empire. (Jones 1980)

Yet the tribune himself is only too sensitive to the call of 'the remembered things of origin and streamhead, the things of the beginnings, of our own small beginnings'. He ends by celebrating his fellowship and brotherhood with his men, those 'Soldiers of our greater Europa, saviours of our world-hegemony': 'See! I break this bread, I drink with you.' Thus a sense of true community, and indeed communion, is found amongst, and because of, the stubborn insistence on difference and demarcations. Thus too the attempt to impose uniformity, to bring everything to a common level, may be undone by the healthy human urge to remember 'the things of the beginnings'.

Individualism, then, as the poem reminds us, may be a valuable site of resistance to power. And as liberal theory has taught us, it may supply grounds for forms of community that we hold worthwhile. For according to that political theory it is precisely in order to further our individual projects and desires that we combine in various ways with other persons. On the other hand, of course, individualism may serve the interests of power where it is promoted over and above those forms of association that, perhaps even better than individualism itself, resist 'empire'.

These issues of individual and community emerge as of considerable significance when we examine recent attempts to articulate a European policy on teaching and learning, especially in relation to higher education, as well as discussions of the nature and function of higher education in the UK. Although there is a wide diversity in these policy documents and discussions – and I shall have room to refer to only a few in the course of this chapter – and although we find explicit warnings about the pitfalls of individualism (for example, 'an individualism which is not counterbalanced by social obligations is emerging' – European Commision Study Group on Education and Training 1996: para. 10, ii), there is a powerful and worrying tendency, I shall argue, to foreground a narrow and dangerous kind of individualism. The dangers here are two in particular. One is of a serious diminishing of our sense of what is involved in learning. The second is of a thinning of our notion of what it is to be a person: a danger which is a corollary of the first, since persons conceived in this thin way can hardly be capable of learning in any rich sense.

The widespread enthusiasm for the development of a 'learning society' is an especially potent source of confusion here. What could seem more communitarian than a learning society? Yet in both its European and UK versions much that is written about the 'learning society' presupposes an individualism seriously infected by the two dangers identified above. The idea of the learning society is given particular emphasis in what follows since it appears destined to be influential well into the next century.

The first section of this chapter centres its discussion on what I call the 'economic model' of higher education, the idea that the prime purpose of education is to meet the needs of industry and society. The second section is concerned with 'the reduction of learning' and the damaging individualisation of the learner. The last section explores the consequences of trying to repair the deficiencies that I identify by reinstating an ideal of democracy and even 'friendship' at the heart of European higher education.

The Economic Model

In November 1994 the Secretary of State for Education in the UK initiated a review of higher education, making it clear that the first stage of the review would be concerned with the size and shape of the sector. Questions of the appropriate funding and 'student support arrangements' would be addressed later. She recalled the deliberations of the Robbins committee, which in 1963 concluded that there were 'at least four objectives for higher education – to provide instruction in skills relevant to future employment needs, to promote the general powers of the mind, to promote the advancement of learning and research, and to transmit a common culture and common standards of citizenship' (Department for Education 1994). She noted, with some understatement, that recent years have seen, 'with encouragement from the Government', increasing emphasis on skills, and added the customary clause about the workforce having to learn new skills 'to reflect changing needs and more frequent job changes'. The questions the Minister poses as central to her review are these:

1. What is the purpose of higher education? How should it support society in general? What role should it play in underpinning a modern, competitive economy?
2. What are the implications for the future shape of higher education – for example, as between initial and continuing higher education, between vocational and non-vocational higher education, between diploma, Honours degree, and Masters degree level courses, and between teaching and research?
3. What are the implications for the future size of higher education?

One response, or set of responses, to these questions has been formulated under the aegis of the Learning Society programme, an Economic & Social Research Council programme set up to determine what a 'learning society' is and how we might move more quickly towards one in the UK. The Director of this programme, Professor Frank Coffield, brought together 'a number of researchers who had specialised in Higher Education to review existing evidence with the aim of responding to the questions which the Secretary of State had posed' (Coffield 1995: p. 2), that is, the questions above.

These responses seem to me to illustrate well a number of unfortunate tendencies in the direction that thinking about higher education is beginning to take in the UK. Three caveats must be noted from the outset. First, these responses were formulated with the explicit intention of addressing 'pressing concerns which merited a more immediate response from the academic community'. My comments and this chapter in general, it could be said, are about more fundamental and enduring issues and thus can afford the luxury of a different kind of language and a different perspective. Second, the agenda had been set by a particular set of questions emanating from government and so it is hardly surprising if the responses were couched in the same terms as the questions. After all, our ability to influence politicians is unlikely to increase if we continually tell them they are asking the wrong questions. Third, it may be said that the demand for accountability and 'quality control' in higher education is now such that we must speak a certain kind of language, on pain of being told that education has no right to be funded from the public purse – a metaphor which immediately encourages us to prejudge the issue – unless the educators are prepared to show how they have used the money. These three points invite certain replies, in turn, and I shall touch on them all below. However, I mention them here as part of making the general point that the 'Responses' which I am discussing, and as I shall refer to them from now on in the interests of brevity, are in no sense egregious or unthought-out instances of a particular way of thinking about higher education.

It will probably come as no surprise to find that the Responses justify higher education in largely economic terms. In his 'Introduction and Overview' Coffield writes that 'Arguments in favour of lifelong learning are usually couched in terms of the "economic" rather than the "democratic imperative", which requires social cohesion and political freedom as well as economic prosperity' (Coffield 1995: p. 8). We need a 'learning society', of course, primarily because the UK and the European Union as a whole are losing their share of global markets. In a significant paragraph Coffield himself appears to endorse this view of education: 'Education can be seen either as an investment whereby individuals or whole societies seek to improve their economic performance ... or it can be viewed as just another consumer good in the marketplace which can be bought to enhance the quality of life. A third approach is to view education as a positional good, which points out that the rate of return from investment in education in order to obtain a scarce and coveted job declines as more and more people make the same investment'(Coffield 1995: p. 16). Other respondents follow the same 'economic imperative'. Robin Middlehurst has no problem with a notion of 'quality' in education defined as 'fitness for purpose where purpose is determined in large part by the identification and satisfaction of customer requirements' (Coffield 1995: p. 41). David Robertson believes we cannot justify the state's investment in higher education (at current levels, anyway) in terms of personal individual development, the growth of human potential or 'elevated images of Higher Education as the unfettered pursuit of truth' (Coffield 1995: p. 49). Governments look rather to 'more precise indicators of the overall social (and of course economic) rate of return on the investment' (Coffield 1995: p. 49).

At this point we might notice an odd shift or feint in the Responses, one at the same time quite obvious yet easy to miss. In tackling questions about the nature and function of higher education, Responses imports the substantive notions of the 'learning society' and of 'lifelong learning', treating them as interchangeable. There is then a marked tendency to move between these terms and talk of higher education as if there was no difference (see especially Coffield 1995: pp. 8–9). Yet the idea of the learning society which is being put about is one wholly based on economic considerations and it presupposes an economic model of the purposes of learning.

This can also be seen clearly in the European *White Paper on Education and Training: Towards the Learning Society* (European Commission 1995). This avowedly 'takes forward the White Paper "Growth, competitiveness, employment", which stressed the importance for Europe of intangible investment, particularly in education and training' (European Commission 1995: p. 1). In its conclusion, 'Teaching and Learning' compares the challenges facing Europe today with those it faced in the Middle Ages and the post-medieval period. Then the 'struggle' was with the Byzantine, Arab, and Ottoman spheres of influence: now it is with 'America, Japan and soon China' (European Commission 1995: p. 53). The economic threat of the so-called Pacific Rim looms here, as it does too in the Responses. It is interesting to note how the language of economic competition and threat carries militaristic overtones, echoing those education rallying-calls in the U.S.A., *A Nation at Risk* and *America 2000*. As Eisner (1996) observes, the language takes on the tones of an international arms race.

It is no part of my thesis to suggest that in an ideal world the benefits of education would be emphasised without reference to economic consequences. What I am concerned to question is the nature of the connection drawn between the two and the excessively, and unnecessarily, individualistic slant given to that connection. In this respect pages two to three of the European White Paper are very instructive. The objective, we are told, is to make the European Union into 'a just and progressive society based on its cultural wealth and diversity… There needs to be permanent and broad access to a number of different forms of knowledge. In addition, the level of skill achieved by each and everyone will have to be converted into *an instrument for measuring individual performance*' (original bold). From the just and culturally rich society we move easily to the idea that this is based on the atomistic separation of individuals in order to measure and grade them. Or take the following claim on page two. The new opportunities, it is said, require everyone to adapt, 'particularly in assembling one's own qualifications on the basis of "building blocks" of knowledge acquired at different times and in various situations. *The society of the future will therefore be a learning society*' (original bold). So this is the meaning of the 'learning society': it is a society in which discrete and disaggregated bits of knowledge and skills are put together by individuals for specific employment purposes. It comes as no surprise to find that 'individuals become the principal constructor of their own abilities' (European Commission 1995: p. 14), carrying a 'personal skills card' which allows them 'to have their knowledge and know-how recognised as and when they are acquired' (European Commission 1995: p. 35).

One further, striking example of this individualising tendency: the UK's Department for Education and Employment (DfEE) maintains a Webpage entitled 'Welcome to UK Lifelong Learning'. This declares that it is the 'home-page of the Individual Commitment Division of the DfEE'. It is probably unnecessary to add that there does not appear to be a Communitarian Division to balance it.

In an interesting and rewarding chapter in the Responses, Ronald Barnett offers a similar analysis of the way the 'learning society' is being conceived: 'The learning society is a society which takes learning seriously. This is not because the learning society 'loves' learning as such. Fundamentally, learning takes centre stage because it is felt that learning is a necessary condition of economic regeneration and economic competitiveness' (Coffield 1995: p. 69). As he notes, in this conception learning is essentially the business and responsibility of individuals, the transformations in them summing to constitute the changes in society and the economy, so that the learning of the 'learning society' is simply a function of the accumulation of the learning of its members (Coffield 1995: pp. 70–71). At the same time, paradoxically, the notion of the enduring individual self becomes increasingly problematic, since the economic and social milieu lacks the constancy in which the durability of the self would make sense: 'This is to put a considerable burden on individuals, existentially and ontologically. Their being is put in question. Their hold on life is put at naught' (Coffield 1995: p. 70).

The Reduction of Learning

The emergent 'learning society', whether of the UK or of Europe, displays all the workings of what Jean-François Lyotard has described, in *The Postmodern Condition: A Report on Knowledge* (1984) and elsewhere, as the 'performativity principle'. The performativity principle dictates a logic of optimising any system's overall performance on the criterion of efficiency, of managing, packaging, and commodifying thought in the new technologies that, Lyotard says, apply capitalist rules to language. Those technologies allow the gathering of information in increasing quantities, which legitimises their function and their further growth: 'Since the amount of information is the key (in the sense that more information means more can be proved, hence a greater degree of legitimation), the computerization of the society goes hand in hand with the process of legitimation in so far as the computer is the most efficient instrument for information processing' (Nuyen 1995: p. 45). The implications for higher education are, according to Michael Peters, that: 'The goal for the university becomes its optimal contribution to the best performance of the social system. This goal demands the creation of two kinds of skills indispensable to the maintenance of the social system: those necessary to enhance competitiveness in the world market and those necessary for fulfilling the need for its internal cohesion'(Peters 1995: p. 35). Lyotard's analysis is prophetic of the European and UK documents I have been examining, so much so that it is almost tempting to wonder if it has been taken as blueprint rather than critique. Yet his delineation of the 'performativity principle' needs to be pursued into its implications for our understanding of learning itself.

The individualised learners of the 'learning society' become above all the bearers of skills and competencies. It is worth emphasising that the tendency to elevate skills and competencies to pride of place – a tendency which I take it is familiar enough to need no illustrating, and is thoroughly in evidence in the Responses – is one of the most individualising factors at work in current thinking about education. For to cast qualities and abilities as skills is precisely to decontextualise them. If semiliteracy, for example, is a matter of having poor reading skills then responsibility is thereby removed from the family that treats books with hostility if not suspicion, and from a society that increasingly seems to regard them as either a hurdle on the road to qualifications or means of escapism, not qualitatively different from a computer game, and attributed to the individual who has failed to acquire the relevant skills. If being a half-reasonable mother is a question of 'parenting skills' and not a function of the complex interrelationships between a woman, her children, and the world they live in, then she ought to solve the problem by going off to acquire the skills she personally lacks, irrespective of the stressful conditions under which she lives that might be connected with her lack of patience – perhaps she has no stress management skills? – or the politicians who add guilt and anxiety to the demands of being a single mother.

Skills and competencies, moreover, seem to be something we locate in the individual to a greater extent than is the case with other ways of conceiving whatever it is that we get out of education. Take, for example, the last three of Robbins's 'purposes of Higher Education': 'to promote the general powers of the mind, to promote the advancement of learning and research, and to transmit a common culture and common standards of citizenship'. The last is by definition not an individualistic matter. The second is clearly to do with learning and research in the academy in general (perhaps as a 'community of scholars', to use a phrase not often heard any more). The first, the promotion of 'the general powers of the mind', examples of which might be the powers of creativity, analysis, breadth of vision, and so on, I shall return to below. Older ideas of what higher education is for, conceptions such as the education of sensibility, for example, move still further away from individualistic notions and approach the idea of the *community* of tact, delicacy, and so on which the development of sensibility in the individual presupposes.

Part of what seems to be happening now is that we are losing interest in what might be called the *process of learning*, or that there has occurred a degeneration in the idea of such process. Simultaneously we have lost faith in the possibility of psychology telling us very much about how people learn and may be helped to learn better, and become impressed by ideas, largely deriving from management theory, about how to make organisations more effective. Thus our interest shifts to the criteria of effectiveness (the 'performance indicators', of course) from which we can construct league tables – other interests come into play here, notably the obsession with quantification and ranking – as well as to planning, which increasingly is the way in which individuals show that they are aware of the *organisation*'s goals. Between planning and outcomes the 'thing in the middle', learning itself, drops out of the picture.

What I have called the 'economic model of higher education', then, of which certain notions of management and management theory are part, has a deeply damaging effect on our conceptions of learning. To be clear: it is not just that the economic model declares education to be for the sake of the needs of industry and commerce, ignoring richer notions of personal development or the fulfilment of individual potential. It is not simply that 'skills talk' is objectionable for this kind of reason. It is rather that this model ties learning to the individual, and does so *in such a way* that the richer and more complex notions of the process of learning become harder and harder to entertain and articulate with any plausibility. It is then beside the point to attempt to add these richer and more complex notions back in, as the Responses try to do, often emphasising, for example, that we need to move from a culture of teaching to a culture of learning (see Robertson, *passim,* in Coffield 1995: especially p. 59). The irony needs no pointing up. Why should the new 'culture of learning', suffering as it does from the deficiencies that other commentators (such as Barnett) and I have identified, be any more stimulating than the supposedly authority-centred and transmissional culture of teaching that it replaces? The richer and more complex notions cannot be bolted back on to a model which fundamentally excludes them.

A crucial aspect of the 'individualising' that is going on here is that our conception of individuals themselves is becoming thinner and thinner. This is a corollary of seeing learning essentially in terms of skills, for as several writers on this subject have noted (for example, Lasch 1984) insisting on seeing the great range of human qualities and capacities as *skills* is to see them as only accidentally connected with the persons who bear them. That which is a skill is something I can lack, or have, without it saying anything significant about *me*. If I could not do something it was just because I did not have the skills. Lasch even goes so far as to suggest that our preference for 'skills-talk' is a way of protecting our fragile selves in troubled times: we hold our skills at arms-length and what reflects badly on them does not reflect badly on our 'essential selves'. By the same token, however, the acquisition of skills, conceived thus, cannot nourish our essential selves either. We simply 'take skills on board', in that most revealing of modern phrases, as temporary cargo, and the vessel itself is unaffected.

There was a time when education made connection with the essential attributes of the person. There was a kind of schooling appropriate for children of a certain class or caste, for children from a particular geographical area (projects on 'our town', railways, coal-mining), children of a certain intelligence (seen as a semi-permanent quality), even an education appropriate for girls rather than boys (needlework and citizenship respectively). Now of course we are alert to the limitations of such a way of distributing education and regard such attributes as merely contingent and (for the most part) as no legitimate grounds for the differential allocation of education. But what picture does this leave us with of the 'self' being educated? Thus it is that, increasingly, all that there is left to 'match' education to is the pupil's or student's current – and evanescent – level of *achievement* and his or her *preferences* or *choices*. In the way that Sandel (1982) has prepared us to see, the self diminishes to the point of the (Kantian/deontologically-inspired) lonely choosing will. I am what I choose: my identity is constituted by my (consumer-) preferences.

At the same time, then, that the self is too separate from its (contingently connected) skills for them to be experienced as sources of empowerment, the self is also too closely identified with its capacity for choosing. Here we have precisely the two ways of dispossession which Sandel identifies: too much distance between the self and its ends (the skills held at arm's length) and too little (I exist in that I am a chooser). And that second deficiency is to be remedied cognitively, as Sandel notes, by reflexivity, where 'the self turns its lights inward upon itself' (Sandel 1982: p. 58). It is tempting here to suggest that the besetting faults of modern individualism are locked in a kind of *folie à deux*. We shall be bound to think of reflexivity as a skill, thus immediately reducing its power and scope. Meanwhile the deficiency of removal (too much space between the self and those highly provisional skills) is to be repaired by 'agency in its voluntaristic sense' (Sandel 1982: p. 58), where I choose to think of some of those skills not just as mine but as constituting me. This is the more difficult, however, insofar as I have come to see my identity as given by my capacity for choice, by my being a chooser, rather than by any particular choices that I make.

Further illustration of this point may make it, and its importance, clearer. It comes again from the European White Paper: 'Everyone is convinced of the need for change, the proof being the demise of the major ideological disputes on the objectives of education.' Here the possibility of reflecting on ends or 'objectives' at all is consigned to the dustbin of history (compare the section on page 24, entitled 'The end of debate on educational principles'). Thus the reflective relation between the self and its ends is not merely distant but stretched to the point where it is broken. In another sense the self's educational end is simply given, as change: arrived at not through reflection or debate with others (that, and disputes, are silenced) but somehow known *a priori*. I change, therefore I am.

The individual as changer and chooser – perhaps he or she will also be skilful in (another modern shibboleth) 'the management of change' – has indeed grown very thin.

It is worth noting at this point the tendency for higher education, in the UK at any rate, to be threatened with the loss or diminution of those of its arms that treat students as the bearers of more than skills. The training of teachers and probation officers, for example, both threatened by government with removal from higher education in favour of 'on-the-job' training out in schools and probation departments, challenges the educationally narrow idea that universities are more than anything else organisations that transmit information and skills, once upon a time via the old-fashioned lecture but now and in the future more and more brilliantly, and of course effectively, via the Internet and other technology. Work with social workers, probation officers, teachers, nurses, lawyers, or managers of all kinds reminds us that many different educational relationships take place in universities. As well as knowledge or skills all manner of other qualities are at issue in these forms of university teaching: values, outlooks, understanding, even wisdom can be cultivated and refined throughout formal education.

Democracy

The relentless individualism, as I have depicted it, of the 'economic model' is a clear threat to any sophisticated notion of democracy. This point, an inversion of one of the classic insights of de Tocqueville, can be made in shorthand by quoting Barber (1984), who reminds us that democracies have tended to erode 'gradually from within, consumed unprotestingly by complacency in the guise of privatism, by arrogance in the guise of empire, by irresponsibility in the guise of individualism, by selfishness in the guise of obsessive rights, by passivity in the guise of deference to experts, by greed in the guise of productivity'. When we say that the 'economic model' is undemocratic, we are saying that democratic theory seems to hold out better possibilities of understanding, and so resisting, the individualism of the 'economic model' than does theory of learning. Perhaps learning theory, being institutionally in the hands of psychologists, who thus define themselves in contrast with sociologists and political theorists, will always tend (despite obvious counter-examples) for the most part to conceive learning in individualistic terms.

At any rate, democratic theory has of course developed in part as an extensive critique of the kind of thin individualism that I have already identified as implied by the 'economic model'. It is above all

John Dewey in modern times who best articulates the connection between democracy and 'freed intelligence', the role of our social and political lives in cultivating the qualities of mind that we bring to choice and debate. We are not to be thought of as bringing our pre-formed selves and their choices into the public realm, as if freedom of action there was all we needed to be autonomous agents in a mature democracy. Rather is it the case that the kind of public realm we have – the society which Margaret Thatcher famously declared not to exist – shapes our selves and our choices. Democracy does more for us than just enable us to pursue our individual choices and ends more successfully since we enjoy the cooperation of our fellows. A democratic society is the forum which stands to enrich our sense of what those ends and choices might themselves be. Thus is the concept of the individual given substance, and the implications of the 'economic model' of education effectively countered.

Thus too a theory of democracy turns out to be a theory of learning. The idea of a 'learning society' turned out to be neither about learning (but about accreditation) nor about society in any but a negative sense, since it was so heavily individualistic. The idea of democracy by contrast has from the first (for example, from Thucydides's account of Pericles's funeral oration in Book II of his *History of the Peloponnesian War*) been of a society where since all could speak all could be learned from, and where the toleration of all kinds of opinions and styles of life – the Athenians live free 'from any jealousy, touching each other's daily course of life; not offended at any man, for pleasing himself', in Hobbes's translation of Thucydides, II.37 – mean there is a rich diversity of resources and examples.

To think of democracy in this way is to think of it as more than just a style of government. Here it is helpful to distinguish between what are often called (for example, by Habermas, in Benhabib 1996) the liberal, republican, and deliberative models of democracy. The first two are essentially styles of government, liberalism content to adjudicate between diverse interests on the part of its citizens or groups of them without itself standing for a particular conception of the common good, while republicanism represents a substantive vision of how communal life should be lived. The deliberative model, in contrast with the other two, conceives democracy as a kind of institutionalisation of the public use of reason and argument, along the lines of what might be said to be its original meaning as sketched by Pericles/Thucydides. On this model, which makes democracy more a mode of *being* – and certainly one that includes learning – than simply a mode of government, an important function of higher education will be to educate young citizens in appropriate deliberative procedures, the right use of reason, and argument.

Of course this conception appears vulnerable to the charge that it presupposes a naive Enlightenment ideal of universal reason. The problem we have in late modernity (so the charge runs) is that even within Europe citizens (of Serbia and Bosnia, say) do not always accept that their claims must be submitted to the same tribunal of reason. The objection is made that the deliberative model, even in its elaborated, Habermasian form, commits us to a homogenising notion of identity which is at odds with the way that millions of Europeans, as well as other inhabitants of the planet, experience their lives.

The point about the nature of that experience is often made in terms of 'the politics of identity/difference'. Although there is a world-wide trend towards democratisation, in the sense that more nation-states than ever before are recognisable as liberal democracies, there are also, and increasingly, powerful 'oppositions and antagonisms asserting themselves against this trend in the name of various forms of "difference" – ethnic, national, linguistic, religious and cultural' (Benhabib 1996: p. 3). One worrying aspect of this challenge is the prevalence of attempts to maintain identity by the *elimination* of difference and otherness (of which events in the former Yugoslavia supply a grim example); another is the demand for separate, sovereign statehood in order to express cultural or ethnic homogeneity and identity (for example, Catalonia). The crucial question then becomes, as Benhabib puts it (Benhabib 1996: p. 4), how we are to achieve 'the negotiation, contestation, and representation of difference *within* the public sphere of liberal democracies' (author's italics). And to take difference seriously, Honig (1996: p. 258) insists, is 'to affirm the inescapability of conflict and the ineradicability of resistance to the political and moral projects of ordering subjects, institutions, and values'. We have to 'give up on the dream of a place called home' (Benhabib 1996: p. 258), a place free from conflict, a refuge from the signs and tensions of difference.

The 'economic model' of higher education, as I have analysed it, is an especially powerful device for denying difference, for it threatens to reduce our conception of persons and to homogenise them to the point where they are little more than exercisers of (groundless) choice and bearers of competencies, proffering their personal skills cards to the subsidiaries of Europe plc. The exponents of the 'politics of identity/difference', however, remind us that difference is not so easy to suppress: that it emerges, and will continue to emerge, in ever more damaging forms unless we learn to 'negotiate, contest and represent' it. How is European higher education to contribute to that learning?

There is no blueprint to be offered here, rather some remarks on tendencies and pitfalls. First, higher education is already playing a valuable role in articulating and studying the experience of 'difference': in the UK, for example, through the inclusion on the university curriculum in recent years of Black Studies, Women's Studies, Celtic, and Cornish Studies (*inter alia*). These marginal curricular voices are constantly threatened by those who would deny difference, frequently in the name of rigour and academic standards – the supposition apparently being that anything called 'Studies' is *ipso facto* academically second-rate. (Hostile critics make much of the emergence of Equine Studies and Golf Studies and damn all Studies by association.) We might note too that many of these new subjects originated in liberal adult education, which in the UK has been one of the first victims of the rush to replace understanding by spurious 'skills' and to replace learning by accreditation. Where university adult education courses do not lead to accreditation they no longer attract funding.

A rather more subtle threat to the critical study of 'difference' comes from its assimilation to the idea of 'heritage'. Where the study of Cornish or Catalan language and culture becomes a matter of 'safeguarding and developing' aspects of 'European Cultural Heritage' (*Commission of the European Communities* 1991: p. II) it begins its journey from the university to the theme park. I have written elsewhere (Smith 1993) of the way that 'heritage' denies difference, purveying the comforting myth of an undivided nation or culture, something which is ours from long ago but lost in the intervening years – and which we can have back, *at a price*. The idea of heritage is thoroughly at home in the economic model of higher education.

Second, recognition of the importance of 'difference' does not mean that deliberation about ends has to be abandoned. This dimension of the Enlightenment Project is perhaps not wholly beyond redemption, even if we are sceptical of the claims of universal reason. If we cease to deliberate and argue about ends we shall have confirmed the claim articulated in the second section of this paper that debate on educational principles is over and done, and may as well throw in our lot with the economic model of higher education forthwith. Rather than giving up on critical argument, deliberation, and deliberative democracy we need what Iris Young (Benhabib 1996: p. 120) calls 'an expanded conception of democratic communication'. She argues that 'Greeting, rhetoric, and storytelling are forms of communication that in addition to argument contribute to political discussion'.

I suggest another form of communication here, which is friendship. Through friendship 'we can know a good in common that we cannot know alone', in the words with which Sandel finishes his critique of the thinness of individualism in *Liberalism and the Limits of*

Justice (Sandel 1982). He observes that friendship is intimately connected with self-knowledge. Friendship is 'a way of knowing as well as liking... Our friends may know us better than we know ourselves... To deliberate with friends is to admit this possibility, which presupposes in turn a more richly-constituted self than deontology allows' (Sandel 1982: p. 181). We might compare here the way that Aristotle in the *Nicomachean Ethics* finds it necessary to connect his analysis of practical wisdom – that is, of a rich kind of learning – with an account of friendship. Only an age as dislocated as ours would think it strange to find in friendship the possibilities of a solution to both the impoverishment of our sense of persons and our need for an expanded conception of democratic communication.

The implications of conceiving *friendship* as an important basis for European higher education – for its joint research projects, its student exchanges, etc. – cannot be pursued further here. They would, I have suggested, prove a helpful way of reintroducing rich and defensible conceptions of learning and of democratic deliberation to an area where their lack is becoming very clear. The language of friendship is, of course, not likely to commend us to Secretaries of State and committees of the European Union. But, as this chapter has argued, the 'economic model', even if we embrace it only for political purposes, to recover our access to the ears of the powerful, carries in its train a set of reductions so devastating and so powerful that the consequences of being listened to in these terms may be more damaging than those of being ignored or thought eccentric, marginal, or 'different'.

We must deliberate together about ends, but we must also celebrate 'the blessed differences', 'the remembered things of origin and stream-head' (David Jones, *The Tribune's Visitation*). They are easily obliterated in a world of homogenising power and economic imperatives. 'These tributary streams we love so well make confluence with Tiber and Tiber flows to Ostia and is lost in the indifferent sea'.

CHAPTER 11

LEAVING HOME FOR HIGHER EDUCATION:
'HOW MUCH *HEIMAT* DOES A HUMAN BEING NEED?'

Bas Levering

It is a striking feature of higher education that for many it involves leaving home. For young people this can be a traumatic though highly enriching experience, a key factor in their education. It presents them with a time of change when their very identity is called into question. At a crucial stage in their lives it causes them to reflect on, and to react to, their home and cultural background, to reconsider their relations with others, and to question who they are to become.

This typical experience of many young people in Europe at the end of the twentieth century coincides with broader changes in the political landscape. The processes of European unification have occurred at the same time as revivals of nationalism, especially of the nationalism of nations within nations whose identity has long been partially submerged. How far these revivals are a good thing is not easy to say. Plainly any evolution from nationalism to internationalism is not a natural process; nor is there any natural moral order between nationalism and internationalism. It is too quick to dismiss nationalism as such as a bad thing: there are oppressive internationalisms and liberating nationalisms. On the one hand, there are cogent arguments for the nation-state as the bearer of parliamentary democracy, social welfare, and constitutional security. On the other, there are the disasters that blinding nationalism has caused throughout Europe's history, from the birth of the nation-states some centuries ago to the genocide in the former Yugoslavia in the 1990s; and there is the increasing subversion of the nation-state's autonomy effected by globalisation. What European identity is or could be, given this background, is hard to define. The kinds of answers we give to these questions are implicated in the structure and the substance of higher education while the university in its turn refocuses those problems. These matters have their bearing on the kind of experience of leaving home that the university is to provide.

In this chapter the figure of the student leaving home provides a motif for examining the themes of nationalism and identity in terms of their relation to the idea of home. Its approach derives from an essay of Jean Améry, who wondered, in 1966: 'How much *Heimat* does a human being need?' Jean Améry was the pseudonym of the Austrian Jewish writer and philosopher Hans Mayer (born in 1912) who in 1938 was forced to flee from the National Socialists to Belgium. From 1943 until 1945 he was held captive in Auschwitz, Buchenwald, and Bergen-Belsen. After the war he settled in Brussels, but he found himself still linked to a nation which disgusted him. One of the ways he tried to get rid of these emotional bonds was by anagrammatising his name from the German 'Mayer' to the French-sounding 'Améry'. The change of name, however, hardly succeeded in cutting his ties: one cannot rid oneself of one's mother tongue.

Améry's title is an intriguing one and for this reason it is included unchanged in the title of this chapter. It is intriguing in the way it presents a seemingly impossible question; his own failure to answer it is something he readily admits. But the fact that there are no (easy) answers here points to the need for rethinking. The oddness in the question evokes something of the ambivalence and paradox at the heart of the idea of home. What seems to be needed is some sense of the existential roots and of the psychology of this idea. Something other than conceptual analysis must be undertaken to help us chart the territory here. We need to survey and to rethink the landscape of nationalism and of home.

There are complex interconnections and differences between 'home' and 'homeland' and their Dutch and German cognates. This chapter will not address these differences systematically but will allow the terms to occur in the text according to their appropriateness to context, always remembering nevertheless the complexity and special importance that *Heimat* has. The word *Heimat* is an equivocal one: for all its positive connotations it is freighted also with a negative sense, with a fear of imperialism and hostility to strangers. In philosophical literature the word has a long pedigree but it undoubtedly became more widely known with the broadcasting of the German television series '*Heimat*'. This series followed the life of a rural village from the early years of the twentieth century. The way of life depicted at the start of the series suggested something of the arcadian idyll. Although supposedly about what has typified German experience, the series powerfully evoked a sentiment that is more widely shared: the feeling of nostalgia, of longing for a lost home.

The themes of *Heimat* and of home will lead us at the end of this chapter to problems of nationalism in relation to higher education. Before that, however, we need to consider the way that the psychology of the idea develops. This will be illuminated by remembering the experience of the student leaving home. Let us begin by considering the fate of the idea in the work of the German philosopher of education and phenomenologist O.F. Bollnow.

Bollnow's *Heimat*

Writing in reaction to the existentialism of the early fifties, Bollnow develops his ideas concerning *Heimat* in *Neue Geborgenheit*. The title here, suggestive of a new belonging and security, signals the direction that his analysis takes. Bollnow sees the situation of modern man as that of the drifter, the fugitive who, separated from others, has no prospect of a fatherland. The livability of the home, essential to the idea of *Heimat*, can only gain substance where individuals are immersed in relationships with real others. Bollnow takes the view that the individual is nothing in abstraction from such social relationships. The intimate and the familial constitute the basis for relationships in general. Man is dependent on his fatherland for his very being. Just as one needs home as a retreat from daily cares, so one cannot live without a fatherland. For modern man, however, a fatherland is not simply given; it is something he has to acquire. And even once obtained, this is not an eternal possession: the fatherland is always necessarily under threat. To paraphrase the words of the New Testament, one must have as if one has not, in order to cope with eventual loss.

Heimat and home perhaps turn out to be less concrete and material than they seemed at first glance. That nomads also can have a fatherland weakens the assumption of the connection with place. The supporting order of life is formed by the social structure with its framework of values, and this can be carried while travelling. Notwithstanding the experience of the wandering nomad, however, the sense of *Heimat* seems to connect above all with a certain land and landscape. When the link with tangible circumstances is stressed the connection between *Heimat* and *Heim* is more evident; ancient associations of the word are recalled – with the ground that is fenced in, with the marking of a boundary. These words connote, first, feelings of being at ease. Second, they suggest a kind of freedom and lack of constraint. But it is a third more emotive meaning which, for Bollnow, is the heart of the matter: the feeling of being safe and secure. The idea of the integrity of the home shades into the Englishman's 'My house is my castle', dating from the late seventeenth century (see Coke 1823: p. 161), when the institution of private property and its protection was beginning to shape reflection on society. Protection from hostile strangers is evident also in the etymology of 'bourgeois' and 'citizen', derived respectively from *bourg* and *citadel* (see De Saint-Exupéry 1948).

In fact, much of Bollnow's analysis returns unquoted in Améry's essay. There is perhaps a blatant absurdity in the suggestion implicit here that the *Heimat* a human being needs could be quantified. It is exactly that aspect, however, which makes the question intriguing in the way that has been suggested above and that enables it to evoke these rich connections. Just as Bollnow sees modern man as a kind of exile, so Améry focuses on the experience of the fugitive. At the beginning of his essay he ponders the thought that the less a human being can carry *Heimat* with him the more he will be in need. To do without *Heimat*, one has to have it. Being ultimately without *Heimat* is a deep deprivation.

Elsewhere, in *Mensch und Raum*, Bollnow follows Binswanger in connecting *Heimat* with the place where love between people starts. More clearly than Binswanger, however, Bollnow interprets this love in terms of the growth of community. It is clear that we are close to a sentimentalisation here – one perhaps encouraged by thoughts of the young student leaving home for the first time, to go to university. To redress the balance, let us turn to the deeper insights achieved by certain twentieth century Dutch poets.

The Idea of Home in Modern Dutch Poetry

The bonds of community are forged in the home. The connection between home and the beginnings of love which preoccupied Bollnow is nicely expressed in a poem by Rutger Kopland. The enigmatic title 'An empty space to stay' is suggestive of the way Kopland draws attention to aspects of home in such a way as to disturb a whole metaphysical perspective. If Bollnow's home is a place of security and safety, the threats against which it is a protection now seem to be certain understandings of space and time themselves. The first and last stanzas of the poem run:

> We had closed the windows and doors,
> we did not want to be robbed and enslaved

by spongers and clock makers. Our secrets
were our House and the Stationary Time
...
We then had a space, a time which did not pass
in our house, they were ours and
we dreamt that we would never awake
but that we were cured without knowing of what.[1]

The 'Stationary Time' found in the home is a respite from the urgencies of clock-time, from the urgent demands of our diaries and careers. Unlike linear clock-time, this time is relational to our being. Home provides also a closing off of space to provide the place where one can live. This is not determinable in terms of the coordinates of measurable space; rather the meanings generated in our family and community provide a *topos* – a meaningful place in which we gain our bearings. The house shared in love is spaceless and timeless, and is free from the thriving profiteers whose exploitation of our lives is a metonym for that calculative metaphysics that the poem calls into question. The perhaps impossible 'dream[ing] that we would never awake' further disrupts the habits of our thinking. The achievement of the release for which we long, so the poem suggests, involves a forgetting of the very condition which occasioned that longing: we are cured without knowing.

While space and time are rethought in Kopland's poem, a further consideration, also disturbing to our accustomed metaphysical picture, concerns the indissoluble connection of native language with home. In Herman van den Bergh's 'An Emigrant' (1979) this is explored through the figure of the emigrant. The poem addresses the emigrant, a Dutchman busily absorbed in the long American working day. For all his busy preoccupation, however, his words occasionally call him back in homesickness to 'a foggy bargetrain on the Lek / or a Saxon village square in Twente'. The thought of return here is not without contradiction and pain:

your native tongue catapults you back-
wards
but steals your soul –
and if America will be a day for you
where never a night is released
then a growing thirst betrays
a writhing in the heart
a homesickness that is love

and never was there
love leaving a greater star in the sky.[2]

When Heidegger spoke of language as 'the house of being', he might have implied in part the way that language conditions thought for the emigrant in this poem. The emigrant who adopts the American way of life and language has, the poem's imagery suggests, almost annihilated himself by putting his homeland behind him. The language that he thought he had taken with him is taken for granted and perhaps forgotten, like a comfortable piece of clothing. But, in dreams and at night, it comes back to him with the surreptitious violence that catapults him back to those connections with his homeland. This language speaks his thoughts; it speaks something close to his identity. Feelings for home offer comfort, but this hides a deeper and uncanny ambivalence. One is drawn back to home, perhaps in spite of a dislike of the physical home where once one had to live. Not uncommonly, insistent memory takes us back with regret and irritation. With each visit home the student comes perhaps more clearly to scorn the narrow-minded dull conventionality of the place where she once lived. In 'Homecoming' by Jean-Pierre Rawie (1992), the speaker wishes that the 'boring town' where he spent his childhood would disappear from memory. Yet the memory is indelible. He is 'occupied' by every detail of the place:

> But look, I still know the names of every street,
> every path, of every nook and cranny.
> All that has been has stationed itself
> in my conscience, with just as much remorse.[3]

Feeling for home is bound up with complex resentments and a sense of the impossibility of fully breaking free. Yet come the time to visit his parents, the speaker becomes the dutiful son and *says*, at least, that he is glad to be home. Memory is weighted with remorse. Your home is with your parents, whether you like it or not.

These poems connect home with feelings for the particular place of one's birth and upbringing, in all its physical detail. There are some people, however, who are not-at-home from the start. Then freedom from home ceases to be the problem; rather, there is the sense that home is always somewhere else. In the 1934 poem 'Homelessness' Jan Slauerhof (1978) tests the idea of homelessness to its limits. Aversion to home is even more evident than in Rawie's poem. The possibility of renouncing the very idea of home is expressed ironically as a kind of project. The poet begins by declaring that he has never found home other than in his own writing. Of his original home and hearth he says: 'A tent was blown away by a storm.' In the second stanza he expresses a tentative confidence that no harm will trouble him as long as he can always find shelter. But the final stanza sounds a dark note which undermines the apparently sanguine spirit created thus far:

> It will take long, but the time shall come
> When before the night saps me of my strength
> And pleads in vain for those more gentle words
> With which of old I could build, and the earth
> Must harbour me and I must bow to the
> Place where my grave breaks open in the dark.[4]

Archetypal and dream-like images – of the tent blown away, for example – point to the way the confidence the poet feels in his self-sufficiency is riven with doubt and disturbance. So also, we have come to see, the idea of home incorporates its apparent opposite: what we should know best comes to seem uncanny. So also the student leaving home will suffer oscillating contradictory feelings, wanting to leave behind her childhood for the world beyond but then overwhelmed by a longing for family and home.

These poems have helped us to consider the powerful and complex feelings which the idea of home evokes and to see how the physical details of language and place are deeply involved. The poets speak about a concrete fatherland, but in doing so they express something universal. These ideas connect in some ways with Bollnow's *Heimat*, but they lead beyond this towards a greater complexity and expose a deep ambivalence, absent in Bollnow's promise of belonging and security. The concrete detail vividly evokes the kinds of contradiction evident in a different way in the experience of the student leaving home. They help to lead us to an idea of home which is psychologically more convincing. In trying to understand this we have used the word 'uncanny'. In the light of this we now move to the place of this idea in Freud.

Freud's *Unheimliche*

In her book *Strangers to Ourselves* Julia Kristeva (1988) argues that the need for a homeland is determined by fear of the stranger. This fear, however, does not originate in fear of something else but rather in a fear of something inside ourselves. Kristeva's book is strongly influenced by Freud's essay '*Das Unheimliche*' of 1919.

Freud's analysis proceeds from a consideration of the term *unheimlich* itself. While it is obvious that *unheimlich* has a negative meaning, Freud is struck by the partially negative connotations – of secretiveness – of its positive correlate *heimlich*. If we risk translating the terms into English we find something similar: while 'uncanny' is clearly negative, the term 'canny' is tainted with suggestions of slyness. What might be thought a superficial linguistic phenomenon turns out to point towards a problematic relationship between the conscious and the subconscious. People possess a fundamental fear of the unknown within themselves, the origin of a need that cannot be satisfied. And this offers an explanation for xenophobia.

Freud's essay has a clear structure. In the first part, he traces the development of the word's meaning. In the second, he pursues the psychological explanation of the feeling. In the third, he examines the discrepancy between actually experienced 'uncanniness' and the feeling of the uncanny evoked in fiction – the aesthetic experience.

How do both *unheimlich* and *heimlich* come by their negative meaning? *Heimlich* (or *heimisch*) has two meanings. In the first place it has the positive sense of familiar and comfortable. But the word can also mean covert and secretive. *Unheimlich* derives its negative sense from the opposing (positive) sense of *heimlich*. The *Unheimliche* corresponds with the uncomfortable, the strange, and that which evokes distrust. After the clarification of the contrast between the *Heimliche* and the *Unheimliche*, Freud points out that both terms are connected with one another in a special way, a way that defies the straightforward opposition of positive and negative: 'Thus *heimlich* is a word the meaning of which develops in the direction of ambivalence, until it finally coincides with its opposite, *unheimlich*. *Unheimlich* is in some way or other a subspecies of *heimlich*' (Freud 1981: p. 226). This clarification of the notion, however, is not sufficient to explain the strange relationship between the *Heimliche* and the *Unheimliche*. And we will certainly not find an explanation for this strange relationship if we remain on the surface of the language. Therefore we must pursue Freud's argument to a deeper level.

Every affective emotion that is repressed, Freud claims, is converted into fear. Fear is the return of that which has been repressed. The *Heimliche* can in this way pass into the *Unheimliche*. The *Unheimliche* is not that which is strange: the *Unheimliche* is repressed familiarity, the familiar that has become strange.

There is no doubt that we must interpret Freud's essay in the light of the drastic changes coming about in his thinking at that time. The terrible reality of the First World War is the background to this change. Up to that point Freud had believed that everything was to be explained in terms of repressed libido, this repression returning as anxiety. In the 1920 essay 'Beyond the Pleasure Principle' Freud tries to render plausible a more fundamental principle beneath the libido: the repetition compulsion. This repetition compulsion is an impulse that does not drive at something new but at restoration of the past. The original dualism in Freud's theory consisted of ego-drives focused on the individual and on libidinal-drives-urges focused on the preservation of one's own kind. This initial dualism disappears because both drives seem to merge with one another. Both impulses are summed up in the life-drives. The dualism in Freud's later theory is made up by the life-drive, on the one hand, and the death-wish, on the other. The death-wish is the repetition compulsion at its optimum. It is focused on restoration of the most original past. This fundamental change in Freud's theory, which is fully presented in 'Beyond the Pleasure Principle', introduces itself unmistakably in his essay '*Das Unheimliche*'.

In his interpretation of the death-wish Freud adopts the idea of 'intellectual uncertainty'. This intellectual uncertainty exists, according to Freud, because biology has not determined whether death is a necessary fate of living beings or something recurring but avoidable. The repetition compulsion cannot be overcome. We have an uncontrollable urge to try to explain all kinds of coincidences and recurrences in life; this is the origin of the demonic. We think about someone and a letter arrives. A special significance is awarded to a number that reappears. It is the unmeant repetition that makes the innocent *uncanny*.

In the third and last part of his essay, Freud pays attention to the *Unheimliche* in aesthetic experience. He does this by comparing the actually experienced *Unheimliche* with that which is conjured in fiction. The actually experienced *Unheimliche* materialises when repressed infantile complexes are relived, or when primitive convictions that had been overcome are reconfirmed. In fiction a lot is not *unheimlich* that would be *unheimlich* in real life. This means that people adopt a certain attitude towards fiction: they enjoy horror stories. Fiction powerfully evokes the *Unheimliche* and can reinforce the actually experienced *Unheimliche*. As has been said, uncanniness can develop as a regression to that which has been conquered. The *Unheimliche* that develops from actually repressed complexes is in all cases more resistant.

It has become clear that language can be a crucial indicator of the way we are strangers to ourselves, in Kristeva's phrase. As was apparent in a different way in van den Bergh's poem 'An Emigrant', language is central to one's connection with one's cultural background. The significance can be expanded more fully if we turn now to autobiographical accounts of the experience of two emigrants.

The Feeling of *Heimat* as a Quasi-Emotion

In 1956, when she was eleven years old, Vera Illés fled with her parents from Hungary to Holland. When she was interviewed at the age of forty-eight, she was working as a journalist:

> We kids learned to speak Dutch very quickly, I think that you really have to be backward not to learn the language within a few months

> if you are under fourteen, and for me it went much too slow anyway. If you don't know the language as a child, boredom is the worst, because you just can't do anything. . . Yes, of course I wanted to eat our food the Dutch way, boiled potatoes every night and so on, and I wanted to speak Dutch perfectly, but you could hear the accent for a long, long time, and I disliked it very much if somebody asked me 'Where are you from?' The assimilant that I was wanted to do it completely right. You don't want to be recognized as a stranger. . . For me, language is the essence of assimilation. When you tell me how good my Dutch is, I feel insulted. I consider it a humiliating remark, a condescending compliment, because to speak a language well is still a sort of achievement and not something self-evident. My Hungarian is poor. . . So, for me there is nothing else but Dutch.. . . In fact I speak a foreign language all the time. I speak it tremendously well and in a way it is the only language I can speak, but it is not my mother tongue. There has to be something, contact with a language, for people who have been speaking their native language all the time and right from the beginning. That's a feeling I don't know. Except for those moments I see or taste milk, and then think of the Hungarian word for milk. Some words have more depth, more colour, do you understand? (Schouten 1994: pp. 240–42; trans. Diana Leigh)

Illés's words here underscore with force the connections of language, home, and cultural identity. As an immigrant in Holland, she has the sense that for people who have been speaking their language right from the beginning 'There has to be something . . . a feeling I don't know.' The sense of dispossession here extends to a kind of psychic amputation in the reflections of Eva Hoffmann. In an interview about her book *Lost in Translation: A Life in a New Language*, she suggests that one is, as an emigrant, robbed not only of one's home but also of one's personality: 'I was robbed of every language (gone from the Polish enclave in Vancouver to study literature in Houston) in that period. My Polish disappeared, because nobody understood it, and my English was, even if I could manage, too poor to express myself in. If you do not know certain aspects of a language, you lose the same parts of your personality. It is a kind of psychic amputation. A number of qualities of your character end up down the drain and if you do not watch out, they stay there. Something you develop later on in a language is for instance a sense of humour. There are many emigrants who have given up that aspect unwillingly'.

These examples help to expose the variety of ways in which one might think of *Heimat*, and the ways one might live without it. *Heimat* is certainly more than being accustomed to a certain way of life, the kind of familiarity which Illés manifestly has. Nor is it sufficient to assert the importance of language unless one recalls the resonant 'thick' sense which this acquires. As she sees or tastes milk, Illés involuntarily recalls the Hungarian word.

Rom Harré (1986) has described the feeling of *Heimat* as a quasi-emotion. Quasi-emotions are characterised by terms that have a double meaning – as feelings and as descriptions of external realities. The things people like about their own homeland are often commonplace and at first sight even completely unimportant. Yet those unimportant things become invested with enormous significance. Part of *Heimat*'s extraordinary value is rooted in a kind of exclusiveness. It excludes the other, and to this extent it needs the other. The other is not able to understand the special significance of ordinary things – of *these* things *for us*. The exclusion may not be intentional but this happens nevertheless, and indeed can surprise us. Every now and then in contacts with close friends from different cultural backgrounds, an apparently minor difference opens a gulf, and the other seems to be from another world. Not surprisingly then quasi-emotions differ from culture to culture not just in intensity but in the kinds of inclusion and repression they involve. They can be present in one culture while absent in another. Harré compares the English word 'cosy' with the Dutch *gezellig*. 'Cosy' and *gezellig* refer to similar states but they are not identical: one cannot be *gezellig* alone. And there are more significant cultural differences: there is no word for 'cosy' in Mediterranean languages (see Harré 1986: p. 11). It is salutary to remind ourselves then of the asymmetry between the terms *Heimat*, 'home', and 'homeland', words we have intentionally used with a certain promiscuousness in the present chapter. But just as *Heimat* is appropriately seen in this way, so also the quasi-emotional quality not just of 'home' and 'homeland' but of 'nation', of 'culture', and of 'identity' itself perhaps come into view.

Nationalism and European Higher Education

The revivals of nationalism referred to at the start of this chapter raise questions to do with *Heimat* and questions regarding the kind of internationalism that the EU seeks to promote through its higher education. This internationalism involves an openness that pulls away from the longing for home. Our student who has left home for university is poised at a critical point to realise this. Her higher education involves an encounter with the other, with another place and other people in the institution of the university. It is there in what she studies – in those ideas and perspectives beyond the present and particular that are enshrined in the university (in a dominant paradigm, at least – see Smeyers in this volume). This happens at a stage in her development when she is newly interested in 'the stranger'.

If the student is so inclined, she may be one of that comparatively small minority of students who take advantage of the opportunities for mobility that the EU has promoted. Such opportunities are, it might be supposed, exemplars of internationalism in education: direct experience of other countries fosters appreciation of other cultures. In such schemes – as perhaps in vacation travel – students even develop a new kind of subculture, which seems to thrive on the openness and flexibility of young people and in itself has the hallmarks of a kind of internationalism. Globalisation has its effects here too, however, where media-driven desires lead to a bland sameness of style and values, and where appreciation of difference reduces to a kind of cultural window-shopping. This can displace the very sense of home and cultural identity that makes the leaving of home significant: one cannot go abroad – intellectually or otherwise – without a point of departure. On the face of it, and in obvious ways, the fostering of the feeling of *Heimat* is a concern less for higher education than for the child's initial upbringing – the kind of cultural location in which learning a first language is essential. We can imagine the new European itinerant scholar who takes full advantage of credit transfer and modularity and who, having studied at a variety of institutions in different countries, completes a composite degree. Systematisation and standardisation bring benefits of mobility but they can undermine the locatedness that is richly significant for our intellectual lives. In contrast, the university can be the *alma mater*, and thus for many a significant point of departure.

These questions of mobility, then, scarcely touch the deeper implications of our discussion. For we have suggested that the intellectual and emotional challenges that the student faces be seen in parallel to those larger dislocations that the new nationalisms aim to redress: both are symptoms of the need for living with the ambivalence of home and of culture. Attachment should not lead us back to an idealised home, nor is it simply to be superseded in a sophisticated internationalism. What is required is an encounter with strangeness where this helps us to recognise and live with – rather than to overcome – the uncanniness of our home. It may be that Europe, a continent where new claims for cultural recognition manifest the burdens of the past, can become a place where people gain the potential to go beyond nostalgia to a new openness to others. Attachments to home will then be off-set against an appreciation of otherness, an exchange in which those attachments are revealed in relief. Where notions of home and culture and identity are invoked, thinking must be taken forward to the beneficent ambivalence by which these ideas are destabilised.

Sensitivity to the *Heimliche* and the *Unheimliche* can inform the manner and ends of European identity that are at stake in university education. From the things shared to the differences, the important and the unimportant ones. From anxiety in the face of the stranger to discovery of the value of the other conferred by difference.

Notes

1. All translations are by Diana Leigh. Rutger Kopland, 'Een lege plek om te blijven' (1975):

 Wij hadden de ramen en deuren gesloten,
 we wilden niet worden beroofd en geknecht
 door uitvreters en klokkemakers. Onze geheimen
 waren ons Huis en de Stilstaande Tijd

 . . .

 Wij hadden toen in ons huis een ruimte, een tijd
 die niet voorbij gingen, ze waren van ons en
 we droomden dat we niet meer zouden ontwaken
 maar dat we genazen zonder te weten waarvan.

2. From Herman van den Bergh, 'Een emigrant':

 je moedertaal katapulteert je achteruit
 maar rooft je ziel –
 en als Amerika jou een dag zal zijn
 waar geen nacht uit verlost
 dan verraadt een stijgende dorst
 een krimpen in 't hart
 een heimwee dat liefde is

 en nooit was er
 liefde die groter ster liet aan de hemel

3. From Jean-Pierre Rawie, 'Thuiskomst':

 Maar kijk ik weet van elke straat, elk pad,
 van elke hoek, elk gat, nog hoe ze heten.
 Al wat is geweest heeft in mijn geweten
 als evenzoveel wroeging postgevat.

4. From Jan Slauerhof, 'De woningloze':

 Het zal lang duren, maar de tijd zal komen
 Dat voor den nacht mij de oude kracht ontbreekt
 En tevergeefs om zachte woorden smeekt,
 Waarmee 'k weleer kon bouwen, en de aarde
 Mij bergen moet en ik mij neerbuig naar de
 Plek waar mijn graf in 't donker openbreekt.

CHAPTER 12

THE SPIRIT OF THE UNIVERSITY AND THE EDUCATION OF THE SPIRIT

Paul Standish

> 'to develop the European dimension in studies at all levels so as to strengthen the spirit of European citizenship, drawing on the cultural heritage of each Member State.' (Commission of the European Communities 1994, Article 3, obj. i)

Is it significant to speak of spirit here? Those concerned with higher education policy for the twenty-first century may prefer to move on to what seem more pressing matters. They may take the view that the term offers nothing more than a rhetorical flourish; beyond this it leads to fanciful speculation, useless if not harmful for good practice. It is true that discussion of education and spirit tends to be mired in a conceptual morass (see White 1995). Analysis, however, may not be enough. Whether the focus is on the ethos of an institution or whether it is on the personal growth of the individual – the spiritual being taken, like the physical, intellectual, and moral, as a facet of development – the analytical approach tends to be inappropriately restrictive of this elusive word. But dismissal ignores the strange intrusion of the idea in diverse ways of thinking. Both the decision to ignore the term and the attempt to tidy the concept up are likely to effect a kind of repression, a refusal to ponder the term's insistent recurrence. To understand this it is necessary to explore its intrusive play. Accordingly this chapter will let the term link a number of themes germane to our project. What is the fate of a liberal higher education in a culture characterised by instrumentalism? The pluralism within the diverse nations of Europe raises questions of access and of curriculum in which problems of personal and cultural identity interweave. The oblique approach to questions of spirit requires us to consider how we have gained our bearings on these matters and the kind of orientation that higher education in Europe must now have.

The Spirit of the University

In Lisbon, at the extreme west of Europe, a monument to the discoverers, the Padrão dos Descobrimentos, marks the point from which the great explorers set sail. Impossibly thin, tall, sculpted like the prow of a sailing vessel pointing out across the water, it is, as it were, watched over from the opposite bank of the Tagus by the gigantic statue of the Cristo Rey. In Barcelona, Columbus stands on a column looking towards an imaginary west. To some this heading out to sea has seemed built into the very geography of Europe. It is as if, looking west, Europe turns its back on the larger land mass of Asia, from which it comes. Europe is the headland, as Jacques Derrida has it, the *Finisterre*, head (*caput*) and leader, capital and centre, capital and wealth (Derrida 1992). The headland makes a point: force is gathered in an assumption of purpose, of a necessary direction, of leading the way as the most advanced societies might do. What spirit of Europe led to, or found itself in, this direction? What spirit was thereby exported? Under what terms *can* we speak of spirit here? A part of this spirit and this export must be the university.

Enough of the picturesque, enough rhetoric perhaps, though rhetoric will have its place here. 'Spirit' – *Geist*, *esprit*, *aande* – is an equivocal word and one we might be inclined to do without. 'Vitality', 'mind', 'soul', 'spook' it says to us: it will always defy easy classification. But although we might avoid the term it will haunt the ideas to be considered. These opening rhetorical words suggest one sense of spirit. I want to invoke at least two. If the first relates to a matter of culture, the second has to do with a more personal quest. Both throw light on the university.

The second sense of spirit can be traced through what we might call a kind of perfectionism. Allan Bloom finds origins of this quest in the Delphic injunction: 'Know thyself'. (Bloom 1987) It is a part of Bloom's lament that democratic relativism joins forces with a certain kind of conservatism so that the orientation towards perfection is suppressed, and idealism comes to be characterised as a sentimental failure to face up to reality. But if the real world is the world of free market capitalism we should not lose sight of the part played in this by media stereotypes and the images of advertising. Realism, Bloom suggests, is an easy way out which can be deadly: 'As it now stands, students have powerful images of what a perfect body is and pursue it incessantly. But deprived of literary guidance, they no longer have any image of a perfect soul, and hence do not long to have one. They do not even imagine that there is such a thing'. (Bloom 1987: p. 67) The orientation of the human being, the quest, the voyage, must be towards perfection: 'This longing for completeness is the longing for education, and the study of it is education'. (Bloom 1987: p. 133) Whether there can be a perfect soul, whether perfection is possible, as Bloom implies, is displaced in those most poignant expressions of perfectionism, the *Symposium* and the *Phaedrus*: the state of wholeness is something to be longed for, striven for, perhaps prayed for, but never finally to be attained. This is evident in Emerson and in Stanley Cavell. The message is not of a perfectibility, of a realisable perfection, nor yet of that more modest and practical teleological thinking that Jorge Arregui discusses in this volume in connection with Aristotle. The implication is rather of an essential incompleteness, something to which we should aspire. This, as something that has no ordinary being, as something beyond the natural, is appropriately seen in terms of spirit. It is intimately connected with education, especially where this is seen as aspiration to what is higher.

In J.H. Newman's eulogy to liberal learning the supernatural is present as an attractive force: 'We attain to heaven by using this world well, though it is to pass away; we perfect our nature, not by undoing it, but by adding to it what is more than nature, and directing it towards aims higher than its own' (Newman 1931: p. 47). A century later, as Karl Jaspers rekindles ideas of Newman, there is something of the ghost that beckons in his words: 'Spirit [*Geist*] lives and moves wherever our striving for clarity is a striving for fullness of insight. Without ideas there is no such insight. Ideas impel us from within and at the same time beckon to us as the goal we can never reach' (Jaspers 1960: p. 44). In the eyes of Michael Oakeshott, the teacher must be entrusted with an initiation of the learner into an inheritance that is something different from an acquaintance with dead authors: 'to make "civilisation" available to a pupil is not to put him in touch with the dead, nor is it to rehearse before him the social history of mankind. Death belongs to nature, not *Geist*.' This man-made imperfect inheritance is a historic achievement 'put together not by designers but by men who knew only dimly what they did. It has no meaning as a whole; it cannot be learned or taught in principle, only in detail' (Oakeshott in Fuller 1989: pp. 48–49). It is to the rectoral address of Martin Heidegger (in 1933) that we must turn, however, for the most explicit presumption of the spiritual purpose of the university. As the opening words state, 'The assumption of the rectorate is the commitment to the *spiritual* leadership of this institution of higher learning.' By the end of the paragraph the sinister reason for the notoriety of these words has become apparent because the leaders of the university must themselves be 'led by that unyielding spiritual mission that forces the fate of the German people to bear the stamp of its history' (Heidegger 1985: p. 470). The beckoning spirit is quickly solidified in a grotesque incarnation. This spirit is fatefully tied, however explicitly in opposition, to a naturalism it purports to transcend.

Spiritual missions then can be for good or ill. It will not be without relief, though with an inevitable bathos, if we now turn from the high rhetoric of these views to the bureaucratic and consensual language of contemporary Community documents, itself, of course, a further rhetorical form. In the new Europe it may be that this solidification of cultural spirit is structurally resisted: in education Community action is to complement and support action taken at national level. The principle of subsidiarity requires that decisions be taken at the most appropriate level, ideally at the level of the individual (Treaty on European Union: Article 3b). Promoting the focal point of the European dimension of education, however, is emphasised as 'a necessity for efficiency in the face of internationalisation and to avoid the risk of a watered-down European society' (European Commission 1995). What, it might be asked in response, would European society be like if taken neat?

Without solidification, spirit is non-natural, non-present, out of reach, and inclined to defy measurement. The perfectionist commitments expressed above, and the prospects for personal growth that they harbour, have not always coincided with the cultural spirit that has characterised the university, in the idea of the university that has developed and been exported. Setting aside for the moment the imperial contexts within which this has occurred, a range of assumptions has gathered in this self-conscious projection. The Enlightenment faith in reason and in the transparency of things to reason has been accompanied by the spectacular rise of empirical science and technology. The elements of universality in the Kantian conception of human being and of morality have been underpinned by a commitment to reasoning from universal principles to particular cases. There are attitudes to history and to self-determination. In the universities at their best such values have been celebrated and enshrined. These forces have even perhaps shaped a certain conception of identity itself, of identity understood in terms of exemplarity of the universal. It may be that the term 'university' itself echoes this possibility in assumptions of an ultimate and unified relation to truth.

For the inheritors of these traditions of the university it becomes natural – is built into the principles – that they should be passed on. The university survives through a tradition. It is a tradition to be maintained, something like a mission, a spirit with a direction, a point built into it. At times it will seem important to assert the perfectionist spirit, and the times that prompt this may be times of crisis. As Derrida puts it: 'In a period of "crisis," as we say, a period of decadence and renewal, when the institution is "on the blink," provocation to think brings together in the same instant the desire for memory and exposure to the future, the fidelity of a guardian faithful enough to want to keep even the chance of a future, in other words the singular responsibility of what he does not have and of what is not yet' (Derrida 1983: p. 20). It is to this combined uncertainty and responsibility to past and future that we must now turn. This will involve a questioning of some of the presuppositions of the cultural spirit.

Critique and Crisis

In the profile and projection of Europe, Paul Valéry saw the special importance that France had had and the way this involved coming to a certain kind of awareness: 'our special quality (sometimes our ridicule, but often our finest claim or title) is to believe and to feel that we are universal – by which I mean, men of universality. . . Notice the paradox: to specialise in the sense of the universal' (Derrida 1992: p. 74). Derrida in effect juxtaposes Heidegger's exploitation of the idea of spirit and his explicit belief in Germany's destiny with the contemporaneous explorations of Valéry. While Heidegger contemplates the desolation of the European spirit (the spirit as essentially European) compressed between America and Russia, Valéry defines the crisis of spirit as the crisis of Europe in the interwar years (Derrida 1992: p. 34). Heidegger is perhaps the most profound twentieth-century critic of the nature of technology. Much of his sense of crisis is driven by his interpretation of the mirror effects of technology in the respective capitalism and communism of the nascent superpowers. A common metaphysics, which, as Heidegger claims, has roots ultimately in the Greek world but which has crystallised in the 'progress' and destitution of the modern era, brings together these apparent opposites. Its instrumentalism puts pressures on higher education from both extremes and there are untold further ways in which it jeopardises the perfectionist spirit of the university.

The perception of crisis has occasioned some of the most memorable declarations of faith in the idea of the university. Indeed, borrowing words from Newman, Jaroslav Pelikan takes as a title for the second chapter of his re-examination of the idea of the university 'The Storm Breaking upon the University: The University in Crisis' (Pelikan 1992). Newman wrote his seminal work, as Pelikan points out, against the threat of the growing forces of utilitarianism and an instrumental conception of education. Jaspers's echoing of Newman's title a century later served to reclaim an idea of the university in the wake of the devastation of Germany as a result of Nazism and the Second World War. Oakeshott's defence of the idea of the university, around the same time, was written in defiance of a climate of growing utilitarianism and vocationalism.

The common refrain in these defences of the university is the idea of a liberal education; instrumentalism is the common target. For Oakeshott, the origins of the threat lie in the ideas of Francis Bacon. The growing prominence of industry in people's lives shaped the threat 'from the North' (of England) to which Newman responded. The modern growth of technology has reinforced, though rendered more subtle, a techno-rationality characterised by programmatic thinking. Means separate tidily from ends to draw attention away from the ends, taking these as unproblematic, and onto the efficiency of the means.

In spite of the development of mass education, modern consumerist society has in some ways deepened the effects of this way of thinking. Noble aspirations – towards democracy and autonomy, for example – have been distorted by their subjugation to consumerist notions of choice and the artificial stimulation of desire. Marketing extends to a manufacturing of identities (or 'lifestyles') to which 'customers' are encouraged to aspire. The pervasive influence of the mass media exacerbates these tendencies with levelling and homogenising effects. These are results of the maximising of availability and the erosion of distance, and the consequent blurring of the distinction between the public and the private. They work through a projection of attitudes and opinions that channels and normalises the way people think. Alongside, and perhaps because of, these media creations there is the presumption of that Europeanised conception of identity – identity with itself to the neglect of a disparaged and derivative otherness, the imagining of oneself as the exemplar of a universal kind. Of course, as Derrida points out, the feeling of being 'men of universality' is not reserved for the French, nor even for Europeans (Derrida 1992: p. 75). Nevertheless, in a culture of self-promotion, marketing makes this identity something to be consciously hyped.

In the prevalent reductive conception of democracy, the foregrounding of consumerist choice to the neglect of other forms of participation can be a source of disempowerment. In spite again of noble aspirations, it can foster – in a certain blinkered interpretation of principles of equality, perhaps – a politics of envy to the detriment of justice. Consumerism tacitly accepts a naturalistic ethics of commensurability, anathema to the sort of perfectionism discussed above. What needs to be added to the natural, being immeasurable, is ruled out of the picture. The erosion of distance through the mass media creates new centres of domination, new kinds of capital. The power of a media tycoon such as Rupert Murdoch is but an example of the power of the multinationals (for whose success communications technology is essential) to shape the opinion and circumstances of masses of people. This is a new imperialism of remote control, providing unprecedented channel-hopping choice but, through surveillance and the normalising of thinking, paradoxically disempowering the person.

While Derrida speaks of a 'totalitarian dogmatism that, under the pretence of putting an end to capital, destroyed democracy and the European heritage', he reserves a special contempt for 'a religion of capital that institutes its dogmatism under new guises' (Derrida 1992: p. 77). In *Specters of Marx* (1994) this contempt is addressed especially to Francis Fukuyama's triumphalist celebration of the 'end of history'. Derrida despairs at the 'imperturbable thoughtlessness that consists in singing the triumph of capitalism or of economic and political liberalism, "the universalisation of Western liberal democracy as the endpoint of human government," the "end of the problem of social classes"? What cynicism of good conscience, what manic disavowal could cause someone to write, if not believe, that "everything that stood in the way of the reciprocal recognition of human dignity, always and everywhere, has been refuted and buried by history"?' (Derrida 1994: p. 78). The phrases quoted are not those of Fukuyama, however, but – surprisingly and inconsistently – of Bloom! (Derrida's note tells us that, according to Michel Surya, Bloom was Fukuyama's 'master and laudator'.) The 'end of history' levels things in a stabilised present, silencing those spectres and spirits from the past – an exorcism effected, so it would seem, with the collapse of the Berlin Wall. Such spirits are untimely, out of joint with the times, and hence all the more *necessary*. Like Hamlet's father's ghost, they knock from beneath the stage of our present interminable economic debates. This disjointure will be seen to be not only the condition of language but the condition of ethics.[1] Failure to recognise this involves the denial of the very conditions of language and thought in a metaphysics of presence. It is precisely the embeddedness of Derrida's cultural criticism in his analysis of the sign and his exposure of this metaphysics that gives it more than rhetorical power.[2]

These are homogenising forces bringing with them a normalisation and presumption of universality. Faith in consensus becomes linked with a concern for transparency. These in turn become masterwords in dominant ideas of management and planning. In the following passage Derrida links these 'best intentions' to a certain sanitised conception of pluralism. In this, many apparent virtues are shown to be subjected to the levelling effects of a uniform discourse:

> The best intentioned of European projects, those that are quite apparently and explicitly pluralistic, democratic, and tolerant, may try, in this lovely competition for the 'conquest of spirit(s),' to impose the homogeneity of a medium, of discourse norms and models.
>
> This can happen, surely, through newspaper or magazine consortiums, through powerful European publishing enterprises. There is a multiplication of such projects today, and we can be happy about this, provided that our attention does not lapse. For it is necessary that we learn to detect, in order to resist, new forms of cultural takeover. This can also happen through a new university space, and especially through a philosophical discourse. Under the pretext of pleading for transparency (along with 'consensus,' 'transparency' is one of the master words of the 'cultural' discourse I just mentioned), for the univocity of democratic discussion, for communication in public space, for 'communicative action,' such a discourse tends to impose a model of language that is supposedly favorable to this communication. Claiming to speak in the name of intelligibility, good sense, common sense, or the democratic ethic, this discourse tends, by means of these very things, and as if naturally, to discredit anything that complicates this model. It tends to suspect or repress anything that bends, overdetermines, or even questions, in theory or in practice, this idea of language. (Derrida 1992: pp. 54–56)

If in this passage there is a presumption of univocity in Habermas and across the range of analytic philosophy, this is excessive, indeed mistaken, as the chapters by Blake and Mendus in this volume should respectively make clear. This does not, however, undermine the general contention here that certain trends in philosophy lie behind contemporary developments in educational policy and practice. The passage above is threaded through with phrases connoting the themes that are our concern. Educational policy and practice have proved to be barometers of crisis and the recent obsessiveness in the language of management is evidence of a change of pressure.

Education has long included a discourse of directionality – of aims, objectives, projects, targets. Yet in recent years the scale of this has been cut down to the terms of manageable and reachable targets offering maximum flexibility: 'Everyone is convinced of the need for change, the proof being the demise of the major ideological disputes on the objectives of education. The central question now is how to move towards greater flexibility in education and training systems, taking take [*sic*] account of the diversity of people's demands. Debate within the union must now focus on this priority issue'(European Commission 1995: p. 21). Narrow specialised training along Taylorist lines is explicitly rejected in favour of a 'solid and broad knowledge base which is literary, philosophical, scientific, technical and practical', and this does not concern only initial training (European Commission 1995: p. 9). There is a danger that that broader conception of knowledge, which might have been the source of complications and resistances, is here incorporated into a transparent and univocal discourse. The well-intentioned happy consensus over the objectives of education leaves the way clear for the homogenising medium of managerialism with its 'hard eyes' of surveillance and its discourse of performance indicators, of measurable outcomes, and quality control. One might cite here mechanical systems of staff appraisal. One might cite programmatic modes of learning or competence-based assessment. Let us consider that expression of purpose, and something like spirit, rapidly becoming *de rigueur*, it seems: the university mission statement.

Five claims for mission statements suggested by Graham Peeke (1994: pp. 9–11) are italicised below and set against the possibilities of cultural takeover that Derrida implies:

i. *They give a clear sense of purpose, enabling firm direction.* Yet the uniformity of this suppresses any deviation.
ii. *They facilitate both decision-making and facilitate communication between strategy formulators and strategy implementers.* But this reduces educational practice to the terms of instrumentality, attention being subtly shifted onto the efficiency of means, and aligns decision-making with prescribed programmes. It imagines a univocal discourse of communication in which everything can be made transparent.
iii. *They aid the evaluation of performance.* But this will be achieved through an increased systematisation which overrides curricular difference and routinises assessment with a denial of complications.
iv. *They clarify marketing strategy.* But this has the effect of submitting the institution in advance to modes of thinking determined by the media.
v. *Finally, as a general combined effect of the above, they promote organisational change.* The presupposition that change is neces-

> sarily for the good is, however, a further dimension of a managerialist cultural takeover. The autonomy that seems to be promised is illusory insofar as these precepts are shaped by techno-rational thinking.

The underlying assumptions locate higher education within a particular framework of practice heavily determined by matters of accountability and funding: there is a logic of rules determined and then applied to particular cases; information technology and a certain conception of psychology are promoted as key disciplines because of their potential application to learning method and management. As Derrida observes, 'The concept of information or informatization is the most general operator here.' It integrates the rational within the technical in a principle of calculability:

> 'Information' in this sense is the most economic, the most rapid and the clearest (univocal, *eindeutig*) stockpiling, recording and communication of news. It must instruct men about the safeguarding [*Sichererstellung*] of what will meet their needs, *ta khreia*. Computer technology, data banks, artificial intelligences, translating machines and so forth, all these are constructed on the basis of that instrumental determination of a calculable language. Information does not inform merely by delivering an information content, it gives form, '*informiert*,' '*formiert zugleich*.' It installs man in a form that permits him to ensure his mastery on earth and beyond. (Derrida 1983: p.14)

The concept of delivery (*Zustellung*) itself, rendered normal in contemporary curriculum discourse, forms part of a *Gestalt* revealed in the German cognates for representation (*Vorstellung*) and safeguarding (*Nachstellung*).[3] This metaphysical constellation brings everything into a problematics of representation and the subject-object relation.

To see the poverty of this trend we might attend also to the different voice of Michael Oakeshott who, in 1950, showed remarkable prescience when he spoke with concern of the way talk of the mission of the university was spreading (Oakeshott in Fuller 1989: p. 96). It is a mistake, Oakeshott argued, to suppose that having a mission in life involves determining a goal and then calculating how to act to realise that goal. Rather it is the other way about: it involves knowing how to behave in a certain way and trying to behave in that way. 'Mission' will then be a kind of shorthand expression of this knowledge and behaviour; it will not be a *programme* – or the basis of a programme – of action. The point is underscored by the famous analogy between educational practice and a kind of conversation. The good conversation is not praised for its end result so much as for its intrinsic quality. A university is not a contrivance of some sort with a particular function, appropriately stipulated by a statement of intent. To see it in such terms is already to have thrown something valuable away.

Oakeshott's words may cause us to reflect on the possibility that the historic achievement of our higher education was put together by men 'who dimly knew what they did', beckoned on by aims higher than they could easily imagine, seeking a perfection of human nature by adding to it what is more than nature, and directing it towards aims higher than its own. These are uncomfortable and untimely thoughts for the current discourse of European higher education.

In the light of the criticisms, and in resistance to the metaphysics of calculability, questions in educational practice are opened up to a non-systematic ethics. Questions that currently arise in circumstances of wider participation make this especially poignant. For here it is necessary to limit the urge to systematise in recognition of the infinite asymmetry of the relation to the other. This is a space not for a calculative distributive justice but for a justice irreducible to the law. It is a space in which the responsibility of decisions becomes apparent. Let us turn to the circumstances of difference that a just higher education system must now confront.

The New Old World

> Europe's cultural diversity, its long existence and the mobility between different cultures are invaluable assets for adapting to the new world on the horizon. (European Commission 1995: p. 48)

We began by thinking of ships setting out from the ports of Europe. At a later date other ships came back to these ports – revenants of a kind from those colonising voyages – and the people they carried were different. In his celebrated *The Black Atlantic: modernity and double consciousness* Paul Gilroy traces these passages across the Atlantic (Gilroy 1993). Gilroy uses this imagery to vivify the historical memories indicated by the 'black Atlantic'. It also suggests that idea of 'double consciousness' that was shaped in the early years of the twentieth century by such works as W.E.B. Du Bois's *The Souls of Black Folk*. Du Bois's characterisation of post-slavery experience recognised the black man's 'twoness, – an American, a Negro; two souls, two thoughts, two unreconciled strivings; two warring ideals in one dark body whose dogged strength alone keeps it from being torn asunder' (Gilroy 1993: p. 126). Gilroy suggests that Du Bois's insight is not applicable only to the black American.

Something of this must be deeply marked in the experience of many people of colour in contemporary Europe. While we ponder the recognition that such experience might require of higher education, it is to be remembered that the diversity of the cultural heritage that the Community tends explicitly to celebrate is indigenous rather than that of these new Europeans.

The special circumstances faced by such people are in no doubt. But might this not be related to something broader and more pervasive and become the source of a deeper insight about identity. The experience of dividedness can be seen in terms of an otherness to oneself, perhaps a lack of wholeness. The aspiration towards wholeness requires the sense of this lack; in dividedness then it is perhaps most poignantly felt. But the forms of wholeness that a solidified cultural spirit might offer – forms of cultural takeover – need to be resisted. How can education meet this need?

Perhaps we can pursue this by imagining Pauline, an Afro-Caribbean student from an inner-city area in England entering university for the first time. Think of Pauline as a single parent of twenty-eight. She left school at sixteen and has had few jobs and prolonged periods of unemployment. Only two years ago she was persuaded to go to her local college for a 'Return-to-Learn' course. Gaining confidence and surprising herself by enjoying studying, Pauline progressed to an 'Access' course. Success on this provided her with alternative qualifications for university. Pauline hopes to get a job one day but quite what this might be she does not know. What she does know is that in some of her studies she is discovering something in herself and beyond herself – a voyage out and back – that answers to a deep longing. It is not primarily that she has gained new skills or that she is better able to assert herself: she is able to see things differently and be fascinated by things as never before, and she has an unquenchable desire to know and understand more.

We might think also of Sarbjit, a Sikh woman of thirty-two, the victim of domestic violence, now divorced and disowned by her family, and living alone with her children. She was persuaded to join a 'Women Returners' Course' and this opened a new range of possibilities to her. She also now finds that university provides her with a sense of achievement: she is empowered through the confidence and employability she has gained. But she has gained also something of a more ineffable kind. It is not that she has become fluent in the prevailing language of power or that she can now see her circumstances from the safe standpoint of a universal reason. Rather the differences in her experience – perhaps in anyone's experience – are revealed in greater depth. She partially overcomes the desire to synthesise and reduce and can live the better through this difference: it can enrich her life.

We should also remember Jackie. Now in the final year of her degree course, through which she has struggled with something like a perfectionist desire for education and not without considerable difficulty, Jackie at last begins to sound more relaxed. No longer does she worry whether she can do the work, whether she understands, because now she has seen through it all. Her lecturers, if they are any good at all, are rushed off their feet with increased workloads and endless bureaucracy, and plainly weighed down with low morale. Others are pretentious or unscrupulous; grades are awarded according to favouritism and favour; and one returns essays awarded the lower grades with a MacDonald's application form attached. For Jackie it would just be an absurd game if it were not an insult. Now at last she knows that she will soon be free from it all.

It is edifying to ponder the problems that these students face and to consider the humble perfectionist yearning that they experience. But one should also think of other new forces within the university, revivals of a very different spirit, as the following extract from *The Guardian* indicates: 'In April the NUS [the National Union of Students] Conference passed a motion condemning the activities of Hizb ut Tahrir in British universities. Literature distributed by the group has demanded the death sentence for homosexuals and invoked the Koran in calling for war between Muslims and Jews' (*The Guardian* 1994, 1 November: p. 3). The motion met a predictably hostile response from certain quarters: 'Muslim students have seen through the West. . . When Muslims first came to Britain they liked the new freedoms that they found here. But now they have found out the truth – the West had a policy against Islam. They have realised that there is something wrong with the society they are living in and they need an alternative' (*The Guardian* 1994, 1 November: p. 3). In the article these comments are balanced against those of moderate Muslim students and set in the context of the contrast between the relatively relaxed attitude of British universities towards fundamentalist Muslims and that prevailing in French institutions at the time of the headscarves case. But it is clear that the kind of solidified cultural spirit that is given some rein here is at odds with the kind of liberal education in which perfectionism might flourish.

These cases do no more than gesture towards some of the forms of difference that multiculturalism presents to higher education. The challenges that these examples represent pose the question how far otherness can be welcomed. Pondering this we should recall the uniformity of the discourse that now shapes higher education policy. And we must ask how far we can recognise the ways in which our presumptions and presuppositions stand in the way of our recognition of and response to others without acceding to a fashionable and ultimately reductive relativism.

Passages across the Atlantic suggest a Continental breathing out and in – expiration and inspiration (*udaande* and *inaande*), a possibility of spirit (*aande*). It is desirable, as Derrida puts it, to offset our commitments to the canons of a Eurocentric logic with a writing that extends beyond these shores: 'Not only in order to look – in the way of research, analysis, knowledge, and philosophy – for what is already found outside Europe, but not to close off in advance a border to the future, to the to-come [*à-venir*] of the event, to that which comes [*vient*], which comes perhaps and perhaps comes from a completely other shore' (Derrida 1992: p. 69). These words point towards a way in which the presumption of universality might be overcome and ethics reconceived. Education must acknowledge the inheritance where this is not limited to a canonical list of Great Books: education is different from an acquaintance with dead authors because death belongs to nature, not *Geist*. The responsibility is to what is not present, to spirits that are not simply to be conjured nor preserved in Great Texts but recognised always as still to be convened. The responsibility must be maintained to the possibility of books, from here and from other shores, in a way that remains open to their future. Here the interweaving of personal and cultural identity can be seen most clearly: 'What I require', as Stanley Cavell puts it, 'is a convening of my culture's criteria, in order to confront them with my words and life as I pursue them and as I may imagine them; and at the same time to confront my words and life as I pursue them with the life my culture's words may imagine for me: to confront the culture with itself along the lines in which it meets in me' (Cavell 1979: p. 125).[4] Unlike the implicit closure of recollection of dead authors, texts must be recalled from the past to new possibilities in the future. Derrida' s reading of Valéry might point a way: 'For perhaps responsibility consists in making of the name recalled, of the memory of the name, of the idiomatic limit, a chance, that is, an opening of identity to its very future' (Derrida 1992: p. 35).

But these words, for all their suggestiveness, are still elusive. How can a way be found in education between Great Books and a reductive relativism, a way in which the responsibility to the past and the future is honoured? Can this question relate to the rather different terms of the *Memorandum*: 'The training given in higher education is one which should seek not only to impart the highest standards in the mastery of professional skills but also to foster independent judgement, creativity and "esprit critique" and to confer the ability to range across the boundaries of disciplines, cultures and countries' (Commission of the European Communities 1991: p. 2)? Or will this reduce to tokenism? Let me press the point by addressing the question of the kind of curriculum in which this might be done.

We are to avoid monological adherence to a canon or to an uncontested paradigm. On the other hand, a 'democratic' access to texts from everywhere leads to a kind of cultural Esperanto. With the former the student's eyes remain blinkered; with the latter, in its egalitarian, uniform, levelling gaze, what is at stake never comes into view. With institutions modelled on one or the other principle the metaphor might be extended to suggest respectively a rigidity of viewpoint in a kind of orthodoxy and a transparent availability with maximal modularity and transferability. Derrida recalls Aristotle's reference to sklerophthalmic animals, animals with no eyelids. Human beings can close their eyes, sometimes the better to listen, remember, and learn. The hard eyes of sklerophthalmic animals, in contrast, like the hard eyes of surveillance cameras, never stop seeing. Unrelenting and severe, such eyes are disturbing. The partial and interrupted vision of human beings intimates a subtler and more inward form of thought. The vision of hard eyes might suggest purely representational thought in a regime of calculability, accounting systems, and observed performance. In contrast to the kind of grasp and mastery that such an image implies, Derrida suggests: 'no experience in the present allows for an adequate grasp of that present, presentable totality of doctrine, of teachable theory. But the crushing sense of that inadequacy is the exalting desperate sense of the sublime, suspended between life and death' (Derrida 1983: p. 6). What is required is a willingness to hear: the word and the call are heard and not seen. The word suggests not a regime of observation and mastery but a dispensation of openness and interpretation where things are always already meaningful but never finally determined, where understanding is never complete. Are there eyelids to the university to allow such thought? Or is learning in the institution – now with its lights on all hours to maximise availability and resource utilisation – under systematic thorough scrutiny and fully managed?

The path between the uncontested paradigm and indiscriminate availability of texts requires an initiation into a cultural heritage. But this must be disturbed or made to tremble, and a minimal condition for this is to be derived from difference itself. This might be realised within a subject by teaching two paradigms, two versions, or two stories, as indicative of multiplicity, teaching each, that is, in depth and with commitment. We might thereby avoid not only monological critique but a dialogue of solipsists. If there are two (at least) this will open a space of incommensurability and resistance to translation, involving border crossings, preserving tradition *with* transgression, dwelling with texts but resisting hagiography. In the space of uncertainty between traditions, in the space beyond the programme and the rule, there is the possibility of a kind of vibration: this can be both the space for creative power and for ethical responsibility, where the law and the rule are no longer enough. We cannot communicate, we must communicate: this might be indicative of the subject itself but also exemplary for democracy.

There are three levels of difference here. While the above concerns difference between paradigms within a subject, the argument for integrated curricula to educate reflective experts, which Weijers pursues in this volume, suggests a bringing together of disparate subjects. A further possibility of 'turning conflict into community', in Gerald Graff's phrase, is perhaps to be found where education includes different languages. The multiple languages of Europe are of special significance here and this is partially recognised by the White Paper. Proficiency in three languages is held to be a key to the feeling of being European with all its cultural wealth and diversity and to understanding between the citizens of Europe: 'Learning languages also has another important effect: experience shows that when undertaken from a very early age, it is an important factor in doing well at school. Contact with another language is not only compatible with becoming proficient in one's mother tongue, it also makes it easier. It opens the mind, stimulates mental agility and, of course, expands people's cultural horizon. Multilingualism is part and parcel of both European identity/citizenship and the learning society' (European Commission 1995: p. 41). It is acknowledged that the command of other languages or bilingualism increase one's employability, and further that they aid intercultural understanding. But beyond these points, perhaps implied by the suggestions of openness of mind and expanded cultural horizons, they realise a difference within thought, of the order of a vibration between paradigms.

Multiculturalism is only one aspect of Europe in the era after the Second World War, a Europe gradually leaving behind its empires, if not their ghosts. The detailing of the wider dimensions of the social upheaval of this period – of increasingly rapid social change, of internationalisation and globalisation, of new technology, of unemployment and social exclusion, of the gradual erosion of allegiance to church and state – goes beyond the present account. But they have their obvious bearings on the university. The new commitment to mass provision reflects a democratising impulse and an inclination to attend to other voices. Pauline and Sarbjit and members of Hizb ut Tahrir are part of this. More dominant responses to these changes, however, have clearly tended towards that instrumentalism that in the past has been seen to put the university into a state of crisis. In part this reflects a preoccupation with the growth of the economy, in part a concern over the funding of higher education. In an age of mass participation what role then can there be for a perfectionist liberal education? Should this be the preserve of the elite?

Educating the Spirit. Whose Spirit?

Beyond the 'sample' of Bloom's study, 'the kind of young persons who populate the twenty or thirty best universities' (Bloom 1987: p. 22), there is a host of new students. As such cases as Pauline's and Sarbjit's imply, in the United Kingdom the proportion of mature students has increased dramatically and students are drawn from an increasingly wide social spectrum. The educational background of such students is different from, and probably less steadily successful than, that of their traditional counterparts. Probably most are, by most criteria, less able than Bloom's elite. Many of them might otherwise have been humbly labouring at Newman's 'mechanical arts' so that the few could pursue the liberal arts. But new systems of production create both unemployment and new possibilities of leisure, perhaps making possible something like a new *schole*. To what extent does this manifest itself in an age of mechanisation and equal opportunities?

The common fear is of a decline in standards with mass participation. As the White Paper expresses this: 'How can the development of schooling and access to higher education for more people, be reconciled with maintaining quality in education?' (European Commission 1995: p. 22). There are, of course, real gains of an instrumental kind that are brought by policies that equalise opportunities. Whatever good standards were achieved in the past resulted from drawing from a very limited pool with the obvious waste of human resources. Some widening of the pool should be compatible with maintaining and probably improving standards. There is no doubt that this is the European Union's intention, though perhaps largely for reasons of social utility.

But a deeper point of a non-instrumental kind has to do with what a liberal education is all about. For in Bloom's view this is centrally tied to that kind of ineffable perfectionist quest traced at the beginning of this essay. What should be asked, as the following passage is considered, is how far this type of education is inappropriate for that growing mass of people who enter higher education:

> A liberal education means precisely helping students to pose this question to themselves, to become aware that the answer is neither obvious nor simply unavailable, and that there is no serious life in which this question is not a serious concern. Despite the efforts to

> pervert it . . . the question that every young person asks, 'Who am I?', the powerful urge to follow the Delphic command, 'Know thyself,' which is born in each of us, means in the first place 'What is man?' And in our chronic lack of certainty, this comes down to knowing the alternative answers and thinking about them. Liberal education provides access to these alternatives, many of which go against the grain of our nature or our times. The liberally educated person is the one who is able to resist the easy and preferred answers, not because he is obstinate but because he knows others worthy of consideration. Although it is foolish to believe that book learning is anything like the whole of education, it is always necessary, particularly in ages where there is a poverty of living examples of the possible high human types. And book learning is most of what a teacher can give – properly administered in an atmosphere in which its relation to life is plausible. Life will happen to his students. The most he can hope is that what he might give will inform life. (Bloom 1987: p. 21)

My own answer, regarding the growing numbers of people in higher education, is that *this* 'book-learning' is not so much inappropriate as inaccessible to many of them. Unschooled intelligence and limited will render difficult those great texts in which Bloom's question is most richly asked. But it is not clear that these difficulties make less desirable the addressing of the question; perhaps they make it more so. And it is not just for 'mute inglorious Miltons' that a liberal education is needed. Indeed the need of others may be all the greater because their lack of education and social deprivation make them more vulnerable, more exposed, more subject to the anti-educational forces that in so many ways dominate contemporary European society. If what counts as success here is referred back to this spiritual need, it is not clear that a liberal education devoted to such students is any the less important. At the other extreme, it is plainly wrong to assume that those who gain places in elite universities will necessarily be asking the question beyond the perfunctory form in which it is required by their programmes of instruction and examination – some will, some will not. Bloom romantically eulogises the youth of these elite students. For many it is precisely this that will stand in the way of their liberal education. The often negative experiences of mature students, in contrast, can bring them to university with a greater readiness and a commitment to respond: life can inform education. If perfectionist longing rather than cleverness is the guiding light of liberal education as Bloom conceives it, it is not clear why any lesser 'academic ability' or advancing years should be allowed to prevent its pursuit.

Yet how quickly Bloom shifts ground from the rather sentimental characterisation – what 'every young person asks' – to the concession that many young students will not respond, and to the aspiration to produce students who stand out from the crowd as noble exemplars:

> Most students will be content with what our present considers relevant; others will have a spirit of enthusiasm that subsides as family and ambition provide them with other objects of interest; a small number will spend their lives in an effort to be autonomous. It is for these last, especially, that liberal education exists. They become the models for the noblest human faculties and hence are benefactors to all of us, more for what they are than for what they do. Without their presence (and, one should add, without their being respectable), no society – no matter how rich or comfortable, no matter how technically adept or full of tender sentiments – can be called civilized. (Bloom 1987: p. 21)

There is no doubt that one can find examples of the exceptional autonomous spirits Bloom has in mind and, as stars to guide our personal voyages, they do perhaps have a special role in the cultural life of a society. Yet for all the non-natural emphasis of Bloom's description it is not clear that the creation of these models of achievement is entirely the point of a liberal education. Models of this kind might be subject to a kind of academicism or to solidification in the cult of the intellectual. The better indicator of what such an education is about is perhaps the book itself. Of course, not any book will do here, not pulp fiction or drab empirical research but the kind of rich writerly text with which Bloom is concerned. Unlike the lauded presence of these 'models of the noblest human faculties' the essential non-presence that the written text (fore)shadows is a better indicator of that incompleteness that is at the heart of the perfectionist quest. In the book there is always something still to be received. The book, like ourselves, forever stands in need of an appropriate spiritual readiness. It conjures spirits from the past to whom it is our duty to respond. Reading the book has a duration and an end; but at a deeper paradoxical level its reading is never complete.

What the book symbolises is something that can be passed on to many in that broader constituency of the new university. With the need for more supportive teaching and guidance in the confrontation with difficult texts, such an education will not be cheap. This is not the kind of learning that can be systematically managed (though this is not to deny other ways in which new technology can richly contribute). This would be a fitting schooling of intelligence and a development of literacy in the deepest sense.

Not all higher education can be like this, and neither is this Bloom's suggestion. There are crucial instrumental functions to higher education and it is proper for the European Union to be concerned with these. But an over-tidy distinction between intrinsic and extrinsic value is often unhelpful. It is possible to find instrumental arguments for a liberal higher education. It may be advocated on the grounds of the range of usefulness of a general education. It might be imagined to pass on transferable skills in contrast to the obsolescence of some technical training. The university might, as Pelikan has observed, be our best staging ground for the achieving of peace and international understanding (1992: p. 16). And it might be recognised that it is cheaper than more technical alternatives. A liberal education may have social utility; a vocational education may incorporate a perfectionist spirit. The White Paper is right to hope for a compatibility of employability and personal fulfilment. But it is a disservice to both to imagine that any specification of 'core skills', competences, or knowledge base can capture what is most important.

Echoing the words of Newman, Pelikan makes the point that knowledge and virtue are not identical and that 'the expulsion of ignorance by knowledge will not be enough to deal with the spiritual realities and moral challenges of the future' (Pelikan 1992: p. 21). If the perfectionist conception of liberal education is to be taken seriously, the university seems already to have spiritual commitments. The frustration of the spiritual aspirations of its students – and perhaps this is the frustration of education – may indeed have implications for that future 'spiritual reality'. Even the perfectionist imagery of the *uni*versity and of *higher* education suggest some such aspiration. Reminding ourselves of this then, and eschewing instrumentalist arguments, may help to balance our tendency to address those pressing economic problems that the European Community undoubtedly faces with a recognition of the sort of perfectionist education that higher education can be. At a time when our thinking is dominated by technology and when higher education is dramatically expanding, this is perhaps especially important.

Notes

1. *Specters of Marx* explores the theme of the ghost in *Hamlet*. It will be remembered that, in contrast to the spirit of his father, Hamlet's flesh is 'too, too solid', or, as some texts have it, 'sullied'.
2. In recent writings Derrida seems to be drawing out the practical implications of his earlier work on language and thought (see, for example, Derrida 1974).
3. Heidegger notes the connection with the delivery of mail. It is perhaps no accident, as Richard Pring has pointed out, that improved curriculum delivery in England and Wales has recently been entrusted to Sir Ron Dearing, the former director of the postal system (Pring 1995: p. 106).
4. I have tried to pursue the rich implications of this passage in a different way, but with a similar concern with perfectionism, in 'Postmodernism and the Idea of the Whole Person' (Standish 1995).

Part V

Higher Education in a European Context

Higher Education in a European Context

Some Recommendations and Conclusions

The contributors to this project have drawn attention to what is at stake for higher education in the new Europe in overlapping, if sometimes divergent, ways. What follows from these arguments for policy and practice? In this final chapter we present twelve recommendations or statements drawn from the above arguments.

1. The Vague Use of Language, Especially Lack of Clarity Concerning Central Concepts, Creates Confusion and Contributes to a Fudging of Important Issues

It is clear that greater clarity is needed in the use of central terms such as 'identity', 'nation', 'citizenship', and 'culture'. It is claimed that higher education systems should play an 'active part' in helping to achieve 'the goals of European integration', and that 'passing on the European cultural heritage' is a key element in the process of European integration, the foundation of which is basically cultural. The 'European Dimension' is held to be an important means of confirming 'European Identity', importantly related to the development of European citizenship: higher education should cultivate a 'European affiliation' in students. The truth of such assertions is reported to be 'obvious' and to have received no dissent. But what does this amount to? The criticism here, advanced by McLaughlin, is not that these claims are necessarily false or unjustifiable. It is rather that they are underanalysed and underexplored by the respondents, and in discussion of European higher education in general. These claims and concepts are potentially rich in implication for European higher education but much depends on how they are interpreted. They have implications for the content of the curriculum and curriculum continuity, balance, and control, and in addition for such matters as access, student location, and mobility. Their implications extend also to the sorts of outcomes that should be expected of higher education institutions both directly and indirectly, and the sorts of roles they should play with respect to society. As long as such an analysis is lacking, the claims and concepts that have been discussed are apt to function merely rhetorically in the discourse of the European Dimension. Terms such as these can be emotive and volatile. Often they have the character of what Rom Harré has called 'quasi-emotions', terms that have a double meaning – as feelings and as descriptions of external realities, as Levering has demonstrated. If the European Dimension is to have positive influence in higher education, it is imperative that these matters are made clear. The preponderance of such terms and lack of clarity in their use mean that difficult points of conflict can be fudged.

There are conflicts within European policy on higher education and these need to be recognised. For example, better integration within a stronger European identity is advocated even as the importance of the recognition of local identities and support for difference is recommended. It is not incoherent to work towards both these ends but clarity of purpose is not helped where such conflicts are covered over platitudinously.

2. Better Account Needs to Be Taken of the Diversity of Higher Education in Europe

Greater clarity should involve greater sensitivity to the character and ethos of different institutions: a new caution about subsuming these under generalisations that may well undermine that character is needed. The debate has tended blithely to assume that there is a consensus in favour of secular liberal humanism. The very assumption of consensus here seems to legitimate, and certainly gives further impetus to, the tendency to systematise and regulate. This can subdue those differences in education that have contributed so much to Europe's cultural vitality. There is a dynamics to the scale of the consultation exercise and perhaps to the functioning of the committee system that creates a propensity towards the establishment of consensus. This carries with it certain assumptions of cultural significance permitting a surreptitious denial of difference detrimental to politics and culture. Critical judgements are likely to be muffled by bland consensus and a lack of expressed disagreement.

Structural and organisational questions concerning the age of students, their mode of attendance, the location of the institution in relation to their home, and their mobility between countries need to be re-appraised. The role of part-time continuing education, which is set to increase, should be recognised. Systematic planning should not lose sight of this diversity.

3. It Is Better to Look Not for Consensus But for Ways of Living with Ineliminable But Acceptable Conflicts

With a number of concepts germane to these matters, a distinction can fruitfully be made between 'thick' and 'thin'. As Mendus has shown, the apparently 'thin' conception of culture and of secularism invoked by the respondents to the Memorandum may have a 'thicker' backdrop than at first appears: the very rejection of thickness (associated especially with religious determinations of society) may itself be an indirect way of thickening the conception of secularism. By advocating secularism, and by explaining it through reference to a conception of people as instigators of action, we marginalise what is given in people's lives. The kind of culture that we then transmit is a culture that has a democratic political order at its heart. This movement from a narrative to an entrepreneurial understanding of the self is not merely a movement from the backward-looking to the forward-looking; it is also a movement from a (broadly) social and religious understanding to a political understanding of culture. The thin conception may be difficult to sustain, not only because it carries its own baggage with it, but also because, by renouncing historical understandings of culture, it is forced to adopt instead a political understanding. Culture then becomes something to be 'created', not something to be acknowledged and received. The history of modern liberal societies is, however, a history of learning to live with conflict, not a history of replacing conflict with harmony. It is perhaps better, therefore, not to look for consensus in society, but for ineliminable and acceptable conflicts, and for rationally controlled hostilities as the best condition of mankind from the moral point of view.

4. A Positive Conception of Cultural Pluralism is Needed

There is a further reason why the attempt to remove conflict via the creation of a common culture might not be appropriate. Arregui has argued that it is a negative conception of cultural pluralism that is based on assumptions concerning the imperfect nature of our rationality and knowledge. If our knowledge were perfect, on this view, if we were capable of comprehending reality and ourselves at a glance, there would be no grounds for pluralism. But because we are historical and intrinsically temporal beings, the idea of one absolute cultural expression, one objectivisation of subjective spirit, is inappropriate. Our subjectivity is formed through the unending process of cultural objectifications. The plurality of cultural objectifications, however, proceeds not from poverty – the imperfect nature of our rationality and knowledge – but from the wealth of what goes into them. It is not that the human intellect is deficient; rather both it and reality are rich. The wealth of human nature requires multiple forms of expression: there is no place for uniformity.

5. Sympathetic Engagement with the Lives of Citizens of Other Countries Needs to Grow from Local Attachments

Part of the positive impulse behind the European project derives from revulsion at the destructive effects of local loyalties. But such loyalties are of a quasi-natural kind and are not to be simply reasoned away. Indeed any positive sense of belonging to a larger human community may need to be grounded in such local allegiances; and these can be the source of a positive orientation towards other peoples, as Williams has argued. There are possibilities within a nation-centred civic education, appropriately conceived and designed, for the promotion of a sympathetic imaginative engagement with the lives of citizens of other countries. Rather than seeking to replace local allegiances by the cosmopolitan ideal of the 'New Europe', national and ethnic sentiment can be educated to an enlarged sense of human sympathy. The promotion of imaginative sympathy beyond the boundaries of the nation-state is likely to be more pedagogically effective if it has its basis in the local and the particular rather than in the benevolent but rationalistic cosmopolitan ideal underlying the European project.

There can be a constructive tension between local allegiance and internationalism where the latter pulls away, but does not cut itself off, from attachment to home. The very experience of going *away* to university may be a crucial element in this, as Levering has shown. Studying in higher education involves an encounter with the other, with another place and other people in the institution of the university. This happens at a stage in her development when the student is newly interested in 'the stranger'. In the increasingly international milieu of the university, in opportunities for mobility and for vacation travel, students even develop a new kind of subculture, which seems to thrive on the openness and flexibility of young people and in itself has the hallmarks of a kind of internationalism. But one cannot go abroad – intellectually or otherwise – without a point of departure; where this is lacking internationalism is of a superficial kind. Yet the attachment needed should not lead back to an idealised home. What is required is an encounter with strangeness where this helps us to recognise and live with – rather than to overcome – the uncanniness of our home. Europe, as a continent where new claims for cultural recognition manifest the burdens of the past, can become a place where people gain the potential to go beyond nostalgia to a new openness to others. Attachments to home will then be offset against an appreciation of otherness, an exchange in which those attachments are revealed in relief.

The White Paper's aim that students become proficient in three languages is very relevant to this end, and this is held to be a key to the feeling of being European in all its cultural wealth and diversity and to understanding between the citizens of Europe. Direct teaching, student mobility, and other types of exposure may all help to bring this about, without drastic distortion of the main substance of students' courses. (The belief that this could be achieved will undoubtedly require less optimism in some countries than in others!) One of the traditional grounds for studying a foreign language, as Dunne has observed, is precisely the perspective that it offers on the distinctive outlook of a people as articulated in the idiom of the language and its literature. This realises a difference within thought, a realisation that the world can be seen in different ways and that there is no external measure with which these differences can ultimately be resolved – there is no such thing as a perfect translation. Far from being incapacitating, however, there is then a kind of vibration between these differences, stimulating mental agility, opening the mind, and expanding cultural horizons.

6. Higher Education Must Not Become the Instrument for the Creation of a New European Culture

The obvious place for the transmission of a culture is an educational institution, and respondents to the Memorandum recognised the dangers of instrumentalisation that this might harbour. Inasmuch as the concern is with the passing on of a pre-existent European cultural identity, this is no great threat as there is no such uniform identity, as Mendus has pointed out. If the anxiety has to do with the *creation* of such an identity, however, this amounts to the injunction to educators to serve a political purpose – and a politically contentious one at that since it assumes that conflict can be eradicated. The realisation of a united Europe becomes a predetermined end with education the means for achieving this. The artificiality of this ideal, which many citizens do not aspire to, causes the European project to be conceived in manipulative, means-ends terms, and it causes education to be seen instrumentally rather than as internal to that ideal.

7. It Needs to Be Questioned How Far the European Dimension Should Affect the Curricula of Higher Education

In the task of educating the imagination and resisting ethnocentricity, many subjects have their place. Apart from the study of languages, history, geography, literature, religion, and philosophy all have an obvious role. While such a range of subjects may be prominent, albeit in different ways, in the schooling of children and young people in Europe, in university study, as Smeyers has argued, this is not the case. Although any one of them might constitute the central focus of study, they may not figure at all. It cannot be assumed then that higher education will necessarily have the kinds of effects gained from a study of these subjects that might reasonably be sought in the case of schooling. It would be paternalistic and oddly parochial to suppose that it should.

The more a society becomes multicultural, it might be argued, the more multiculturalism needs to be evident in the curriculum of schools. But higher education is in that respect quite different. It is the logic and content of the discipline that must guide criteria for the content of courses. University subjects are already international, irrespective of boundaries of language and culture. Higher education above all leads beyond the present and the particular. The study of any subject at a higher level involves an encounter with what is other. Typically the presentation of a paradigmatic method, together with sets of problems and solutions, demonstrates how research in a discipline is properly pursued. Over the centuries the European project of the university has taken different forms and has led in diverse directions. For the most part, however, the university has remained a place where attention is turned away from the immediate locality, beyond the boundaries of the commonplace and of common sense. Its unchanged first responsibility remains to initiate (at an advanced level) students into the ongoing conversation of mankind, in Oakeshott's celebrated phrase, so that students are able to continue this for themselves. The European Dimension should not impinge on this fundamental task. In this light preoccupation with the differences between the peoples of Europe in the present day would seem misplaced, a distraction from this larger and more broadening commitment. Ironically it would amount to compromising those traditions of university education that have played so rich a part in Europe's cultural life and achievement and that have been enabled a turning of the attention beyond Europe's most immediate (and Eurocentric) concerns.

8. The Place of Tradition and Criticism in the Curriculum Needs to Be Re-thought

The fact that universities in several countries are opening their doors to wider sections of the population has raised again questions about the appropriateness and indeed the legitimacy of curricula. Famously such concerns are acute in the case of subjects whose paradigms have been shaped by canons of Great Books. The study of a canon involves the convening of a succession of cultural artefacts; but, the objection runs, the memories these products evoke are culturally relative and increasingly unrepresentative of the expanding student population. The case for such a tradition depends on the intrinsic worth and breadth of influence, actual and potential, of the works it comprises – on their ability not to impose ideas and values but rather to provoke an enlivening and interrogative response, disturbing settled ways of thinking. A canon enables, and ultimately requires, a practice of reading that always maintains the possibility of more rich interpretations, in which students' critical powers are formed and developed. This need neither supersede nor be impeded by those same students' diverse cultural backgrounds.

For all the emphasis on criticism internal to this idea of tradition, however, it is necessary to realise the extent of the difference that an approach firmly based on a particular canon or settled paradigm will be inclined to overlook. The alternative is not a curriculum relativised endlessly to the diversities of different cultural needs. The alternative, as suggested by Standish, is to maintain the tradition but in parallel to different paradigms. In the end a tradition develops best when it is confronted with what is beyond it. And the kind of energising uncertainty that is generated between different paradigms can be a source of creative power even as it is a condition for ethical responsibility. Students educated in this way are not limited by a reductive relativism, where the curriculum relates exclusively to their needs. Neither are they wholly absorbed into the regime of the uncontested paradigm where difference is obscured. The need to communicate, to understand across borders, might be indicative of the life of a subject itself but also exemplary for democracy. Culture (in its richest sense) must incorporate these destabilisations and crossings, and tradition (in its best sense) critical possibilities of change.

9. The Vocational and Industrial Commitments of Higher Education Need to Be Released from an Incapacitating Instrumentalism

However it recognises the liberal imperatives of the European university tradition, the EU is inevitably preoccupied with more immediate matters of the economy. Amongst academics and administrators there is often a wary stand-off between those who advance these seemingly rival commitments. More than in the past, educators and administrators find themselves called upon to account for their use of the investment that society makes in higher education. Whatever the seductive force of simple ready-made answers, whatever the pressures of the market and the imperatives of profit, a university needs to affirm itself as a place that fosters independent judgement and creativity.

Much higher education must be vocational. But this must not be only instrumental in nature: it must initiate the learner into what has been found to be most valuable within a disciplined practice. The tendency to conceive of such practices in exclusively instrumentalist terms, however, obscures the possibility of a more rounded understanding of technical expertise.

A first way that this might be achieved is through a reconceiving of the vocationally educated person in terms of the responsible and reflective expert, as Weijers has argued, such a person considers what her expertise involves, both in its cognitive and in its social aspects. Her training is orientated towards a deepening assessment of her own expertise – the exercise of critical thinking in her specialist practice, the adoption of problem-solving strategies that are relevant for the kinds of problems in her field, continual reflection on learned strategies, reconsideration of her know-how. This means constantly raising the capability of the student to reflect on the practice, to articulate the principles embedded in it, and thus to bring the theoretical to the surface. Such a rich practical expertise is not achieved by a fragmentation of studies in numerous subspecialisations, by the addition of ancillary components to a core discipline. Rather it requires an adjustment of the character of those specialist studies themselves: to make them more reflective will indeed be to make them more 'philosophical', more 'historical', and more sensitive to their social context. The educational aim of creating the reflective expert offers a much-needed alternative to the individualistic and functional vocational training that characterises current trends.

Indeed ultimately such narrow vocational training is counterproductive. For with the impoverishment of education it effects there comes a failure to recognise the crucial role of networks of understanding and shared experience. It is this kind of knowledge base that provides the tacit capability essential for innovation, as Blake has shown. Establishing the conditions where such networks can flourish is then a second way in which narrow instrumentalism must be resisted. Tacit capability not only relies on but in large measure consists in a conversationally constituted shared experience. A well-managed institution then must attend with care to the conditions under which the construction of shared experience is best fostered. Utilitarian forms of management are not only morally objectionable but are, in the long term, destructive of the very knowledge capital, the tacit capability, that a healthy growth economy requires. Shared knowledge, shared experiences, and normative structure help to create the kind of community that is focused on a particular industrial aim. Managerial innovation involves changes of working relationships and attitudes. A social structure of pre-defined and closely interknit functional roles is the least appropriate to sustain such changes. The interaction of academics, in contrast, approximates to conditions in which talk of extraneous constraints is minimised and rational debate given its freest rein. These, surely, are the ideal conditions for the innovative thinking that industry requires. Innovative firms look to higher education not for the provision of specific knowledge but for a wider base of knowledge creation and skills. What has been overlooked, therefore, is the central role played in this base by the understanding graduates acquire at university of the ideal conditions of discourse and their point and purpose. This understanding used to typify higher education and here are strong practical reasons why it still should. In its deep commitment to economic growth in a globalised world, Europe has to be on its guard not so to pressurise higher education as to pre-empt its creation of local networks of tacit capability.

10. A Narrow Conception of Teaching and Learning Will Undermine Europe's Higher Education and Democracy

If tacit capability is appropriately described as a 'thickened' form of knowledge and understanding, there are multiple forces that conspire to 'thin' this down. Narrow and dangerous kinds of individualism and entrepreneurialism, as Smith has argued, are often promoted that diminish our sense of what is involved in learning. They etiolate our notion of what it is to be a person. Widespread enthusiasm for the development of a 'learning society' is a response in part to the economic threat of the so-called Pacific Rim. The learning society is envisioned as a society in which discrete and disaggregated bits of knowledge and skill, perhaps with pretensions to transferability, are put together by individuals for specific employment purposes. Individuals become the designers of their own developing skill-profiles, their accumulating knowledge and know-how being recorded bit by bit on personal skills cards which they carry with them. But for teacher and student alike the skills and competencies that allegedly are the outcomes of learning displace the sense of what it can amount to. Dominated by ideas derived from management theory, such an instrumental frame dispels faith in the possibility of a psychology that might genuinely cast light on the way people learn and how they may be helped to learn better. Interest shifts obsessively to the 'performance indicators' of effectiveness – to quantification, ranking, and league tables, and to planning in the light of predetermined goals. It is not just that this economic model declares education to be for the sake of the needs of industry and commerce, ignoring richer notions of personal development or the fulfilment of human potential. It is that learning is tied inextricably to the individual in such a way that richer and more complex notions of the process of learning become harder to entertain and to articulate with any plausibility. It is then beside the point to attempt later to reintroduce these more complex notions, as the Responses try to do – as, for example, where they emphasise that we need to move from a culture of teaching to a culture of learning – for with this 'thin' conception of the individual such a possibility is already foreclosed.

Moreover, this is dangerous from the point of view of democracy itself. For it obscures the original impulse to the idea – of a society where, since all could speak, all could be learned from, and where the toleration of diverse opinions and styles of life ensured that there was a rich variety of resources and examples. To think of democracy in this way is to think of it as more than just a style of government, a means of regulating the actions of individuals; it is to revive a notion of democracy in which the idea of friendship is not out of place: we can know a good in common that we cannot know alone. Europe's joint research projects and its student exchanges, it is no exaggeration to say, create new possibilities precisely of friendship: they enable us better to deliberate about ends and more spontaneously to celebrate differences, differences all too easily obliterated by the homogenising power of managerialism and economic imperatives. These conceptions of democracy and friendship can enrich higher education enormously, and enable it in turn to give renewed resonance to the very idea of community.

11. The Development of Citizenship is Dependent on an 'Exchange of Memories'

In something like a spirit of friendship also there can be an exchange of memories, indicating not just the psychological faculty through which we recall the past but more profoundly the structuring of our whole way of being in time – hence the constitution of our very identity. In the context of Europe this whole theme is transposed, Dunne has suggested, from the level of individual persons to that of nations and cultures – on the assumption that one can speak meaningfully of collective memory and that the identity of a group, culture, people, or nation, is not that of an immutable substance, nor that of a fixed structure, but that, rather, of a recounted story. In the case of a nation, the story will profile 'founding events' that, because they are primordial and have been much commemorated and celebrated, tend to hold the story in a fixed mould, to the point even of generating an identity that is not only immutable but also deliberately and systematically incommunicable. In relation to founding events or generative moments in the life of a nation one should look neither for abandonment nor for amnesia but for an effort of plural reading. Reinterpretation can bring liberation not *from* the past but *of* the past, or rather of the frustrated potential of the past. The exchange of memories involves an attempt by people of one nation to enter imaginatively and sympathetically into the story or stories of another people, while at the same time allowing one's own story or stories to be reconfigured through the impact of this recognition of the other. Recognition and reconfiguration are ethical in kind, invoking what Ricoeur calls the model of forgiveness. The search here is indeed for a kind of citizenship and patriotism. But this must not be vitiated by the sense of blood and belonging. And it must not be subsumed under the kind of cosmopolitanism that may fail to meet people's needs for identity – by this failure helping to open the door to the very xenophobic nationalism that it wishes to repudiate. It involves an exchange that is not economic and offers nothing that could properly be called union. It is an exchange without commensurability.

This appreciative recognition of otherness between the nations of Europe may not, however, prevent xenophobia from reasserting itself within a new European identity. Standish has explored the need to take account not only of influences from beyond Europe's boundaries, especially in view of its complex history of exploration and discovery, but also of ethnic minorities who have settled in Europe bringing with them different pasts that need to be acknowledged and read again. The extension of access to higher education for such groups should be seen as an aspect of the European Dimension. This is a dimension of Europe that demands the active involvement of such groups in higher education.

12. The Political Realm Needs to be Reconceived to Embrace Multiple Strands of Allegiance and Commitment

Though there remains the possibility of a European xenophobia, it is not clear that this is complemented by any robust sense of European citizenship. Nor is any such consolidated identity desirable. To approach the possibility of a different kind of political identity it is appropriate to consider the derivation of the concept of citizenship in our western democracies, as Crawley shows. On the one hand, this has developed from the modern idea of the individual as free and autonomous; on the other hand, it has been used equally to indicate members of a nation who, by birth and lineage, share a common origin and a common ethos. These two very different notions of citizenship interweave in the history of Western democracies. The question whether there can ever be such a thing as European citizenship arises at the moment one looks for the possibility of active participation by 'European citizens' in supranational or transnational political decision-making processes. Habermas's proposal of a 'communicative pluralism' is intended to foster a particular concept of European identity: if there is a chance for a future European citizenship it lies in the possibility of individuals maintaining their attachments to the identities of the nation's prepolitical cultural artefacts and values while effective communication networks are established for the expression of a common political will at the European level. The idea of a European state and European citizenship is constructed on the back of firmly ingrained histories, artistic expressions, and national identities that are not easily loosened from their attachment to linguistic expression and locality; indeed these form the substance of some academic subjects.

Recalling the emphasis on diversity with which these recommendations began, we find here further grounds for believing that over-systematic planning is inherently inhibitive of cultural exchange and development. We need to realise a political life in which different strands of attachment and commitment, cooperation and association, traverse our identities, one which supersedes, yet relieves the pressures of, a supposedly settled allegiance to the nation-state. What the strands of European citizenship would then amount to is not to be immediately settled. It is clear nevertheless that they would include the formal, characterised by the politico-legal commitment to Europe Union, and the more concrete, arising from local cultural attachments. This would be to incorporate both a recognition of the continuing importance of different cultural histories and an acceptance, in the face of globalisation and the incipient anachronism of the nation-state, of the need for larger structures for cooperation. Interaction with multiple others in the daily lives of millions of Europeans presents a dynamic for change. The critical traditions of Europe's universities provide sources for the kind of politics that is needed. The re-membering of Europe depends on a recovery and exchange of different histories integral to the understanding and enactment of citizenship in member-states: of what citizenship amounts to and of what it can become.

Bibliography

Allen, W. (1958). *The English Novel*. Harmondsworth: Penguin Books.

Améry, J. (1992). Hoeveel 'Heimat' heeft een mens nodig? *De XXIe Eeuw*, 2: 95–117. (Original work published in 1966)

Anderson, B. (1983). *Imagined Communities: Reflections on the Origins and Spread of Nationalism*. London: Verso.

Anderson, P. (1996, 4 January). Under the Sign of the Interim. *London Review of Books*, p. 16.

Appleton, N. (1983). *Cultural Pluralism in Education*. New York: Longman.

Arendt, H. (1958). *The Human Condition* (part 5). Chicago: University of Chicago Press.

Arnot, M., Araujo. H., Deliyanni-Kouimtzi, K., Rowe, G., and Tome, A. (1996). Teachers, Gender and the Discourses of Citizenship. *International Studies in Sociology of Education*, 6: 3–35.

Arregui, J.V. (1988). El Papel de la Estética en la Ética. *Pensamiento*, 44: 439–51.

Arrow, K.J. (1973). Higher Education as a Filter. *Journal of Public Economics*, 2: 193–216.

Association of Teacher Educators in Europe *Actes de Palerme: sur la Prise en Compte de la Dimension Européen dans l'Education*, Brussels, 1989.

ATEE News (Association for Teacher Education in Europe), 38/39, December 92/March 93, p. 23.

Baggen, P., and Weijers I. (1995). *De toekomst van de Universiteit*. Amsterdam: Amsterdam University Press.

Bailey, C. (1984). *Beyond the Present and the Particular. A Theory of Liberal Education*. London: Routledge and Kegan Paul.

Barber, B. (1984). *Strong Democracy: Participatory Politics for a New Age*. Berkeley: University of California Press.

Barnett, R. (1990). *The Idea of Higher Education*. Buckingham: SRHE/Open University Press.

Barnett, R. (1992). The Idea of Quality: Voicing the Educational. *Higher Education Quarterly*, 46: 3–19.

Basombrío, M. (1997). Hermenéutica y Ciencias del Hombre en P. Ricoeur. *Themata*, 17.

Beck, U. (1992). *Risk Society: Towards a New Modernity*. London: Sage.

Becker, G.S. (1968). *Human Capital. A Theoretical and Empirical Analysis with Special Reference to Education*. New York: NBER.

Bender, T. (1993). *Intellectuals and Public Life: Essays on the Social History of Academic Intellectuals in the United States*. Baltimore: Johns Hopkins University Press.

Benhabib, S. (1996). *Democracy and Difference: Contesting the Boundaries of the Political*. Princeton: Princeton University Press.

Bergh, H. van den (1979). *Verzamelde Gedichten*. Amsterdam: Querido.

Berlin, I. (1990). Alleged Relativism in Eighteenth Century European Thought. In I. Berlin (ed.), *The Crooked Timber of Humanity: Chapters in the History of Ideas* (pp. 70–90). London: Murray.

Bernstein, R. J. (1983). *Beyond Objectivism and Relativism*. Oxford: Basil Blackwell.

Blake, N.P. (1995). Truth, Identity and Community in the Universities. *Curriculum Studies*, 3, 263–81.

Bloom, A. (1987). *The Closing of the American Mind*. London: Penguin.

Boileau-Despréaux, N. (1939). *Epîtres. Art poétique. Lutrin*. Paris: Société les Belles Lettres. (Chant premier, v. 48)

Bollnow, O.F. (1955). *Neue Geborgenheit*. Stuttgart: Kohlhammer.

Bollnow, O.F. (1963). *Mensch und Raum*. Stuttgart: Kohlhammer.

Borghans, L., de Grip, A., and Heijke, H. (1989). *De Aansluiting Tussen het Hoger Onderwijs en de Arbeidsmarkt: Een Theoretisch Kader*. Maastricht: Researchcentrum voor Onderwijs en Arbeidsmarkt.

Bowles, S., and Gintis H. (1976). *Schooling in Capitalist America. Educational Reform and the Contradictions of Economic Life*. London: Routledge.

Bowser, P., Jones, T., and Young, G.A. (eds.). (1995). *Toward the Multicultural University*. Wesport: Praeger.

Boyce, D.G., Brady, C., and O' Day, A. (1996). *The Making of Modern Irish History: Revisionism and the Revisionist Controversy*. London: Routledge.

Boyle, N. (1995). Hegel and the End of History. *New Blackfriars*, 76(891): 109–19.

Brady, C. (1994). *Interpreting Irish History: the Debate on Historical Relativism, 1938–1990*. Dublin: Irish Academic Press.

Brecher, B., Fleischmann, O., and Halliday, J. (eds). (1996). *The University in a Liberal State*. Aldershot: Avebury.

Brennan, E. (1995). Reflections on a New Ethos for Europe. *Philosophy and Social Criticism*, 21(5/6): 3–13.

Brown, C. (1994). The Ethics of Political Restructuring in Europe. In C. Brown (ed.), *Political Restructuring in Europe: Ethical Perspectives* (pp. 163–84). London: Routledge.

Burms, A. and De Dijn, H. (1986). *De Rationaliteit en Haar Grenzen: Kritiek en Deconstructie*. Leuven: Universitaire Pers.

Callaghan, D.F.O. (1993). Part two: Synthesis of Principal Responses to the Memorandum. In European Communities, Commission Brussels (ed.), *The Outlook for Higher Education in the European Community: Responses to the Memorandum* (pp. 27–57). Luxembourg: Office for the Official Publications of the European Communities.

Callan, E. (1991). Pluralism and Civic Education. *Studies in Philosophy and Education*, 11: 65–87.

Callan, E. (1992). Finding a Common Voice. *Educational Theory*, 42: 429–41.

Callan, E. (1994). Beyond Sentimental Civic Education. *American Journal of Education*, 102: 190–221.

Cantwell, J. (1995). Innovation in a Global World. *New Economy*, 2: 66–70.

Cavell, S. (1969). *Must We Mean What We Say?* New York: Charles Scribner's Sons.

Cavell, S. (1979). *The Claim of Reason: Wittgenstein, Skepticism, Morality and Tragedy*. London: Oxford University Press.

Cavell, S. (1982). *The Senses of Walden. An Expanded Edition*. Chicago: University of Chicago.

Choza, J. (1988). *Manual de Antropología Filosófica*. Madrid: Rialp.

Choza, J. (1990). Reflexión Filosófica y Desintegración Cultural en la Antropología de G.B. Vico. In J. Choza (ed.), *La Realización del Hombre en la Cultura* (pp. 163–94). Madrid: Rialp.

Clark, G. (1983). *The Identity of Man as Seen by an Archeologist*. London: Methuen.

Coffield, F. (1995). *Higher Education in a Learning Society*. Durham: University of Durham.

Coke, E. (1823). *Institutes of the Laws of England, or a Commentary upon Littleton*. London: Worrall.

Commission of the European Communities. (1991). *Memorandum on Higher Education in the European Community* (Document COM(91) 349 final). Luxembourg: Office for the Official Publications of the European Communities.

Commission of the European Communities (1993a). *The Outlook for Higher Education in the European Community: Responses to the Memorandum*. No. 2 in the series of Studies of the Task Force: Human Resources, Education, Training and Youth.

Commission of the European Communities (1993b). *The Outlook for Higher Education in the European Community: Responses to the Memorandum. Theme Reports: The European Dimension in Higher Education*. Smith, A. & Schink, G. assisted by Kotterman, M.L.

Commission of the European Communities. (1993c). *Green Paper on the European Dimension of Education* (COM(93) 457 final). Luxembourg: Office for the Official Publications of the European Communities.

Commission of the European Communities. (1994, 3 February). *Proposal for a European Parliament and Council Decision Establishing the Community Action Programme 'Socrates'* (COM(93) 708 final). Brussels: Author.

Committee on Institutional Affairs, European Parliament (Rapporteur: Mr. Fernand Herman). (1993). *'Article 3: Citizenship of the Union.' Draft Report on the Constitution of the European Union* (DOC EN\PR\234\234101 PE 203.601/rev 9 September). Luxembourg: Office for the Official Publications of the European Communities.

Convery, A., Evans, M., Green, S., Macaro, E., and Mellor, J. (1997). *Pupils' Perceptions of Europe: Identity and Education*. London: Cassell.

Corson, D. (ed.). (1991). *Education for Work: Background to Policy and Curriculum*. Clevedon: Multilingual Matters.

Couloubaritsis, L., De Leeuw, M., Noel, E., and Sterckx, C. (1993). *The Origins of European Identity*. Brussels: European Interuniversity Press.

Council and the Ministers of Education Meeting within the Council (1988). Resolution of the Council and the Ministers of Education Meeting within the Council of 24 May 1988. *Official Journal of the European Communities*, 31(N° C 177/5, 88/C/177/02).

Cuypers, S. (1992). Is Personal Autonomy the First Principle of Education? *Journal of Philosophy of Education*, 26: 5–17.

Cuypers, S. (1996). A Community View on Personal Autonomy. In M.G. Amilburu (ed.), *Education, the State and the Multicultural Challenge* (pp. 119–33). Pamplona: Ensua.

Davies, N. (1996). *Europe: A History*. Oxford: Oxford University Press.

De Tocqueville, A. (1982). *On Democracy, Revolution and Society*. Chicago: University of Chicago Press.

Delanty, G. (1995). The Limits and Possibilities of a European Identity. *Philosophy and Social Criticism*, 21(4): 15–36.

den Boer, P. (1993). Europe to 1914: The Making of an Idea. In K. Wilson and J. van der Dussen (eds.), *The History of the Idea of Europe* (pp. 13–82). London: Routledge.

Department for Education (1994). *Higher Education in the 1990s*. London: DFE.

Derrida, J. (1974). *Of Grammatology* (G.C. Spivak, trans.). Baltimore: Johns Hopkins University Press. (Original work published in 1967)

Derrida, J. (1983, Fall). The Principle of Reason: The University in the Eyes of Its Pupils. *Diacritics*.

Derrida, J. (1989). *Of Spirit: Heidegger and the Question* (G. Bennington and R. Bowlby, trans.). Chicago: University of Chicago Press. (Original work published in 1987)

Derrida, J. (1990). Les pupilles de l'Université: Le principe de raison et l'idée de l'université. *Du droit à la Philosophie* (Collection La Philosophie en Effet; pp. 461–98). Paris: Galilée.

Derrida, J. (1992). *The Other Heading* (P.-A. Brault and M.B. Naas, trans.). Bloomington and Indianapolis: Indiana University Press. (Original work published in 1991)

Derrida, J. (1994). *Specters of Marx: The State of the Debt, the Work of Mourning, and the New International* (P. Kamuf, trans.). New York: Routledge.

Dilthey, W. (1973–82). *Gesammelte Schriften*. Göttingen: Vandenhoeck.

Duchene, D. (1995). Jean Monnet: *The First Statesman of Interdependence*. New York: Norton.

Dunne, J. (1993). *Back to the Rough Ground: Phronesis and Techne in Modern Philosophy and in Aristotle*. Notre Dame: University of Notre Dame Press.

Dunne, J. (1995a). Beyond Sovereignty and Deconstruction: The Storied Self. *Philosophy and Social Criticism*, 21(5/6), 137–57.

Dunne, J. (1995b). Philosophies of the Self and the Scope of Education. In J. Tooley (ed.), Papers of the Annual Conference of the Philosophy of Education Society of Great Britain (pp. 170–80). Oxford: Philosophy of Education Society of Great Britain.

Dunne, J. (1996). Beyond Sovereignty and Deconstruction: The Storied Self. In R. Kearney (ed.) *Paul Ricoeur: The Hermeneutics of Action*.

Education Guardian. (1994, 1 November). *The Guardian*, p. 3.

Eisner, E. (1996). *Cognition and Curriculum Reconsidered*. London: Paul Chapman Publishing.

Eliot, T.S. (1948). *Notes Towards the Definition of Culture*. London: Faber and Faber.

Elósegui, M. (1991). En Torno al Concepto de Simpatía y el Espectador Imparcial en Adam Smith, o la Sociedad Como Espejo. *Eurídice*, 1: 122–48.

Enslin, P. (1993/94). Education for Nation-building: A Feminist Critique. *Perspectives in Education*, 15: 13–25.

Europa Past Gedecentraliseerd Partnerschap. (1997, 23 February). *De Standaard*, p. 13.

European Commission (1995). *Teaching and Learning: Towards the Learning Society. White Paper on Education and Training*. Brussels: European Commission.

European Commission Study Group on Education and Training (1996). *Accomplishing Europe through Education and Training*. Brussels: European Commission.

European Commission: Study Group on Education and Training (1997). *Accomplishing Europe through Education and Training: Report*. Luxembourg: Office for the Official Publications of the European Communities.

European Communities, Commission Brussels (ed.) . (1993). *The Outlook for Higher Education in the European Community: Responses to the Memorandum*. Luxembourg: Office for the Official Publications of the European Communities.

European Union (1995, 29 November). *Teaching and Learning: Towards the Learning Society. White Paper on Education and Training*. Luxembourg: Office for the Official Publications of the European Communities.

Extraits de l'Entretien Télévisé du Président de la République. (1977, 12 March). *Le Monde*, pp. 8–9.

Feinberg, W. (1995). Liberalism and the Aims of Multicultural Education. In Y. Tamir (ed.), *Democratic Education in a Multicultural State* (pp. 45–58). Oxford: Basil Blackwell.

Follon, J., and McEvoy, J. (eds.). (1992). *Finalité et intentionnalité*. Louvain-la-Neuve: Institut Supérieur de Philosophie.

Frankfurt, H. (1988). *The Importance of what We Care About: Philosophical Essays*. Princeton: Princeton University Press.

Freud, S. (1968). Remembering, Repeating and Working-through. In J. Strachey (ed.), *Standard Edition of the Complete Psychological Works* (Vol. 12: pp. 236–43). London: Hogarth Press.

Freud, S. (1981). The Uncanny. In J. Strachey (ed.), *Standard Edition of the Complete Psychological Works* (Vol. 17: pp. 219–52). London: Hogarth Press.

Frijda, N.H., and Mesquita, B. (1993). Emoties: natuur of cultuur? In N.H. Frijda (ed.), *De Psychologie Heeft Zin* (pp. 196–217). Amsterdam: Prometheus.

Fuller, T. (ed.). (1989). *The Voice of Liberal Learning: Michael Oakeshott on Education*. New Haven: Yale University Press.

Gadamer, H.-G. (1975). *Truth and Method*. London: Sheed and Ward.

Galeotti, A.E. (1993). Citizenship and Equality: The Place for Toleration. *Political Theory*, 21: 585–605.

Galoetti, A.E. (1994). A Problem with Theory. A Rejoinder to Moruzzi. *Political Theory*, 22: 673–77.

Garforth, F.W. (1964). Values in Society and Education. *Education for Teaching*, 64: 22–28.

Geertz, C. (1973). *The Interpretation of Cultures: Selected Essays*. New York: Basic Books.

Geertz, C. (1983). Common Sense as a Cultural System. In C. Geertz (ed.), *Local Knowledge: Further Essays in Interpretive Anthropology* (pp. 79–93). New York: Basic Books.

Gellert, C. (ed.). (1993). *Higher Education in Europe*. London: Jessica Kingsley Publishers.

Gibbons, M., Limoges, C., Nowotny, H., Schwartzman, S., Scott, P., and Trow, M. (1994). *The New Production of Knowledge. The Dynamics of Science and Research in Contemporary Societies*. London: Sage.

Gilroy, P. (1993). *The Black Atlantic: Modernity and Double Consciousness*. London: Verso.

Glaser, R. (1991). The Maturing of the Relationship between Science of Learning and Cognition and Educational Practice. *Learning and Instruction*, 1: 129–44.

Goldberg, D.T. (1994). *Multiculturalism: A Critical Reader*. Oxford: Blackwell.

Government of Ireland, Communicating Europe Task Force. (1995). *Communicating Europe: Report Summary*. Dublin.

Graff, G. (1992). *Beyond the Culture Wars. How Teaching the Conflicts Can Revitalize American Education*. New York: W.W. Norton.

Greenhalgh, C. (1995). Supply Side Puzzles. *New Economy*, 2: 89–93.

Gutmann, A. (1987). *Democratic Education*. Princeton: Princeton University Press.

Gutmann, A. (1992). Introduction. In C. Taylor (ed.), *Multiculturalism and 'The Politics of Recognition'* (pp. 3–24). Princeton: Princeton University Press.

Gutmann, A. (1993). Democracy and Democratic Education. *Studies in Philosophy and Education*, 12: 1–9.

Habermas, J. (1984). *The Theory of Communicative Action: Vol. 1. Reason and the Rationalization of Society*. Oxford: Blackwell.

Habermas, J. (1986). Die Idee der Universität.- Lernprozesse. *Zeitschrift für Pädagogik*, 32: 702–17.

Habermas, J. (1992). Citizenship and National Identity: Some Reflections on the Future of Europe. *Praxis International*, 12: 1–19.

Habermas, J. (1994). Struggles for Recognition in the Democratic Constitutional State (S.W. Nicholsen, trans.). In A. Gutmann (ed.), *Multiculturalism: Examining the Politics of Recognition* (pp. 107–48). Princeton: Princeton University Press.

Habermas, J. (1995). Citizenship and National Identity: Some Reflections on the Future of Europe. In R. Beiner (ed.), *Theorising Citizenship* (pp. 255–81). Albany: SUNY.

Haldane, J. (1991). Political Theory and the Nature of Persons: An Ineliminable Metaphysical Presupposition. *Philosophical Papers*, 20(2): 77–95.

Halstead, J.M. (1994). Moral and Spiritual Education in Russia. *Cambridge Journal of Education*, 24: 423–38.

Hampshire, S. (1989). *Innocence and Experience*. Cambridge: Harvard University Press.

Harré, R. (1986). *The Social Construction of Emotions*. Oxford: Basil Blackwell.

Hartog, J. (1986). Earnings Functions: Beyond Human Capital. *Applied Economics*, 1291–1309.

Haydon, G. (ed.). (1987). *Education for a Pluralist Society*. London: Institute of Education, University of London.

Heidegger, M. (1985). The Self-assertion of the German University. *Review of Metaphysics*, 38: 470–80.

Hellemans, M. (1994). Het wetende niet-weten. In P. Smeyers (d.), *Heeft de school nog een vormingsproject?* (pp. 133–45). Leuven: Acco.

Hoffman, E. (1989). *Lost in Translation. A Life in a New Language*. London: Heinemann.

Hoffman, E. (1994). *Exit into History: A Journey through the New Eastern Europe*. London: Heinemann.

Hone, K. (1995). *Irish Times* 14 October: 9.

Honig, B. (1996). Difference, Dilemmas, and the Politics of Home. In S. Benhabib (ed.), *Democracy and Difference: Contesting the Boundaries of the Political*. Princeton: Princeton University Press.

Hoof, J.J. van, and Dronkers, J. (1980). *Onderwijs en arbeidsmarkt*. Deventer: Van Loghum Slaterus.

Hughes, A., Keeble, D., and Wood, E. (1995). Small Firms, Big Ideas. *New Economy*, 2: 94–98.

Hughes-Warrington, M. (1996). History Education and the Conversation of Mankind. *Collingwood Studies*, 3: 96–116.

Hume, B. (1994). *Remaking Europe. The Gospel in a Divided Continent*. London: Society for Promoting Christian Knowledge.

Hume, D., (1978). *A Treatise of Human Nature* (Ed. L. A. Selby Bigge, 3rd edn. revised P.N. Niddich). Oxford: Clarendon.

Hutchinson, J. (1994). *Modern Nationalism*. London: Fontana.

Ibáñez Martín, J.A. (1996). Multiculturalism, Identity and Unity. In M.G. Amilburu (ed.), *Education, the State and the Multicultural Challenge* (pp. 97–8). Pamplona: Ensua.

Ignatieff, M. (1994). *Blood and Belonging. Journeys into the New Nationalism*. London: Vintage.

Jabès, E. (1989). *Un étranger avec, sous le bras, un livre de petit format*. Paris: Gallimard.

Jacoby, R. (1987). *The Last Intellectuals. American Culture in the Age of Academe*. New York: Basic Books.

Jallade, J.-P. (1993). Participation in and Access to Higher Education. In European Communities, Commission Brussels (ed.), *The Outlook for Higher Education in the European Community: Responses to the Memorandum* (pp. 18–21). Luxembourg: Office for the Official Publications in the European Community.

Jaspers, K. (1960). *The Idea of the University* (H.A.T. Reiche and H.F. Vanderschmidt, trans.). London: Peter Owen. (Original work published in 1946)

Jones, David (1980), The Tribune's Visitation. From *The Sleeping Lord and Other Fragments*. In J. Matthias (ed.), *Introducing David Jones: A Selection of his Writings* (pp. 197–210). London: Faber & Faber.

Kant, I. (1991). *Political Writings* (ed. H. Reiss and H.B. Nisbet). Cambridge: Cambridge University Press.

Kearney, R. (ed.) (1996). *Paul Ricoeur: the Hermeneutics of Action*. New York: Sage.

Kearney, R., and Wilson, R. (1997). Northern Ireland's Future as a European Region. In R. Kearney (ed.), *Postnationalist Ireland: Politics, Culture, Philosophy* (pp. 75–91). London: Routledge.

Keller, H. (1992, 29 August). De uitvinding van Amerika [Interview met Eva Hoffman]. *Vrij Nederland*, 29: 65–66.

Kettle, M. (1993). False Hopes, Lost Dreams. In V. Keegan and M. Kettle (eds.), *The New Europe* (pp. 7–12). London: Fourth Estate.

Kopland, R. (1975). *Een lege plek om te blijven*. Amsterdam: Van Oorschot.

Kripke, S. A. (1982). *Wittgenstein on Rules and Private Language: An Elementary Exposition*. Oxford: Basil Blackwell.

Kristeva, J. (1988). *Étrangers à nous-mêmes*. Paris: Fayard.

Lasch, C. (1984). *The Minimal Self*. London: Picador.

Lennon B.S.J. (1997, 25 February). Forgiveness is Not Enough to Bring about Reconciliation in the North. *Irish Times*, 25, p.14.

Liedman, S.E. (1993). In Search of Isis: General Education in Germany and Sweden. In S. Rothblatt and Wittrock (eds.), *The European and American University Since 1800: Historical and Sociological Essays* (pp. 74–106). Cambridge: Cambridge University Press.

Lluesma, C.R. (1994). *El humanismo comercial de Adam Smith*. Pamplona: Ensua.

Lovejoy, A.O. (1948). *Essays in the History of Ideas*. Baltimore: Johns Hopkins University Press.

Luntley, M. (1996). Renovating the Political and the Autonomous University. In B. Brecher, O. Fleischmann, and J. Halliday (eds.), *The University in a Liberal State* (pp. 53–66). Aldershot: Avebury.

Lyotard, J.-F. (1984). *The Postmodern Condition: A Report on Knowledge*. Manchester: University of Manchester Press.

MacIntyre, A. (1990). *Three Rival Versions of Moral Enquiry*. London: Duckworth.

Magris, C. (1990). *Danube*. Paris: Gallimard.

Marín, H. (1990). *Las formas Epocales del Humanismo*. Pamplona: Ensua.

Marín, H. (1993). *La Antropología Aristotélica Como Filosofía de la Cultura*. Pamplona: Ensua.

Marquand, D. (1993). Heart of the Matter. In V. Keegan and M. Kettle (eds.), *The New Europe* (pp. 16–18). London: Fourth Estate.

Mauss, M. (1990). *The Gift: The Form and Reason for Exchange in Archaic Societies* (W. D. Halls, trans.). London: Routledge. (Original work published in 1925)

McClelland, C.E. (1980). *State, Society and University in Germany, 1700–1914*. Cambridge: Cambridge University Press.

McDowell, J. (1979). Virtue and Reason. *The Monist*, 62: 331–50.

McEwan, I. (1988). *The Child in Time*. London: Picador.

McLaughlin, T.H. (1992). Citizenship, Diversity and Education: A Philosophical Perspective. *Journal of Moral Education*, 21: 235–50.

McLaughlin, T.H. (1995). Liberalism, Education and the Common School. In Y. Tamir (ed.), *Democratic Education in a Multicultural State* (pp. 81–97). Oxford: Basil Blackwell.

Mendus, S. (1992). All the King's Horses and All the King's Men: Justifying Higher Education. *Journal of Philosophy of Education*, 26: 173–82.

Menze, C. (1976). Die philosophische Idee der Universität und ihre Krise im Zeitalter der Wissenschaften. *Vierteljahrschrift für Wissenschaftliche Pädagogik*, 52: 702–17.

Mickel, W. (1986). *The 'European Dimension' in the Classroom – Justification, Documents and Proposals* (ECN- series No 4). Alkmaar: ECN Publication.

Mill, J. S. (1984). Inaugural Address to the University of St Andrews. In Robson (ed.), *Collected Works of John Stuart Mill*, Vol. 21. Toronto.

Miller, D. (1976). *Social Justice*. Oxford: Clarendon Press.

Miller, D. (1993). In Defence of Nationality. *Journal of Applied Philosophy*, 10: 3–16.

Miller, D. (1995). *On Nationality*. Oxford: Oxford University Press.

Miller, L., and Sugden, R. (1995). Small Firm Webs. *New Economy*, 2: 85–88.

Milward, A. (1994). *The European Rescue of the Nation-state*. London: Routledge.

Modgil, S. (ed.). (1986). Multicultural Education. *The Interminable Debate*. Barcombe: The Falmer Press.

Morrell, F., (1996). Continent Isolated. *A Study of the European Dimension in the National Curriculum in England*. London: The Federal Trust for Education and Research.

Moruzzi, N.C. (1994a). A Problem with Headscarves. Contemporary Complexities of Political and Social Identity. *Political Theory*, 22: 653–72.

Moruzzi, N.C. (1994b). A Response to Galeotti. *Political Theory*, 22: 678–79.

Mulcahy, D.G. (1993). International Higher Education in the European Community. *International Education*, 23: 52–64.

Mulhall, S., and Swift, A. (1996). *Liberals and Communitarians*. Oxford: Basil Blackwell.

Naval, C. (1995). *Educar Ciudadanos. La Polémica Liberal-Comunitarista en Educación*. Pamplona: Ensua.

Neave, G., and van Vught F. A. (eds.). (1991). *Prometheus Bound. The Changing Relationship between Government and Higher Education in Western Europe*. Oxford: Pergamon Press.

Newman, J. (1960). *The Idea of a University*. New York: Holt, Rinehart and Winston.

Newman, J.H. (1931). *Select Discourses from the Idea of a University*. London: Cambridge University Press.

Nordenbo, S.E., (1995). What is Implied by a 'European Curriculum'? Issues of Eurocentrism, Rationality and Education. *Oxford Review of Education*, 21: 37–46.

North, J. (ed.). (1987). *The GCSE: An Examination*. Claridge Press.

Nuyen, A.T. (1995). Lyotard and Rorty on the Role of the Professor. In M. Peters (ed.), *Education and the Postmodern Condition*. Westport: Bergin and Garvey.

Oakeshott, M. (1975a). *On Human Conduct*. Oxford: Clarendon.

Oakeshott, M. (1975b). The Vocabulary of a Modern European State. *Political Studies*, 23: 319–41/409–14.

Oakeshott, M. (1981). *Rationalism in Politics and Other Essays*. London: Methuen.

Oakeshott, M. (1989). A Place of Learning. In T. Fuller (ed.), *The Voice of Liberal Learning: Michael Oakeshott on Education* (pp. 17–42). New Haven: Yale University Press.

Oakeshott, M. (1991). *Rationalism in Politics and Other Essays*. Indianapolis: Liberty Press.

O'Day, A. and Boyce, D.G. (1996). *The Making of Modern Irish History: Revisionism and the Revisionist Controversity*. London: Routledge.

O'Dwyer, T. (1993). Foreword. In European Communities, Commission Brussels (ed.), *The Outlook for Higher Education in the European Community: Responses to the Memorandum*. Luxembourg: Office for the Official Publications of the European Communities.

Osler, A., Rathenow, H.-F., and Starkey, H. (eds.). (1995). *Teaching for Citizenship in Europe*. Stoke-on-Trent: Trentham Books.

Pascal, B. (1960). *Pensées*. Paris: Colin.

Pavitt, K. (1995). Backing Basics. *New Economy*, 2: 71–74.

Peeke, G. (1994). *Mission and Change: Institutional Mission and its Application to the Management of Further and Higher Education*. Buckingham: Open University Press.

Pelikan, J. (1992). *The Idea of the University: A Re-examination*. New Haven: Yale University Press.

Peters, M. (ed.). (1995). *Education and the Postmodern Condition*. Westport: Bergin and Garvey.

Plato. *Phaedrus*. In B. Jowett (ed.), *The Dialogues of Plato* (Vol. 3, pp. 379–449; B. Jowett, trans.). Oxford: Clarendon.

Ploeg, S. W. van der (1992). Expansie van het voortgezet en hoger onderwijs: Effecten van veranderingen op de arbeidsmarkt, in gezinnen en in het onderwijssysteem. *Mens en Maatschappij*, 67: 156–76.

Pocock, J.G.A. (1975). *The Machiavellian Moment: Florentine Political Thought and the Atlantic Republican Tradition*. Princeton: Princeton University Press.

Pollit, C. (1987). Measuring University Performance: Never Mind the Quality, Never Mind the Width. *Higher Education Quarterly*, 44: 60–81.

Pratte, R. (1985). Tolerance, Permissiveness, and Education. *Teachers' College Record*, 87: 103–17.

Pring, R. (1995). Educating Persons: Putting Education Back in Educational Research. *Scottish Educational Review*, 27: 101–12.

Putnam, H. (1981). *Reason, Truth and History*. Cambridge: Cambridge University Press.

Putnam, H. (1987). *The Many Faces of Realism*. La Salle, Il: Open Court.

Quality and the Management of Quality [Special Issue]. (1992). *Higher Education Quarerly*, 46(1).

Quint, D. (1979). *The Stanze of Angelo Poliziano*. Amherst: University of Massachusetts Press.

Rawie, J.-P. (1992). *Onmogelijk geluk*. Amsterdam: Bert Bakker.

Rawls, J. (1993). *Political Liberalism*. New York: Columbia University Press.

Rhonheimer, M. (1987). *Natur als Grundlage der Moral. Die Personale Struktur des Naturgesetzes bei Thomas von Aquin*. Innsbruck: Tyrolia.

Ricoeur, P. (1973). Herméneutique et crititique des idéologies. *Archivio di Filosofia*, 2: 25–61.

Ricoeur, P. (1986). *Lectures on Ideology and Utopia*. New York: Colombia University Press.

Ricoeur, P. (1996). Reflections on a New Ethos for Europe. In R. Kearney (ed.), *Paul Ricoeur: the Hermeneutics of Action*. London: Sage.

Ringer, F. K. (1969). *The Decline of the German Mandarins. The German Academic Community 1890–1930*. Cambridge, MA: Harvard University Press.

Rizvi, F. (1986). *Ethnicity, Class and Multicultural Education*. Victoria: Deakin University.

Robson, J.M. (ed.). (1984). *Collected Works of John Stuart Mill* (Vol. 21). Toronto: Toronto Press.

Rorty, R. (1983). Postmodern Bourgeois Liberalism. *Journal of Philosophy*, 80: 583–89.

Rorty, R. (1989). Education without Dogma. *Dissent*, 36: 188–204.

Rorty, R. (1989). Richard Rorty Replies. *Liberal Education*, 85: 28–31.

Rorty, R. (1990). The Dangers of Over-philosophication: Reply to Arcilla and Nicholson. *Educational Theory*, 40: 41–44.

Rothblatt, S. (1993). The Limbs of Osiris: Liberal Education in the English-speaking World. In S. Rothblatt and B. Wittrock (eds.), *The European and American University since 1800: Historical and Sociological Essays* (pp. 19–73). Cambridge: Cambridge University Press.

Saint-Exupéry, A. de (1948). *Citadelle*. Paris: Gallimard.

Sandel, M. (1982). *Liberalism and the Limits of Justice*. Cambridge: Cambridge University Press.

Sanders, J.M. (1992). Short- and Long-term Macroeconomic Returns to Higher Education. *Sociology of Education*, 65: 21–36.

Schouten, M. (1994). *Kleur. Blank, Bruin & Zwart in Nederland. Interviews*. Amsterdam: De Bezige Bij.

Schultz, T.W. (1971). Investment in Human Capital. In M. Blaug (ed.), *Economics of Education* (Vol. 1: pp. 13–33). Harmondsworth: Penguin Books.

Scott, P. (1984). *The Crisis of the University*. London: Croom Helm.

Searle, J.R. (1969). *Speech Acts*. Cambridge: Cambridge University Press.

Skinner, Q. (1979). *Foundations of Modern Political Thought* (Vols. 1–2). Cambridge: Cambridge University Press.

Slauerhoff, J. (1978). *Verspreide gedichten*. Amsterdam: Bert Bakker.

Smart, B. (1993). *Postmodernity*. London: Routledge.

Smeyers, P., and Marshall, J.D. (1995). The Wittgensteinian Frame of Reference and Philosophy of Education at the End of the Twentieth Century. *Studies in Philosophy and Education*, 14: 127–59.

Smith, A. D. (1991). *National Identity*. London: Penguin.

Smith, A., and Schink, G. (1993). The European Dimension in Higher Education. In European Communities, Commission Brussels (ed.), *The Outlook for Higher Education in the European Community: Responses to the Memorandum* (pp. 47–55). Luxembourg: Office for the Official Publications of the European Communities.

Smith, R. (1993). Remembering Democracy. *Studies in Philosophy and Education*, 12: 45–55.

Snow, C.P. (1974). *The Two Cultures: And a Second Look*. London: Cambridge University Press.

Soffer, R. (1987). The Modern University and National Values, 1850–1930. *Historical Research*, 60: 133–46.

Spaemann, R. (1987). *Das Naturliche und das Vernünftige*. München: Piper.

Spaemann, R. (1989). *Glück und Wohlwollen*. Stuttgart: Klett-Cotta.

Spaemann, R. (1991). La Naturaleza Como Instancia de Apelación Moral. In R. Alvira (Ed.), *El Hombre: Inmanencia y Trascendencia* (Vol. 1: pp. 49–67). Pamplona: Ensua.

Standish, P. (1995). Postmodernism and the Idea of the Whole Person. *Journal of Philosophy of Education*, 29: 121–35.
Stehr, N. (1994). *Knowledge Societies*. London: Sage.
Stichweh, R. (1984). *Zur Entstehung des modernen Systems wissenschaftlicher Disziplinen: Physik in Deutschland* 1740–1890. Frankfurt a.M.: Suhrkamp.
Tabatoni, P. (1993). Part One: Main Issues in European Higher Education. In European Communities, Commission Brussels (ed.), *The Outlook for Higher Education in the European Community: Responses to the Memorandum* (pp. 9–26). Luxembourg: Office for the Official Publications of the European Communities.
Tamir, Y. (1992). Democracy, Nationalism, and Education. *Educational Philosophy and Theory*, 24: 17–27.
Tamir, Y. (1993). *Liberal Nationalism*. Princeton: University Press Princeton.
Tamir, Y. (ed.). (1995). *Democratic Education in a Multicultural State*. Oxford: Basil Blackwell.
Taylor, C. (1979). *Philosophy and the Human Sciences: Philosophical Papers, II*. Cambridge, MA: Cambridge University Press.
Taylor, C. (1991). *The Ethics of Authenticity*. Cambridge, MA: Harvard University Press.
Taylor, C. (1994a). *Reconciling the Solitudes: Essays on Canadian Federalism and Nationalism*. Montreal: McGill-Queen's University Press.
Taylor, C. (1994b). The Politics of Recognition. In A. Gutmann (ed.), *Multiculturalism: Examining the Politics of Recognition* (pp. 67–70). Princeton: Princeton University Press.
Taylor, C. (1995). *Philosophical Arguments*. Cambridge, MA: Harvard University Press.
Teichler, U. (1988). *Changing Patterns of the Higher Education System*. London: Jessica Kingsley.
Teichler, U. (1993). Structures of Higher Education Systems in Europe. In C. Gellert (ed.), *Higher Education in Europe* (pp. 23–36). London: Kingsley.
Thurow, L.C. (1979). A Job Competition Model. In M.J. Piore (ed.), *Unemployment and Inflation*. New York: Sharp White Plains.
Tijssen, L. Van Vucht (1991). Hoger onderwijs, voor wie en waartoe? *Comenius*, 38: 256–70.
Treaty on European Union, Together with the Complete Text of the Treaty Establishing the European Community. (1992). *Official Journal of the European Communities*, 35(N° C224, 92/C224/01). Luxembourg: Office for the Official Publications of the European Communities.
Valéry, P. (1957). *Essais quasi politiques, Oeuvres*. Paris: Gallimard.
Vanbergen, P. (1988). *Enhanced Treatment of the European Dimension in Education*. Rapport préparé par P. Vanbergen. Brussels: European Commission.
Vickery, J.B. (1993). Myth. In A. Preminger and T.V.F. Brogan (eds.), *The New Encyclopedia of Poetry and Poetics* (pp. 806–9). Princeton: Princeton University Press.
Von Krockow, C. (1993). *Hour of the Women*. London: Faber.
Wachelder, J.C.M. (1992). *Universiteit tussen vorming en opleiding: De modernisering van de Nederlandse universiteiten in de negentiende eeuw*. Hilversum: Verloren.

Wagner, P. (1990). *Sozialwissenschaften und Staat: Frankreich, Italien, Deutschland 1870–1980*. Frankfurt a.M.: Suhrkamp.

Wagner, P. et al. (eds.). (1991). *Social Sciences and Modern States. National Experiences and Theoretical Crossroads*. Cambridge: Cambridge University Press.

Walters, P., and Rubinson, R. (1983). Educational Expansion and Economic Output in the United States 1890–1969. A Production Function Analysis. *American Sociological Review*, 48: 480–93.

Walzer, M. (1994a). Comment. In A. Gutmann (ed.), *Multiculturalism: Examining the Politics of Recognition* (pp. 99–103). Princeton: Princeton University Press.

Walzer, M. (1994b). *Thick and Thin: Moral Argument at Home and Abroad*. Notre Dame: University of Notre Dame Press.

Weber, E. (1979). *Peasants into Frenchmen*. London: Chatto and Windus.

Weber, M. (1919). *Wissenschaft als Beruf*. Berlin: Duncker and Humblot.

Weber, M. (1972). *Wirtschaft und Gesellschaft*. Tubingen: J.C.B. Mohr.

Weil, S. (1978). *The Need for Roots*. London: Routledge and Kegan Paul.

Weusthof, P.J.M. (1994). *De interne kwaliteitszorg in het wetenschappelijk onderwijs*. Utrecht: Lemma.

White, J. (1996). Education and Nationality. *Journal of Philosophy of Education*, 30: 327–43.

White, J. P. (1995). *Education and Personal Well-being in a Secular Universe*. London: Institute of Education, University of London.

Willey, B. (1940). *The Eighteenth Century Background*. London: Ark.

Williams, K. (1989). The Gift of an Interval: Michael Oakeshott's Idea of a University Education. *British Journal of Educational Studies*, 37: 324–37.

Williams, K. (1995a). Modern Languages in the School Curriculum: A philosophical view. *Journal of Philosophy of Education*, 25: 247–58.

Williams, K. (1995b). National Sentiment in Civic Education [Review of the book *Liberal Nationalism*]. *Journal of Philosophy of Education*, 29: 433–40.

Williams, K. (1996a). Education for European Citizenship: A Philosophical Critique. *Studies in Philosophy and Education*, 15: 209–19.

Williams, K. (1996b). Promoting the 'New Europe': Education or Proselytism? *Studies: An Irish Quarterly Review*, 85: 49–57.

Wittrock, B. (1993). The Modern University: The Three Transformations. In S. Rothblatt and B. Wittrock (eds.), *The European and American University since 1800: Historical and Sociological Essays* (pp. 303–62). Cambridge: Cambridge University Press.

WRR [Scientific Council for Government Policy]. (1995). *Hoger onderwijs in fasen*. Den Haag: Staatsdrukkerij Uitgeverij.

Young, I.M. (1996). Communication and the Other: Beyond Deliberative Democracy. In S. Benhabib (ed.), *Democracy and Difference: Contesting the Boundaries of the Political*. Princeton: Princeton University Press.

Zec, P. (1980). Multicultural Education: What Kind of Relativism is Possible? *Journal of Philosophy of Education*, 14: 77–95.

Ziman, J.M. (1987). *Science in a Steady State: The Research System in Transition*. London: Science Policy Group.